WHEN GOD TURNS

...THE NEXT GREAT AWAKENING

WHEN GOD TURNS
...THE NEXT GREAT AWAKENING
by Charles W. Clark

This book or parts thereof may not be reproduced in any form, stored in a retrieval system, or transmitted in any form by any means—electronic, mechanical, photocopy, recording, or otherwise—without prior written permission of the publisher, except as provided by United States copyright law.

Unless otherwise quoted, scripture quotations are taken from the Holy Bible, New International Version. Copyright © 1973, 1978, 1984, International Bible Society.

Scripture quotations marked KJV are from the Holy Bible, King James Version (KJV).

Scripture quotations marked NKJV are from the Holy Bible, New King James Version. Copyright © 1982, Thomas Nelson, Inc.

Scripture quotations taken from the Amplified Bible, Copyright © 1954, 1958, 1962, 1964, 1965, 1967 by the Lockman Foundation, La Habra. CA. Used by permission.

Scripture quotations marked MSG are taken from THE MESSAGE® Copyright © 1993, 1994, 1995, 1996, 2000, 2001, 2002. Used by Permission of NavPress Publishing Group. Colorado springs, CO. All rights reserved.

Scripture marked ICB is taken from the International Children's Bible® Copyright© 1986, 1988, 1999 2015 by Thomas Nelson, Inc., all rights reserved.

Copyright © 2017, Charles W. Clark
ISBN: 978-0-9991009-1-2

Charles Clark Ministries
20923 E. Girard Dr., Aurora, CO 80013

Phone: 720-244-7732
www.aurorahillschurch.org

ENDORSEMENTS

The Church in America seems to have lost the purpose for which our Lord created it—to GO into the world and tell others about our Lord's love for them, and to proclaim His truth. The Church in America desperately needs a great awakening—revived vigor and boldness to stand for truth.

This timely book gives you some thoughts about how, when, and why God has moved in the past, and why God wants us on our knees praying for revival now. The Church needs to appropriate the authority that Our Lord has given us. It starts with you, the reader, asking God to revive you so you can be bold and proclaim the truth with love, with clarity and with boldness.

Steve Skelton
Founder and President
EKG Ministries
(Experiencing and Knowing God)

As an arm-chair theologian, I try to look between the lines of any book I read to see if there are flaws. *(Flawed theology, after all, is usually a matter of personal preference regarding one's particular bias.)* I didn't do that with Charlie's thesis. Instead, I read with an open heart to listen to his love for Christ, the passion for souls, and the conviction that we must have revival. It's all there.

After you read this book, you may choose not to become a concerned watchman on the wall. However, if you don't, it will not be because you are misinformed regarding the importance and need for Christians of every stripe to become intercessors for our nation. *When God Turns* offers a challenge to and a method for seeking God's face to reverse the course of destruction that faces the United States of America.

Proceed with determination.

Dr. Philip R. Byler.
Founder and President,
C.T.T.M. Ministries
(Coaching, Teaching, Training & Mentoring)

TABLE OF CONTENTS

Dedication vii

Chapter 1 When God Turns 1

Chapter 2 Personal Revival . . . . ,, 21
    Part 1- Approaching God 21
    Part 2 – Separating from Self 26
    Part 3 Maintaining Your Revival 48

Chapter 3 The Elements of an Awakening/Revival 51
    Part 1 – Recent History When God Turned 51
    Part 2 – Elements of Revival 57
        Element 1: Conviction 59
        Element 2: Repentance 61
        Element 2.5: Repenting for the Sins of a Nation . . . 64
        Element 3: Tearing Down Strongholds 68
        Element 4: Transformation 74
        Element 5: Passion for God 78
        Element 6: Prayer 86

Chapter 4 Waking up the Church 91

Chapter 5 Hurdles Facing a GreatAwakening/Revival 111

Chapter 6 Praying for an Awakening/Revival 151

Chapter 7 Equipping the Church for Revival 241

DEDICATION

For the past few years, Steve Skelton (ekgminitries.org)[†] and Terry Appel have met with me at noon each Tuesday to pray for a revival in the Church, and a great awakening in this generation. It was these times in prayerful discussion when many of the ideas in this book were developed. I appreciate their time and input, but what I really value is their love and friendship.

The congregation at Aurora Hills Church has heard me preach through the understandings of this book over the last three years. They have always encouraged me and blessed me, and I am grateful to them all for their support.

Beyond Jesus, what more can a man ask for than people who will stand with you and friends who will sit with you. We do life together.

My wife Jackie and I were fortunate to fall in love and stay in love. We live together and work together, and still we miss each other when we are apart for even the briefest of times. She has probably heard more about this book than she ever wanted to, but she always encourages me. It still amazes me how much she believed in me, even when nobody else did—even when I didn't believe in myself. If God is able to use me today, it has everything to do with how she stood by me through a 40-plus year growth curve.

She calls me a diamond in the rough. I call her priceless. I call myself blessed.

—CWC

[†] Steve Skelton's *ekgministries.org* is a website that is filled with resources for your church's outreach program.

CHAPTER 1

WHEN GOD TURNS

Occasionally, in the course of human history, God deliberately changes that course. Yes, I'm talking about divine intervention. Those specific times when God turns from judgment, punishment, and wrath, which would be the normal consequence of humankind's rebellion against him, and instead God forgives, and with loving kindness he reestablishes himself with people. He revives them and brings new hope. He turns from wrath, and toward mercy, and wonderful things happen when he turns.

But now let's go a step further. I want to consider something radical. Can a believer convince God to turn, to change from his stated course? Can an individual pray, or bring an argument before God, that would cause God to turn away from his current path and take a different direction?

CAN A PERSON'S PRAYERS CAUSE GOD TO TURN?.

My first thought is no. God doesn't change. He has determined in advance how all history will run, and he will not change it, period. God is all-knowing and all-wise. What could any human being ever say or do, that would cause God to redirect his plan? God effects humankind, but do humans effect God? We read in our Bibles about predestination and how God already knows who will choose to believe in him before they are born. No one can change that. Yes, we have free will, but God already knows how we will use it. For us it's a free choice, but God knew how we would choose before time began. How is it possible that anyone could ever talk God into turning?

My second thought, however, is, "I've seen it happen." I have read in that same Bible where people have made their case before God and he has changed course—He has turned! Stay with me, (even if you're a Calvinist) until I reach my conclusions. I think we will find common ground. But first let's look at a dramatic example from scripture where a man convinced God to turn.

In order to say for certain that God has turned from a particular course, we must first know for certain where God was going before he turned. How else can we claim that God has turned unless we know what He has turned from? Fortunately, sometimes, God makes things clear for us. Consider this example.

The scene is familiar to many believers. Moses is on Mt. Sinai. God has finished giving Moses the Ten Commandments, and the rest of the law, the plans for the tabernacle, and all the provision he will need to implement this massive undertaking of launching a formal religion for the Jews. But now God is angry. While he and Moses were meeting on the mountain, the Israelites, whom God had brought out of Egypt with all kinds of miracles, were now breaking all Ten Commandments, and Moses' brother Aaron had built a golden idol which they were worshipping whole-heartedly. Now God tells Moses what he will do about it, and we now get to know exactly what God plans to do.

> *"I have seen these people," the Lord said to Moses, "and they are a stiff-necked people. Now leave me alone so that my anger may burn against them and that I may destroy them. Then I will make you into a great nation."* (Exodus 32:9-10, emphasis added)

God doesn't lie. He was going to wipe out the children of Israel and start over with Moses the way he had once started with Abraham. The Israelites had been whining all the way from Egypt to the mountain. Now they're out of control with sin, and God is a few heartbeats away from their destruction. But Moses, who is known to lose his temper with these people too, instead intercedes for the people with a heart toward protecting God's name.

> *But Moses sought the favor of the Lord his God. "Lord," he said, "why should your anger burn against your people, whom you brought out of Egypt with great power and a mighty hand? Why should the Egyptians say, 'It was with evil intent that he brought*

> them out, to kill them in the mountains and to wipe them off the face of the earth?" (Exodus 32:11-14, emphasis added)

Respectfully Moses is arguing with God. He's making a case for why God shouldn't do what he just told Moses he would do. And now Moses delivers the line that sums up what he wants God to do.

> "**Turn** from your fierce anger; relent and do not bring disaster on your people."(vs. 12b)

This is the key verse, the request that a human makes to the one true God Almighty. Moses is bold yet humble, respectful and yet pleading in tone. He seeks God's best interest and he shows no ego toward becoming the next Abraham. He is lobbying for the life of an entire nation. He's asking God to turn! Then he continues his argument by reminding God of His promises.

> Remember your servants Abraham, Isaac and Israel, to whom you swore by your own self: 'I will make your descendants as numerous as the stars in the sky and I will give your descendants all this land I promised them, and it will be their inheritance forever.'" (vs. 13)

But would it work? Would God turn from wrath to mercy? Would God change the very course he had just stated? The next line tells us.

> Then the LORD relented and did not bring on his people the disaster he had threatened. (vs. 14)

Now, allow me to offer an explanation of what happened here between God and Moses.

First, I believe that God knew everything that was going to happen, and everything that would be said, on that mountain, long before it took place.

- ◆ God was not surprised by what Moses said.
- ◆ Moses didn't tell God something he hadn't thought of before.
- ◆ God knew that Moses would step up.

- God knew, going in, that he would relent.

Second – God doesn't lie, so I am also convinced that he fully intended to put an end to the children of Israel, except that he knew that Moses would talk him out of it.

So why did God go through this whole exercise with Moses if he knew it wasn't going to happen? Why does God orchestrate this confrontation when he knew he was going to relent? The answer is powerful!

You see, I believe that God wants everyone to see in this passage, that this is how God works with his people! He wants us to ask him to spare the lost. God wants us to plead for outpourings of his love and mercy on people who have only earned his wrath. God is looking for those intercessors who will boldly stand before him and cry out for Him to turn from judgment to revival, and for Him to bless those who would otherwise remain in the darkness of their thinking. This is the great lesson of the intercession of Moses, that God, who already knows when he plans to turn, nevertheless calls for his people to ask for him to turn. God wants the partnership. He wants us to participate with him in saving the people of this planet by learning to care about them and pray for them.

> **GOD WANTS US TO ASK HIM TO SPARE THE LOST.**

CONSIDER HUMAN PARENTS

How good does a parent feel when their older child asks them to help the younger child? It shows that they are growing up with a sense of responsibility and family.

Imagine for a moment that you knew that your Dad was about to spank your kid sister Sue for throwing something at your Mom. But you have decided to intervene on your sister's behalf. So you say, "Dad, could we talk about this spanking? Sue has really been struggling lately. Her friends have been mean to her and she feels terrible about herself right now. It just seems to me that this might be a good time to skip the spanking and just love her, and give her a chance to make it up to Mom." What parent wouldn't rethink things at that point, and feel pretty good about the older kid, too.

Of course, God knew what Moses was going to say before he said it. But God went through this to reinforce Moses as a caring leader of the people, and to show us that we should come to God and ask him to reconsider the direction he has allowed things to go, and to turn, and change things.

WHAT HAPPENS WHEN GOD TURNS

And what happens when God turns like this?

The Levites, who were the first to respond to Moses and return to the Lord when he came down from the mountain, became the priests of Israel.

Aaron, the one who crafted the golden calf, became the first high priest of Israel and officiated over the opening of the Tabernacle.

The one million plus people whose lives were saved, grew into a powerful nation that, forty years later, took the promised land and established Israel as a true and lasting nation.

Many great scholars, musicians, artists, and Bible teachers come from this nation, and much of the Old Testament is indeed their story and we are the richer for it.

Most important of all, Jesus was born into these people, and he launched his Church with the help of those few Jews who followed him as the Son of God and the Savior of the world.

This picture of God's turn in response to a pleading prayer is so important to God that he causes a similar scene to play out later in Moses' life, only this time with more details.

Again the Lord tells Moses of his intent to destroy the nation of Israel.

> The Lord said to Moses, "How long will these people treat me with contempt? How long will they refuse to believe in me, in spite of all the signs I have performed among them? I will strike them

> *down with a plague and destroy them, but I will make you into a nation greater and stronger than they."*
>
> *(Numbers 14:11-12, Emphasis added)*

This time we know exactly how God will destroy them, with a plague. And again Moses would become the father of God's new nation. But Moses is again determined to talk God out of it. And we get better details on how he talks with God.

> *Moses said to the Lord, "Then the Egyptians will hear about it! By your power you brought these people up from among them. And they will tell the inhabitants of this land about it. They have already heard that you, Lord, are with these people and that you, Lord, have been seen face to face, that your cloud stays over them, and that you go before them in a pillar of cloud by day and a pillar of fire by night. If you put all these people to death, leaving none alive, the nations who have heard this report about you will say, 'The Lord was not able to bring these people into the land he promised them on oath, so he slaughtered them in the wilderness.'*
>
> *(Numbers 14:13-16, emphasis added)*

Moses is seeking to protect God's reputation among the nations. He wants God to receive glory for all he does, not ridicule. Now, Moses uses God's own words, which is always a good way for believers to pray prayers that resonate with God.

> *"Now may the Lord's strength be displayed, just as you have declared:*[18] *'The LORD IS SLOW TO ANGER, ABOUNDING IN LOVE AND FORGIVING SIN AND REBELLION...' In accordance with your great love, forgive the sin of these people, just as you have pardoned them from the time they left Egypt until now."*
>
> *(Numbers 14:17-19, emphasis added)*

And God again turns from his stated plan, and instead relents, although he is now determined that Israel will wander in the wilderness for a time rather than taking this generation into the Promised Land.

WHEN GOD TURNS

The LORD replied, "I have forgiven them, as you asked." (vs.20)

The similarities of these two events in Moses' relationship with God, highlight and reinforce for us that God wants this kind of prayer and interaction with his children, his leaders, and his Church.

God established this idea, of asking him to turn when things were going badly, in a very direct way in the days of King Solomon.

The temple had been built when Solomon was a young king. It was built in accordance with the plans and the wishes of his father, King David. Right after Solomon had dedicated the Temple, he sent the people home with joy. That night God appeared to him and told him that whenever things were not going well for Israel, there was something they could do.

> *If my people, who are called by my name, will humble themselves and pray and seek my face and turn from their wicked ways, then I will hear from heaven, and I will forgive their sin and will heal their land.*   *(2 Chronicles 7:14, NKJV)*

Let's keep in mind that this promise was given to the nation of Israel, which was also a nation of people who believed in God. The nation and the faith were inseparable and no one could join this nation without converting to the faith and being circumcised—if they were males.

Today I often see Christians apply this scripture to praying for the nations in which they live. But what nation on earth today requires a person to be a Christian in order to join? None?

Therefore I'm not certain we can claim this promise of God for the nations in which we live. Our nations are political organizations, not religious organizations. But there is one nation on earth that is a religious organization, and they do require that any perspective members have to believe in their hearts and confess with their mouths that Jesus Christ is everything he says he is. Which nation am I talking about?

> *But you are a chosen people, a royal priesthood, a **holy nation**, God's special possession, that you may declare the praises of him who called you out of darkness into his wonderful light. Once you*

> *were not a people, but now you are the people of God; once you had not received mercy, but now you have received mercy.*
>
> *(1 Peter 2:9-10, emphasis added)*

I have come to believe that the promise God gave to King Solomon is still valid in these New Testament times. However, it applies not to political nations, but rather to the Church. We are a Holy Nation of people who are called by His name. I'm not saying that God won't answer prayers for the nations we live in. On the contrary, God expects us to pray for our political leaders, and that our nations will be blessed and protected by Him. But the promise of 2 Chronicles 7:14 is for that "Holy Nation", and the land that God will heal is the Church.

WE ARE A HOLY NATION CALLED BY HIS NAME.

With this understanding, the Second Chronicles promise reads, to me, like a call for Christians to pray and ask God to turn from spitting the lukewarm Church out of his mouth, and instead, heal us and revive us until we are on fire for the Lord. And certainly if the Church is revived and energized, then our countries will be impacted with a resurgence of God's love and power, and a new generation will awaken to salvation in Christ Jesus.

Before Moses, God had already given us a hint that he wanted to partner with His people in this way. Abraham once tried to ask God to turn from his wrath. God entertained Abraham's prayer and agreed with his argument to spare Sodom and Gomorrah. Abraham negotiated with God for a long time, and over and over again, God agreed to turn from wrath if Sodom and Gomorrah could fulfill the limited requirements that Abraham pleaded for. Ultimately God's wrath destroyed the cities, but still we see the strong evidence that God listens to prayers that beg him to turn from wrath.

> *The men turned away and went toward Sodom, but Abraham remained standing before the* Lord. *Then Abraham approached him and said: "Will you sweep away the righteous with the wicked? What if there are fifty righteous people in the city? Will you really sweep it away and not spare the place for the sake of the*

WHEN GOD TURNS

fifty righteous people in it? Far be it from you to do such a thing—to kill the righteous with the wicked, treating the righteous and the wicked alike. Far be it from you! Will not the Judge of all the earth do right?"

The Lord said, "If I find fifty righteous people in the city of Sodom, I will spare the whole place for their sake."

Then Abraham spoke up again: "Now that I have been so bold as to speak to the Lord, though I am nothing but dust and ashes, what if the number of the righteous is five less than fifty? Will you destroy the whole city for lack of five people?"

"If I find forty-five there," he said, "I will not destroy it."

Once again he spoke to him, "What if only forty are found there?"

He said, "For the sake of forty, I will not do it."

Then he said, "May the Lord not be angry, but let me speak. What if only thirty can be found there?"

He answered, "I will not do it if I find thirty there."

Abraham said, "Now that I have been so bold as to speak to the Lord, what if only twenty can be found there?"

He said, "For the sake of twenty, I will not destroy it."

Then he said, "May the Lord not be angry, but let me speak just once more. What if only ten can be found there?"

He answered, "For the sake of ten, I will not destroy it."

When the Lord had finished speaking with Abraham, he left, and Abraham returned home.   (Genesis 18:22-33, emphasis added)

You have to love Abraham's humble approach to God. Like Moses, he too was seeking to protect God's name and reputation. He didn't want injustice to be associated with God in any way. He knew that God was so just that he could avoid collateral damage, and Abraham hoped that for the sake of a few, God would relent.

Of course, in this case, God didn't find even ten who were righteous and the cities were destroyed. But the idea that God will listen to a believer who is trying to convince him to turn from wrath, is clear and evident. It seems unavoidable to me. God wants this kind of prayer.

Undoubtedly God's greatest turning began when he sent his son to earth. Israel had suffered long enough trying to keep God's Law. God had established His perfect standard, and the children of Israel had learned just how impossible it was to try to keep the law. So God turned and changed everything for good. He sent his son to establish a new and better path to salvation. About God's Law, Jesus said. "Do not think that I have come to abolish the Law or the Prophets; I have not come to abolish them but to fulfill them" (Matthew 5:17).

Because God turned in such a marvelous way, salvation would be God's free gift to those who believe in His son! Jesus would fulfill the requirements of the law by being the atoning sacrifice for sin, once and for all, on a cross.

But who was it that prayed for God to turn? The evidence shows that many in Israel were praying for a Messiah for centuries. If you want an example, here's one man in scripture who was apparently believing very strongly for God to turn and for Jesus Christ to come.

> *Now there was a man in Jerusalem called Simeon, who was righteous and devout. He was waiting for the consolation of Israel, and the Holy Spirit was on him. It had been revealed to him by the Holy Spirit that he would not die before he had seen the Lord's Messiah. Moved by the Spirit, he went into the temple courts. When the parents brought in the child Jesus to do for him what the custom of the Law required, Simeon took him in his arms and praised God, saying:*
>
> *"Sovereign Lord, as you have promised, you may now dismiss your servant in peace. For my eyes have seen your salvation, which you have prepared in the sight of all nations: a light for revelation to the Gentiles, and the glory of your people Israel."* (Luke 2:25-32)

Simeon wasn't the only one with such a hope and prayer, and certainly, like all of God's other turns, this one had been planned since before the beginning of time. No doubt most Jews of that time were praying for a political and military Messiah who would crush the Roman occupation and give them national freedom. But Simeon seemed to understand that "the Lord's Christ" was about freedom from sin and spiritual salvation, and not just for the Jews, but also for the Gentiles.

TURNS THROUGHOUT HISTORY

This greatest of all turns fuels the Church today. But was this the last big turn of God's, or should we still pray for him to turn? I've already stated that I believe God's promise to Solomon is still valid for the Church today, but what is the evidence that God still turns from wrath to mercy under this new covenant secured by the blood of Christ?

God again changed the course of the world when, of all things, Rome dramatically ended the worship of "the gods" (Zeus, Athena, etc.) and declared Christianity to be the religion of the state! Christians who famously hid in the catacombs were allowed above ground. Christians, who had often been executed, now found themselves in favor. As this awkward marriage between Rome and Christianity worked itself out, the Church had to find it's footing as a legitimate worldwide organization. This eventually led to the establishment of the Roman Catholic Church as well as other Orthodox Christian groups.

> **THIS GREATEST OF ALL TURNS FUELS THE CHURCH TODAY.**

LUTHER

God turned again when Luther launched the Protestant Reformation by nailing his ideas to the Church door. Although Protestant denominations began to flourish in parts of Europe, and over the decades, some countries changed their religion of state from the Catholic Church to various denominations like the Church of England, Europe also experienced a number of religious wars which were driven by the inevitable clashes between Catholics and Protestants.

WHEN GOD TURNS

JOHN AND CHARLES WESLEY

By the early 1700s, many people in Europe were put-off by religious fervor so much that they withdrew from any passionate pursuit of God, and they kept their faith at arms-length. They made faith into an intellectual pursuit, but society largely shunned people who got excited about God and Jesus. God had become, for many, a large impersonal power who had little impact on how they lived.

With this state of affairs in western civilization, which at that time was the home of Christianity in the world, let's look at how God turned and re-established himself in the lives of people in Europe and also in that soon-to-be country, America.

Passion had left the Church. Christianity had become academic. Personal relationship with God was not a goal. Miracles, the Holy Spirit, being sold-out for Jesus, sharing the faith—these things were shunned even by most Christians. Then God turned.

It happened on May 24th, 1738 at a Moravian meeting at Aldersgate Street, London. A frustrated and depressed theologian and pastor who had been sued by a member of his last congregation and was forced to flee back to England, was suddenly and miraculously touched by God. He described it this way.

> "In the evening I went very unwillingly to a society in Aldersgate Street, where one was reading Luther's Preface to the Epistle to the Romans. About a quarter before nine, while he was describing the change which God works in the heart through faith in Christ, I felt my heart strangely warmed. I felt I did trust in Christ, Christ alone for salvation, and an assurance was given me that he had taken away my sins, even mine, and saved me from the law of sin and death."

John Wesley had just found salvation in Christ—he was born again, and the Evangelical movement had begun. Later he would say this about the Aldersgate experience.

> "By a Christian, I mean one who so believes in Christ, as that sin hath no more dominion over him: And in the obvious sense of the

word, I was not a Christian till May the 24th last past. For till then sin had dominion over me, although I fought with it continually; but surely, then, from that time to this it hath not; – such is the free grace of God in Christ."

Wesley and his brother Charles would become the founders of the Methodist movement, the first evangelical denomination, and this movement of passion for God and commitment to walk in the way of Jesus would go against the flow of European culture until their influence grew to reshape the direction of western civilization.

John Newton

On March 10th, 1748, the captain of a slave ship had seen his ship nearly sunk off the coast of Ireland. But when he prayed, the cargo shifted covering a hole, stopping the leak, and the ship drifted calmly to safety. So on March 10th, Captain John Newton experienced an evangelical conversion to Christianity. (Yes, he's the one who wrote *Amazing Grace* with a friend.)

William Wilberforce

But God was far from done. The influence of evangelical Christianity, with it's flair for the miraculous and an uncanny ability to pull truth and logic out of the pages of the Bible, eventually reached the doorstep of a hard partying young genius of a British politician, William Wilberforce.

Wilberforce's mother and grandfather had raised him to refrain from any enthusiasm for the Christian faith, even though he had lived for a few years with an Aunt and Uncle who were Methodists. Like most of the wealthy and elite ruling class of Europe, he too held Christianity at armslength and disdained the cheap emotionalism that he believed to be at the basis of the Evangelical/ Methodist movement.

However, Wilberforce took a long cross-country trip with another genius, Isaac Milner, who had been headmaster of Wilberforce's grammar school. But now Milner had risen to become the most famous and popular professor at prestigious Cambridge University. Wilberforce was amazed and disappointed to find out that his old teacher was not just a born again

Christian, but he was also a well-armed Christian apologist who, over the weeks of their journey, totally destroyed every argument that Wilberforce could generate. By the time he returned to London, Wilberforce had experienced his own evangelical conversion.

It took two years for Wilberforce to recant his former life of drinking, gambling, and frequenting gentlemen's clubs, and to connect with God so that he could understand what God wanted him to do.

Wilberforce met with an old acquaintance, John Newton, whom he had seen at his Aunt and Uncle's house as a boy when he was away from home for a time. Newton convinced him to remain in politics and see how God might use him. Of course Newton was an abolitionist—opposed to slavery.

Finally, Wilberforce knew what God wanted and he wrote these words in his journal, "God Almighty has set before me two great objects: the suppression of the Slave Trade and the Reformation of Manners." Wilberforce would spend his life being true to this call.

By reforming manners, Wilberforce meant reforming society. The disconnection that so many people had with God, meant that people did not live with Christian values. In his book "7 Men" Eric Metaxas writes about the plight of English culture in the time of Wilberforce. He makes these points.

- 25% of all single women in London were prostitutes.
- 5 year olds worked 10 to 12 hour shifts in factories.
- Public hangings and dissections were common.
- Alcoholism was epidemic.
- Prison conditions were atrocious.
- Cruelty to animals was unchecked.

Wilberforce set out to change all this through new laws, and by influencing people as he could, to live and act in more humane and Christian ways. He wanted the love of Jesus to touch his world and heal it. So he prayed, he lived the example, he recruited many others to join him, and he fought with all his considerable talent to change the laws.

To this day, William Wilberforce, and his considerable allies, are credited with:

- Abolishing slavery in the United Kingdom, and influencing much of the rest of Europe to do the same.

- Founding the Society for the Prevention of Cruelty to Animals.

- Improving working conditions for textile workers and chimney sweeps.

- Passing Child labor laws.

- Outlawing dueling.

- Supporting the formation of Sunday schools for children in poverty, which would eventually lead to public education.

- Advancing prison reform and restrictions on capital punishment.

- Founding the Royal National Lifeboat Institution.

- Founding the Society for the Suppression of Vice.

- Founding the Church Missionary Society which sent the very first missionaries into foreign lands to evangelize.

- Writing into the Charter Act of 1813 that the British East India Company would be required to provide teachers and Chaplains to improve the lot of Indians and offer salvation.

This implanting of a Christian conscience in European society and western civilization as a whole (*and America, thanks to those preachers and reformers who carried it here*) had an amazing impact that we still experience today. Before this move of God, the great charities we see today like the Red Cross and the Salvation Army did not exist. But through the Evangelical movement, God made "goodness fashionable".

Now many governments serve their people, and many countries have programs for the poor and sick. Churches are so often involved in charitable works. These things were largely unseen in the world prior to this turn of God. And when God turned in the 1700s, the wave of people who began to return to the love of God and the practice of Christianity changed the world for good.

WHERE FROM HERE?

So where does all this scripture and documentation take us?

We live in a time when western civilization has not seen God turn for almost two generations. Yes, there have been churches, and even regions, that have experienced revival. The underground Church in China seems to be growing mightily, and many parts of Africa have seen awakenings in the last century. But the primary audience I write to has not seen this phenomenon in our lifetime.

> **IT'S TIME TO SEE GOD TURN ONCE AGAIN.**

I don't want to just read about it, I want to see God turn, and I want to influence anyone I can to join me in praying those prayers that God wants. Let us be the next generation to see a turn of God, because we asked.

It's time for the Church to be revived. It's time for our generation to come alive with the life of Christ. I'm not waiting any longer. I'm in, and I pray that you are too. It's a long term investment that will change the face of our nations, and dramatically add to God's family. If it's good enough for Moses, it's good enough for me.

Of course, the rest of this book is aimed at inspiring and growing our understanding so we can prepare and pray with all possible wisdom. Let's pray.

WHEN GOD TURNS

PERSONAL THOUGHTS ON PRAYING FOR GOD TO TURN—

- On what I believe—

I believe it's time. I believe that, as we ask, God will turn from the wrath our nations deserve, show mercy, destroy the enemy's plan, revive His Church, and awaken this generation. I believe it's inevitable. And, I believe that we need to pray for it and prepare for it.

- On who needs prayer—

Let's consider, who is in danger of being destroyed by God today?

Well, billions are in danger of spending eternity in hell.

America and Europe lead the world in some good ways, but we also lead in pornography. We are slowly legalizing drugs and prostitution. We've already legalized adultery. (That's right! It used to be against the law.) Families are falling apart and addictions are growing. People are becoming more and more dependent on governments, and not on Jesus. So our nations could use some prayer.

Christians are quickly being eradicated in parts of the Middle East. Jesus said to pray for our enemies, so we could intercede for those who hate us over there, not to mention those who are being systematically wiped out.

The Church is losing influence and effectiveness. Our divorce rates are the same as non-believers. Missionaries are returning home for lack of funding. Many believers fail to grow in their relationship with God because they lack the discipline and the desire to pray, read their Bibles, fast, and give.

Will God just ignore all this? I think his wrath is building.

- On Numbers—

Sometimes, like with Moses, it seems that God turns on the prayers of one person. Other times, like with the coming of Jesus the Messiah, hundreds of thousands were praying. I'm not too worried about numbers, but I am asking you to join me and pray and prepare.

A Poem

How fortunate are the people who know what God will do
They will not wilt for lack of vision
Nor will they boast in their understanding
They need not shout about it to make it come true
Nor will they be silent.

They speak with a determined assurance
As the sun burns high in a cloudless sky,
they can hear the rain coming
And they pray for it
When they finish praying
They are wet
God has never asked them to waste time

- ◆ On Old Age—

At age 65, I realize I have come to a point in my life where, most of the time, I do what I want to do. More importantly, most of the time, what I want to do is what God wants me to do.

Maybe the greatest advantage of age is the taming of vice;
Or—

Maybe the greatest advantage of age is the refinement of purpose;
Or—

Maybe the greatest advantage of age is the accumulation of wisdom.

I have learned that humility is better for the soul than self-esteem. I do not trust me, but I do trust God to work through me.

Age has the potential, through all of these things, to complete faith. It's not a guarantee, but it can happen.

Abraham demonstrated his greatest act of faith, offering his son to God, at age 113.

WHEN GOD TURNS

John wrote his Gospel and the Book of Revelation toward the end of a long life.

Maybe the worst thing to do in old age is to waste time.

I hope to flunk retirement and remain true to this great purpose for all my life—to beg you, God, to turn.

I know you, God, I know you love me and I love you

Your love is defined by sacrificial actions. I am seldom that good.

But I give you this—I give you my time

THE MAN WHO CAN GET BELIEVERS TO PRAYING WOULD, UNDER GOD, USHER IN THE GREATEST REVIVAL THAT THE WORLD HAS EVER KNOWN.

—LEONARD RAVENHILL
Why Revival Tarries

CHAPTER 2

PERSONAL REVIVAL
PART 1
APPROACHING GOD

I would like for you to have something—your own awakening—your own personal revival. I'm not talking about your salvation. I'm talking about you, the believer who is reading this book. I want you to have more. I want you to be revived and renewed in your faith, and more connected to Jesus than ever. I want you to step into the everyday newness of intimacy with God through Jesus by the Holy Spirit. I'm not trying to judge or insinuate that your walk isn't what it should be, but if you are a true believer in Jesus, then you always want more, and I want you to have it. But what I want is unimportant. What God wants is important, and He always seems to want more too. Paul said that he was always trying to take hold of that for which God had taken hold of him. Paul seemed to know that God always had more for him. (See Phil. 3:12)

(*If you are not yet sure of your faith, please keep reading. Although this chapter initially is addressed to believers, I will come around to your salvation.*)

How can we approach God with faith in hand and with assurance of his response for a turn that will impact this generation if we ourselves are not in revival? Moses had to meet God on the mountain before he could bring Israel to God on the mountain. Paul had to encounter Jesus and believe before he could reach others with the Gospel message. If you are to ask God to revive his Church and awaken a generation, you need to be revived and awake.

Most believers want more of God. We really want intimacy with Him, to genuinely share life with Him. So it seems important for you to have revival yourself.

Be open. Accept challenges. Lead with what you already know about God, and then lean in close. It's what God wants. Why else would God call us His children, and Jesus call us his friends, and along with the Spirit they choose to dwell with us? It must be that God longs for closeness with you. Getting close is everything once you're saved. Don't miss it. Receive it.

(Author's note: Some of this section is devoted to pushing back on sin in your life, becoming less selfish, and making more room for God in your life. Self- examination and repentance are wonderful when they come to us naturally out of our love for Jesus and an overriding desire to move some of our baggage out of the way so we can know Him better. But if you take these things on as a duty, a goal in and of themselves, then you could get trapped in endless cycles of effort and failure, feeling successful one minute, and then crashing when a sin returns the next minute. The goal is not a sin free you. Jesus has already done that. The goal is more of your awareness and connection with Jesus in you. As you consider these points that lead to your personal revival, don't get bogged down if you feel convicted to make some changes. Jesus will always work in your heart, and the Holy Spirit will bring you the power to do it. Remember, the process also brings us closer together with Him. Don't try to improve alone. Wait for the God of heart change. With God, all things are possible. Without God, why try?

I have put other warnings in this chapter because it is so important that you keep your priorities straight, and keep the balance. So let me explain the balance of the Christian walk that helps us to grow in Christ. Here is a common model of how some believers view the process of change in the lives of Christians.)

Change is the goal of the Christian faith, and Jesus is the mechanism of positive change in believers.

This idea has some truth in it, but the ultimate goal is not for a believer to change. The ultimate goal is to know Jesus intimately and completely as Savior, Brother, Friend, and Lord. With this model, Jesus only exists to make <u>you</u> a better person. It becomes all about you, and not Him. Yes, believing in Jesus changes us for the better, but given a choice between changing a bad habit, and knowing more of Jesus, I'll take Jesus every time.

This leads us to a second model.

Jesus is the goal of the Christian faith, and change is the mechanism that brings us closer to him.

Again, this model has some truth in it, but it has caused so much unnecessary pain and wasted effort by Christians who believe that if they change enough, then they can earn more of Jesus. And again, the definition of grace is undeserved, un-earnable, unmerited favor from God. We can't earn more of Him through our efforts. The door to Jesus was opened wide when we first believed and it will not close.

The partial truth here is the reality that as sin retreats in our lives, we do tend to experience more of Jesus. But sin doesn't retreat because we try, it retreats because God in us pushes it out, throughout our lifetimes. The most we can do is cooperate.

> *For it is **God** who **works** in you to will and to act in order to fulfill his good purpose.* (Philippians 2:13, emphasis added)

This brings us to the best model I can generate from my years of following Jesus and studying his word.

More of Jesus is the goal of Christianity. Our love for him and our desire to serve him is the mechanism that draws us closer. The massive changes that occur in our lives as a result of pursuing Jesus are merely a simple by product of that pursuit. These changes are not the goal or the mechanism.

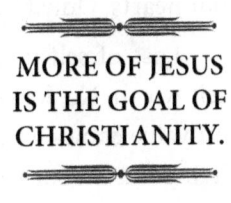

MORE OF JESUS IS THE GOAL OF CHRISTIANITY.

It is so easy to get this one turned around. As you consider things like repentance, sin, being less selfish, and making room for God, remember this model. Hang on to the motivation of love and desire for him and resist the "clean-up-your-act" mentality of trying to earn him, as well as the "Jesus-exists-to-make-me-wonderful" way of thinking.

Unfortunately, the Church has often mistakenly used fear and guilt, as well as offers of worldly recognition and promotion, in the effort to get believers to change. If we could just model love, service, and the desire to know him better, then we would be motivating the way Jesus intends.

- Fear only works as long as the threat remains.
- People grow to resent guilt and rebel against it.
- Worldly recognition and promotion simply feeds pride.

Only the love of Jesus brings about the life God desires in us. Love is by far the greatest motivation, but it takes longer and it requires that both the teacher and the student love Him.

(As you apply this model of love motivation to your walk, you will grow closer to Him. Because we are human, it's not perfect, but it is the way God wants it to work. Amen)

THE LOSS OF SELF

Loss of selfishness is a most difficult and elusive goal to attain. People we admire who have spent their lives blessing others seem to have found it. It is the last and greatest step in personal sanctification. (Sanctification is the walk of becoming more holy, more like Jesus) Only after we have found that place of the loss of self, can we truly walk in the "Kingdom of God" in our hearts. Only then may we be Spirit led.

Loss of self does not mean the loss of our personal identity or our self-worth. No, loss of self is a stepping into the realization that our greatest value comes when we stop living for ourselves, and humbly submit to living this life for Jesus – the one who paid for it. But even though he paid the price for your life, he will not forcibly take it. We must humbly offer it. We must choose to follow. We must pick up our cross, die to self, and follow him. In our weakness, he is at his strongest in us. This is no longer self-worth, this is selfless-worth.

But he said to me, "My grace is sufficient for you, for my power is made perfect in weakness." Therefore I will boast all the more

> *gladly about my weaknesses, so that Christ's power may rest on me.* *(2 Corinthians 12:9)*

Your personal revival, oddly enough, is not rooted in you becoming "great" at all. You see, when God revives, there is an exchange taking place. First he gave his life to save yours, now he wants you to exchange your old life for the life He has for you. So personal revival doesn't make you great, rather it gets you out of the way so He can be great in you.

Let's look further at this exchange.

SPIRITUAL CPR

When a drowning victim stops breathing we perform CPR on them. We force the heart to pump and we breathe air into their lungs. When God revives us, he breathes his life and Spirit into us. The drowning victim isn't dead, but they will die unless their breathing and pulse are revived in them. And we are not dead, but we may be lukewarm, carnal, and compromised, baby believers who are stuck in arrested development until God revives our lives by breathing more of His life and Spirit into us. This puts the old life to death by the Holy Spirit, and revives us to live His life for us—to do the good works he planned for us to do since before the beginning of time!

For someone who has never known Jesus before, the exchange is your mortal life for the immortal life that God gives us as His children.

Jesus' words and teachings exhort people to live amazing lives—vital, purpose-filled lives, dynamic lives filled with both trials and successes. So, why does the Church often seem so common and just like the rest of the people in the world?

Answer: We need revival too! Three days after Jesus' death on the cross, God revived His son, and Jesus was resurrected from the dead. Revival literally means, to bring life back into that which is dead or dying. (The resurrection of Jesus is the greatest revival of all because we can all share in it.) Now, full of resurrection/revival power, Jesus appears to his disciples and immediately pours that revival power into them. Jesus said:

> *As the Father has sent me, I am sending you. And with that He breathed on them and said, "Receive the Holy Spirit."*   (John 20:21-22)

Then he gave them authority to share salvation with others.

This was spiritual CPR! This was personal revival for those men. They went from defeated, depressed, hopeless disciples without a teacher, who had just witnessed the destruction of the Son of God on a cross, to a revived band of evangelists who would soon take the known world for Christ in their generation!

But don't believers get this same Holy Spirit in them when they are first saved? Why do Christians need revival?

PART 2
SEPARATING FROM SELF

FANNING THE FLAME

There was a very young man named Timothy. Paul, who helped to lead the awakening of the New Testament in the Bible, saw himself as Timothy's "Spiritual Father" (See: 2 Tim. 1:2). Paul often sent Timothy to the most difficult churches in the toughest mission fields, because he saw in Timothy a reliable student with the ability to overcome great problems and lead people toward Jesus.

Timothy was a believer, filled with the Holy Spirit. But toward the end of Paul's life, when he knew that the emperor Nero would soon have him executed, Paul wrote an urgent last letter to Timothy. Sensing that the young pastor was burning out and in danger of losing his effectiveness, Paul urges his beloved protégé to pursue personal revival. Paul writes:

> *Fan into flame the gift of God, which is in you by the laying on of my hands. For God did not give us a spirit of timidity, but a spirit of power, of love, and of self-discipline.*   (2 Timothy 1:6)

PERSONAL REVIVAL

Paul took Timothy back to a time when Paul had participated in seeing the Holy Spirit move powerfully in Timothy's life. Paul knew that Timothy could always go back to that certainty, and rekindle it. If you are saved, you have those moments too. To have a personal revival, go back to those moments! Rekindle them. Blow on the flames of the great times when the Spirit infused you with a gift, or when Jesus brought a surprise provision, or when you thought you were alone but He showed up on your side. You know those times. Only you know them. They are personal, and holy, central to your love and growing faith in God. Revisit them, fan them into flame and walk with the strength they provide. It's part of your personal revival and Jesus tells us all to do this.

> **REKINDLE THE FLAMES OF YOUR PAST EXPERIENCES WITH GOD.**

> *But I have this [charge] against you, that you have left your <u>first love[you have lost the depth of love that you first had for Me]</u>. So remember the heights from which you have fallen, and repent [change your inner self—your old way of thinking, your sinful behavior—seek God's will] and <u>do the works you did at first [when you first knew Me];otherwise, I will visit you and remove your lampstand (the church, its impact) from its place—unless you repent.</u>* (Revelation 2:4-5, AMP, underscore added)

Jesus and Paul both tell us that love motivated change comes from the heart, and sometimes we need to go back to when things were strong in our hearts, and build on that truth and that love that once was strong in us, and can be again.

Here in Colorado, every year we have forest fires, and sometimes they come from a campfire that someone thought was out. But, when the wind comes up and the embers blaze again, thousands of acres are burned. You have a forest fire of love and strength in you. So heed the words of Jesus and return to your first love and do the works you first did. This is a strong way for you to step into your own personal revival.

Here, too, we can see that personal revival is not just for the new believer who just found Jesus. It is also for the strongest of believers when they are struggling and fading. Most all of us have blown on the coals of a fire to revive it. And here is our picture of personal revival—to fan into flame the coals of the deposit that God has placed in us. Also, in Paul's picture of revival from Second Timothy, we see the elements of the control of self, the love of God, and the power of the Holy Spirit working in concert as we apply love inspired effort.

So what does it mean to fan the flame of the Spirit in you? It means to get alone for a moment and focus on Jesus and the Holy Spirit in you. Recall... remember them and how they have touched you before. Dwell on those moments in the past when God demonstrated himself to you, when the Holy Spirit moved in your heart, when you first saw Jesus on the cross with your sins on him, when he brought light and love into your darkness. Now apply your faith in Jesus, and your trust in the Holy Spirit to move and draw near to you.

Every Christian needs this intimacy. Wait upon the Lord in remembrance and expectation and be filled with his presence and love. Jesus wants you to remember those times, that's why in the communion service, we quote Jesus' words: "Do this in remembrance of me." (See 1 Corinthians 11:24) We're just getting started.

Reconnecting with Jesus by dwelling on past closeness, and waiting expectantly for more, is fanning the flame. King David practiced remembering God when he was feeling lost and empty.

> *My tears have been my food day and night, While they say to me all day long, "Where is your God?" These things <u>I remember</u> and I pour out my soul within me. For I used to go along with the throng and lead them in procession to the house of God, With the voice of joy and thanksgiving, a multitude keeping festival.*

PERSONAL REVIVAL

Why are you in despair, O my soul? And why have you become disturbed within me? Hope in God, for I shall again praise Him for the help of His presence. (Psalm 42:3-5, NASB, underscore added)

What an incredible inner conversation David's spirit has with his soul. He is remembering the good times with God from his past, and then he says to his soul, "Why are you in despair?" David remembers, and his spirit is ready to go back to praising God, so he chews himself out for being sad. His memories turned him around. He fanned the flame of the deposit God had left in him from earlier times. All Christians have these times, and we must remember them and fan them back into powerful existence within us.

QUIETING THE VOICE OF SELF

There are many ideas in the world today that are well intended, but they often, accidently, feed our own selfishness. For instance, we are taught from childhood to be independent and strong when it comes to peer pressure. "If everyone else jumped off a cliff, would you jump too?"

The implied answer of course is "no". But the rest of the implied answer is "You're too smart for that. You can handle the peer pressure and make your own judgments about what to do with your life. Don't let anyone tell you what's the right thing or the wrong thing to do. You can decide for yourself what's right and wrong for you."

Hidden in all of these affirmations of yourself is the message that you are the most important thing in your life, and you should live your life based on what's best for you. We've all heard these kinds of philosophies that promote self over everything else, because parents and teachers want everyone to have positive self-esteem and a good self-image. The unintended consequence, however, is that we come to believe that we should live for self and believe in self above all else.

"If you can conceive it, and you can believe it, then you can achieve it!" One famous man who promoted this thinking ended up cheating on his wife. His adult son was recently arrested for stealing money.

THE VOICE OF SELFISHNESS IS LOUD!

The voice of selfishness becomes loud. In this inner landscape of self, our appetites lobby strongly, and we try to rely on our self to manage them. But these appetites <u>are</u> us! How long can a self-empowered person say no to self? It is unavoidable that we become selfish, self-centered, and always seeking self-satisfaction.

If you want personal revival, then you may need some help to quiet the voices of selfishness.

Many of the religions in the world today recognize the need to contend with the voices of self. They promote various techniques to quiet the self. Some claim that if we stop eating for a while, we can tame an appetite and learn about self-denial. Some meditate for hours at a time, mastering the voices of self while they empty themselves of all thought, or achieve an "out of body" experience. Some just block out these voices by chanting on and on over the top of them. The fatal flaw in these approaches is that, again, they are trying to use self to control self, and as we have already seen, self only briefly, if ever, says no to self.

It's true that Christians also meditate, fast, and sing, but we don't do these things to simply quiet the voices of self. We use them to slow our lives down so we can reconnect with God, who is the only true source of power over self.

Since our help in quieting the voices of selfishness cannot come from ourselves, how do we get help?

It is God who revives us. It is God who quiets the voices of selfishness. Here is how he does it.

> *For if you are living according to the [impulses of the] flesh, you are going to die. But if [you are living] by the [power of the Holy] Spirit you are habitually putting to death the sinful deeds of the body, you will [really] live forever.* (Romans 8:13. AMP)

The Holy Spirit, in this passage, clearly has the power to help us push back on our sin. We need to appropriate this power by taking deliberate actions against our sin, like turning our back on it, not going there, throwing it out, confessing to an accountability partner, and setting boundaries for ourselves. Also, it is sometimes effective to verbalize this power—to speak out loud this truth. Sometimes I will speak to my sin by simply saying, "I put this (name the sin) to death by the power of the Holy Spirit." In doing this we confess our sin and acknowledge the Holy Spirit's power over it. This kind of practical faith in God's word brings results.

MAKING ROOM FOR GOD

The Holy Spirit is the agent of your personal revival. As we have just seen, the Spirit has the power over self. Therefore revival must involve the constant infilling of the Holy Spirit. But don't Christians already have the Holy Spirit? How can we be revived by the Spirit we already have while we need revival? What made the Spirit go dormant in us?

The truth is painful to hear.

Over time, we grieve and quench the Holy Spirit in our lives until we become insensitive to him. We ignore him, and do what we want until we get used to not paying attention to the promptings and pleadings of the Spirit. It's that simple, and it devastates our spiritual growth.

> *And do not grieve the Holy Spirit of God, with whom you were sealed for the day of redemption. Get rid of all bitterness, rage and anger, brawling and slander, along with every form of malice.*
> *(Ephesians 4:30-31)*

Here in Ephesians is a laundry list of things the Holy Spirit is ready to deal with in the human heart if we will not fail to heed the Holy Spirit and cooperate. We grieve the Spirit when we keep doing these things and refuse to use His power to put sin to death in us.

> *Do not quench the Spirit. Do not treat prophecies with <u>contempt</u>.*
> *(1 Thessalonians 5:19-20, underline added)*

God speaks to us through his Holy Spirit, but when he doesn't say what we want to hear, when he tells us what to do and we refuse to do it... that's contempt.

Simply put, grieving the Holy Spirit is, doing what he tells you not to do, and quenching the Holy Spirit is, failing to do what he tells you to do.

When these two things happen for long enough inside us, then we become insensitive to the Holy Spirit. His voice retreats to the background, and the voices of self, get louder. Your conscience may be at risk of being seared. It's like a scar that heals over but has hardened and lost all feeling.

> *Such teachings come through hypocritical liars, whose consciences have been seared as with a hot iron.* (1 Timothy 4:2)

Is this what's happening in you? Are you disconnected from the Spirit because it's been so long since you followed Him in the tougher areas of your life? There is a solution.

Your personal transformation begins now with repentance. It begins when you are convicted that you should be living a life closer to God, a life more within his will. Personal revival becomes more likely in us when we recognize the specific areas in our lives where we resist God. Then we ask for God's help, turn our backs on that old behavior by the power of the Holy Spirit, and walk away from it and toward Christ.

PERSONAL TRANSFORMATION BEGINS WITH REPENTANCE.

When we do this, we have made more room for God, by moving out the old furniture of our sin lives. So have a garage sale and let God get rid of all that old stuff you don't need any more. If you're just not sure where to start, the Holy Spirit will help with that too. He is the one who will convict you of what needs to go.

> *And He (the Holy Spirit), when He comes, will convict the world concerning sin.* (John 16:8, NASV, parenthesis added)

Initially this statement refers to the sin of not believing in Jesus, but the sins of believers are also dealt with through conviction. In fact, it should come easier to us because we have the Spirit in us. It is in resisting the sin of this world that we begin to be able to hear and understand God's will for us.

PERSONAL REVIVAL

> *Therefore, I urge you, brothers and sisters, in view of God's mercy, to offer your bodies as a living sacrifice, holy and pleasing to God—this is your true and proper worship. Do not conform to the pattern of this world, but be transformed by the renewing of your mind. Then you will be able to test and approve what God's will is—his good, pleasing and perfect will.* (Romans 12:1-2)

Here we can see the principal of making room for a believer's revival clearly. If we will deny self and live sacrificially for God, following the promptings of the Holy Spirit, turning our backs on the sinful parts of worldly living, and allowing God, through his Word and his Spirit, to change the way we think about these worldly things, then we come closer to God and we begin to know his heart and walk with Him in his will for us.

What a tremendous opening this creates for God to move in a person. (Or a church, or a nation)

> *(I must step aside here for a minute, because we are in dangerous territory. One of the classic temptations of the Christian faith is to develop a "works" mentality. This means that we can begin to think that if we try hard enough, we can earn God's blessings—we can give great effort, perform at a high level, and deny ourselves in ways that will please God and cause Him to favor us more, and then He will give us the blessings we need and want. But the wonderful, yet hard to accept truth is, God's favor—His grace—is unmerited and un-earnable. It absolutely can't be earned, because He gives it freely to all who believe in His Son.*
>
> *So if we already have everything God gives, if we have God's undeserved unmerited free grace and favor, and his unending love and his blessings, why should we try so hard to deny self?*
>
> *Answer: because we love Him, because we want to serve Him, because the most meaningful life we can live is the one He has for us, and not the selfish life we would otherwise live. The Bible says "God's kindness leads us to repentance." (Romans 2:4) That's why we deny ourselves, pick up our crosses, and follow the one we love.*

*So don't think to yourself, "I'm going to do this, and then I will be great in the Lord, and I will be fulfilled." Instead, think like Paul, who wrote, **"I want to know Christ"**—yes, to know the power of his resurrection and participation in his sufferings, becoming like him in his death (See: Philippians 3:10).*

Jesus was the first to die to self and Paul wanted to be like Him in that death. This is the desire of a mature Christian. Not to be great or successful or even powerful, but simply to know Jesus by being more like Him. And the more we are like him, the less we are like the old self.)

MOVING FROM SELF TO SOMETHING MORE IMPORTANT

True personal revival is much more than turning from sin and making more room for God. The joy and the goal of personal revival is intimacy with God, the experience of his love, power, and glory, and passion for a life of service that flows out of that increased closeness.

The Apostle Paul, wrote much of the New Testament, and is credited with taking all that Jesus did and taught, and developing around it the theology and practice of the Christian faith. Yet Paul, who was an active grown man when Jesus was preaching and teaching and crucified and resurrected, apparently never saw Jesus. In all of Paul's writings, he never mentions seeing Jesus before that time when he met the risen Christ on the Damascus road, five years after Christ's death on the cross.

Evidently Paul was so consumed with pursuing the chaste life of a Pharisee, in an attempt to gain God's favor by meticulously keeping every detail of the Law of Moses, that he missed God's own Son as he passed by in close proximity.

What a shock it must have been when Jesus appeared to him, and he realized that all of his efforts to be perfect were worthless, because he had

PERSONAL REVIVAL

failed to recognize what God was doing, and who Jesus is. But once Jesus found him, Paul's life became the model of personal revival.

If we consider Paul's writings chronologically, we see that he grew in humility and away from pride and self over the years, and he grew in his passion to experience his relationship with Jesus.

(Most historians place Jesus' death and resurrection in the Spring of 32 A.D., Paul's encounter with Jesus in 37 A.D., and Paul's death was 30 years later, around 67 A.D. Here is a chart of the dates when Paul's letters were written. By knowing when he wrote, we can measure the growth of humility in him, and his loss of self-importance.)

First Thessalonians	52 AD
Second Thessalonians	52 AD
First Corinthians	57 AD
Second Corinthians	57 AD
Galatians	55-57 AD
Romans	57-58 AD
Ephesians	62 AD
Philippians	62 AD
Colossians	62 AD
Philemon	63 AD
Hebrews	64-65 AD
Titus	64-65 AD
First Timothy	64-65 AD
Second Timothy	66-67 AD

Look at the way Paul refers to himself over the years of his ministry with ever greater humility. He journeys from being least among the Church leaders to presenting himself as the worst of all sinners.

WHEN GOD TURNS

1 Corinthians 15:9 – 57 A.D.

For I am the <u>least of the apostles</u> and do not even deserve to be called an apostle, because I persecuted the church of God. (underscore added)

In this early letter, Paul places himself just below the most revered leaders of the early Church. He has some humility, but see how it grows in the books to come.

Ephesians 3:8 – 62 A.D.

Although I am less than <u>the least of all the Lord's people</u>, this grace was given me: to preach to the Gentiles the boundless riches of Christ. (underscore added)

In five years, Paul's ideas about himself have lowered considerably. Although he is now a strong leader in the Church, he sees himself as the Church's lowest member.

1 Timothy 1:15-16 – 64-65 A.D.

Here is a trustworthy saying that deserves full acceptance: Christ Jesus came into the world to save <u>sinners—of whom I am the worst.</u> But for that very reason I was shown mercy so that in <u>me, the worst of sinners,</u> Christ Jesus might display his immense patience as an example for those who would believe in him and receive eternal life. (underscore added)

In eight years, Paul went from being the least of the apostles, to the least of the Lord's people, to being the worst of all sinners! This is not just humility, it is the continuing loss of self. Again, repentance and turning toward Jesus and away from self is just the launch point of personal revival. It's our relationship with God, through Jesus, by the power of the Holy Spirit that brings the overwhelming joy, drive, and commitment, which are the hallmarks of personal revival. Here is how Paul describes it.

PERSONAL REVIVAL

PHILIPPIANS 3:7-14 62 A.D.

But whatever were gains to me I now consider loss for the sake of Christ. What is more, I consider everything a loss because of the surpassing worth of knowing Christ Jesus my Lord, for whose sake I have lost all things. I consider them garbage, that I may gain Christ and be found in him, not having a righteousness of my own that comes from the law, but that which is through faith in Christ— the righteousness that comes from God on the basis of faith. I want to know Christ—yes, to know the power of his resurrection and participation in his sufferings, becoming like him in his death, and so, somehow, attaining to the resurrection from the dead.

Not that I have already obtained all this, or have already arrived at my goal, <u>but I press on to take hold of that for which Christ Jesus took hold of me.</u> Brothers and sisters, I do not consider myself yet to have taken hold of it. But one thing I do: Forgetting what is behind and straining toward what is ahead, I press on toward the goal to win the prize for which God has called me heavenward in Christ Jesus. (underscore added)

Here then is the complete picture of Paul's personal revival. It's the sold-out, all-in idea of faith, where we hold no area of our lives back from God. All is dedicated to him, and our experience of his presence with us is maximized. This is not self–denial for the sake of demonstrating discipline. This is setting self aside for the goal of experiencing ever more of the God who made us, and the Savior who saved us, and the Spirit who spreads his Love all through us.

Do you not want this revival? Do you not want to fan the flame of your relationship with Jesus Christ, the Almighty Son of God? He is the King of Kings and Lord of Lords, who also happens to call you his brother and personal friend? Do you not want all that you can know of Him? Do you not want God to turn, in your personal life, and take you in a new direction, which will be closer to him and his will for your life?

(And I reiterate. I don't want to suggest that we can earn more of God in our lives. Please don't think that you should conquer your sin problem, and then God will reward you with more of himself. It's really the opposite. God wants into your life. He's already in love with you, and he wants the satisfaction of living with you. In fact, for believers, God's already totally in our lives. However, our ongoing infatuation with pleasing ourselves blinds us to his presence and love. Oh for the personal revival that would sweep away self, and leave us in Christ alone, at the foot of the throne of something greater and more important than us—at the threshold of meaningful purpose and in silence before his majesty and glory.)

YOUR REVIVAL COMES FIRST TO YOUR HEART

I have come to believe that our hearts are the closest part of us to God. Would you consider opening your heart to God to receive more of His love, forgiveness, encouragement, and power? It's what God gives to his children. Give me just a moment to explain.

I'm not talking about your physical heart, and, I'm talking about more than just the seat of your emotions. I'm talking about your spiritual heart, which is sometimes spoken about as very close to your own spirit. This spiritual heart is spoken of powerfully by an Old Testament prophet. Here, the prophet quotes God.

> *I will give you a new heart and put a new spirit in you; I will remove from you your heart of stone and give you a heart of flesh. And I will put my Spirit in you and move you to follow my decrees and be careful to keep my laws.* (Ezekiel 36:26-27)

GOD IS MOST CONCERNED ABOUT THE CONDITION OF PEOPLE'S HEARTS.

God is always most concerned about the condition of the hearts of people. A person's good heart is everything to God. So in this scripture, God makes a promise for the future, that he will put a softer heart in his people, which will not be hardened toward Him.

PERSONAL REVIVAL

And, He promises to put His own Spirit in them. This is the promise we live in today. Believers are filled with the Holy Spirit. We see this half of God's promise coming true at the very beginning of the Church when the very first believers accept Jesus as Lord and Savior. Peter had just preached the first sermon ever in the Christian Church era, and he finishes with this altar call.

> *Peter replied, "**Repent** and be **baptized**, every one of you, in the name of Jesus Christ for the forgiveness of your sins. And you will receive the gift of the Holy Spirit.   (Acts 2:38, emphasis added)*

Since this day, this is the truth for believers. We get the Holy Spirit when we believe in Jesus, the very Son of God.

But how does our new heart happen? Consider these heart scriptures

Peter is testifying in Acts 15 how he has seen God give salvation to non-Jews, (which the disciples hadn't really understood even though Jesus had said that his salvation would be for all nations.)

> *God, who knows the heart, showed that he accepted them (non-Jews) by giving the Holy Spirit to them, just as he did to us. He did not discriminate between us and them, for he purified their hearts by faith.   (Acts 15:8-9, parenthesis added)*

A purified heart sounds like a "new heart". These gentiles have just received the promise that God made back in Ezekiel's time of a new soft heart and God's indwelling Spirit. It was so hard for these disciples to grasp it at first.

Paul really understands the new heart and he writes about it often.

> *(God) set his seal of ownership on us, and put his Spirit in our hearts as a deposit, guaranteeing what is to come.*
>   *(2 Corinthians 1:22, parenthesis added)*

The relationship between God's Spirit and our heart is undeniable. This is why our hearts are closer to God than even our minds. Paul continues.

> *For God, who said, "Let light shine out of darkness," made his light shine in our **hearts** to give us the light of the knowledge of God's glory displayed in the face of Christ.*
> *(2 Corinthians 4:6, emphasis added)*

The very light of Jesus, who calls himself the light of the world, is in our hearts. There is no other part of us that is so filled and touched by God. And still Paul adds even more.

> *I pray that out of his glorious riches he may strengthen you with power through his Spirit in your inner being, so that Christ may dwell in your **hearts** through faith.*
> *(Ephesians 3:16-18, emphasis added)*

We have always known that the Father and the Son come to us, when we believe, and they make their home with us (See: John 14:23), but the question was, "where in us do they dwell?" Now we know - Jesus lives in our hearts. Jesus lives in your heart. If Christ revives you, it must start in your heart.

These are pictures of how God keeps the promise in Ezekiel of giving us a new heart. The relationship between our spiritual hearts and the Holy Spirit and Jesus is unmistakable.

If you study the heart throughout the New Testament, you will find that, before salvation, the human heart is deceptive, and the seat of all kinds of wrong thoughts and actions. At other times, the word heart is used in phrases like, "take heart" or "don't lose heart." But if you study particularly the relationship between the Holy Spirit and our own spiritual hearts, I believe that you will discover that our hearts live closer to God than any other part of us. Therefore, when God wants to give us something, it often comes to us from Him into our hearts. This is never more true than when it comes to God's love for us. He downloads it into our spiritual hearts!

PERSONAL REVIVAL

> *And hope does not put us to shame, because God's love has been poured out into our hearts through the Holy Spirit, who has been given to us.* (Romans 5:5)

It seems that our hearts are the conduit of the things of God for us. The spiritual gifts are handed out by the Holy Spirit, and Paul tells us to eagerly desire them. Do we not desire them in our hearts?

The fruit of the Spirit—love, joy, peace, etc.—seem to be things most at home and most appreciated in our hearts. Our conscience, a crucial part of our spiritual heart, was cleansed from guilt by our faith in Jesus.

> *Let us draw near to God with a sincere <u>heart</u> and with the full assurance that faith brings, having our <u>hearts</u> sprinkled to cleanse us from a guilty <u>conscience</u> and having our bodies washed with pure water.* (Hebrews 10:22, underline added)

In fact, our hearts are of such supreme importance to God that He has made our hearts to be the center, the birthplace, the home, of our saving faith in Jesus.

> *But what does it say? "The word is near you; it is in your mouth and in your <u>heart</u>," that is, the message concerning faith that we proclaim: if you declare with your mouth, "Jesus is Lord," and <u>believe in your heart</u> that God raised him from the dead, you will be saved. For it is with your <u>heart</u> that you believe and are justified, and it is with your mouth that you profess your faith and are saved.* (Romans 10:8-10, underscore added)

This is the definition of salvation. All eternal life is decided by the heart condition of humankind. We are not capable of saving faith unless it comes from our hearts. Oh, we can believe things in our minds—logical things, patterns and predictions, technical things, math, science, philosophy, and psychology. But Biblical faith stretches us beyond what is predictable, and requires us to believe in the love of God and his promise of eternal life through His Son. This eternal life will happen in a place we've never seen, with a God we've never seen, and a Son few have ever seen, and a Spirit we cannot see. But in our hearts and our lives, we have seen and felt the evidence, and we believe. Only the spiritual heart inside us can do that.

> *Now **faith is** confidence in what we hope for and assurance about what we do not see.* (Hebrews 11:1, emphasis added)

If revival is God breathing more of Himself into us, if revival is a stronger than ever download of God's love and grace, if revival is embracing the fact that Jesus Christ lives in your heart, if revival is going to inspire and drive and call into being God's life-giving Church in each of its members, then it must come into your heart.

That's right, YOUR heart, the one that has been broken more than once. The one that's sometimes a bit afraid of believing for too much. The one that doesn't quite understand why God does what He does. Your heart, it's a good heart. God gave it to you. It's still soft. It still has the capacity to believe, even for revival—especially for revival.

RESTORATION PRAYER

Here is a prayer I hope you will pray. It's aimed at shoring up brokenness, and restoring the pathway, so the heart can be revived, and get back to receiving all of the things of God.

"The Lord is my shepherd", but God, I still want. I want more of you. I want to feel your touch and hear your voice in my heart. I want closeness Lord, closeness to you. I want.

"He maketh me to lie down in green pastures", but lately Lord I've lost the ability to see colors in my heart. What would make those pastures sparkle green again would be to return to those first days when my heart swelled with your love as the waters of baptism surrounded me, and I knew I was yours and you were mine. No pasture is green until you manifest yourself in my heart again. Less of you is unbearable. More of you is the only thing.

"He leadeth me beside still waters. He restoreth my soul." Oh that the water of life would well up inside of me so that I might thirst no more. Then I would be restored. Then, everything in my life would have meaning.

PERSONAL REVIVAL

"He leadeth me in paths of righteousness for His name's sake." That's right God. For the sake of your name revive me. I am a Christian. I am called by your name. Heal me. I am your child – grow in me.

"Yea though I walk through the valley of the shadow of death, I shall fear no evil, for thou art with me." There are no guarantees in this life Lord. I could go to be with you at any time. I don't doubt my salvation, but I don't want to live another day without growing closer to you, starting now. I know you are with me, but please, don't be invisible. Let me know you.

"Thy rod and thy staff, they comfort me." The rod of correction is your word God, and I will spend more time knowing you there. It comforts me, and so does the staff of your leadership. When I look back I can see that my life has followed your plan, but I wish we had somehow shared it more openly. The rod and the staff together form the cross, which is the basis of all I believe. I do feel that in my heart.

"Thou preparest a table before me, in the presence of mine enemies." Perhaps I've been too slow in believing for your provision when life has turned hard and my heart has been wounded. Perhaps now I could find the faith to celebrate you even while my enemy, the devil, looks right at me. That would be really strong Lord.

"Thou annointest my head with oil. My cup runneth over." I need to be refreshed in the Holy Spirit. I haven't listened to Him as well as I should. It's time to start. The anointing of your call and your Spirit runs like oil down the sides of my head. I will not take it for granted. And I do know your love, and the love of so many you have given to me in this life. Truly my cup runneth over.

"Surely goodness and mercy shall follow me all the days of my life." I'm beginning to feel it Lord. I'm beginning to understand. Every good thing I have ever known in this life comes from you! You have always been that source of goodness. If only the world could see it. And, you have always been there to forgive me—for everything, and put me back together. I will always love you for that.

"And I shall dwell in the house of the Lord forever." I guess I don't have to wait until I die—forever starts today. I'm in. I'm already in! I'm in your house Lord, I'm in your temple, I'm in your Church, I'm in your heart. It's like Jesus said, I'm in you and you're in me, forever. This is everything I need. It's all I want. I'm back. I never left, and yet I'm back. And you, God, are real and true and faithful and good. I belong to you, and you belong to me. After all, I never wanted a personal revival because I earned it. I want this personal revival because that's how much you love me. Amen." (Based on Psalm 23, KJV)

Sometimes it's easy to receive a gift, other times it takes faith to receive it. When God gives you a gift, (like personal revival) you don't have to have faith in the gift. You only have to have faith in the giver to receive it. Here's proof.

*And with that he **breathed** on them and said, "Receive the Holy Spirit."* (John 20:22, emphasis added)

The disciples were still reeling with joy at Jesus' sudden appearance among them, when Jesus, out of nowhere, blasted his Spirit into them. They didn't have time to believe in the gift. It just came to them and they received it because they trusted and believed in the giver. It changed them forever.

You also trust and believe in the Father, the Son, and the Holy Spirit, so receive your personal revival now, in your heart. Feel the flow of God's gentle yet powerful love, and all of the blessings of God as the gradual parade enters your heart and fills all of you. Let your mind be piqued with a thousand new thoughts, and let your soul be at rest in the completeness and certainty of God's plan. Soon enough, you'll begin to walk in the calm assurance that God is tangibly with you, and you have grown closer to Him. This is your personal revival. Receive it.

I want you to have revival for yourself. I pray for you to have it. Christians always want the rest of the world to have what we have because it blesses us so. So I have decided that you have come to this point in my book and you should now have revival.

Will you <u>hope</u> for it now?

PERSONAL REVIVAL

> *But those who <u>hope</u> in the LORD will renew their strength. They will soar on wings like eagles; they will run and not grow weary, they will walk and not be faint.*   *(Isaiah 40:31, underline added)*

Will you ask for it now?

> *"<u>Ask</u> and it will be given to you; seek and you will find; knock and the door will be opened to you.*   *(Matthew 7:7, underline added)*

Will you believe for it?

> *If you <u>believe</u>, you will receive whatever you <u>ask</u> for in prayer.*
>   *(Matthew 21:22, underline added)*

It's not like we're asking for something outside of God's will. Praying that we might experience a revived heart and spirit are central to what God does. We are simply asking God to be God. This is the appetite He wants us to have, and it's the thirst that Jesus died to quench by providing for us living water.

Because you are the righteousness of God…

> ***God*** *made him who had no sin to be sin for us, so that in him we might become the **righteousness of God**.*
>   *(2 Corinthians 5:21, emphasis added)*

…you are at peace with God,

> *Therefore, since we have been justified through faith, we have **peace with God** through our Lord Jesus Christ. (Romans 5:1)*

…and you may have this revival in your heart and spirit.

> *His divine power has given us **everything we need** for a godly life through our knowledge of him who called us by his own glory and goodness.*   *(2 Peter 1:3, emphasis added)*

I need this revival in me, and I need you to have it too. Ask for it now in hope and faith and receive it even right now.

> *Now **faith** is confidence in what we **hope** for and assurance about what we do not see.*   *(Hebrews 11:1, emphasis added)*

What's happening in your heart right now is the miracle of the Christian faith. You are claiming your relationship with your heavenly Father as his child. You know this is true in your spirit, in your heart where Jesus lives.

> The **Spirit** himself **testifies** with our **spirit** that we are God's children. (Romans 8:16, emphasis added)

Remember earlier in this chapter how Paul Told Timothy to fan the flame on the spiritual gift he had received earlier in his life, so he could use what God had given for ministry and not try to do things on his own strength? You are now fanning the flame on the greatest spiritual gift of all – your relationship with God as one of his children. Now blow on those embers, which have been there in your heart since the day you were saved.

> (This next part is for those who wish to accept Jesus into their hearts for the first time. The rest should proceed to "Maintaining Your Revival".)

BELIEVER'S PRAYER OF SALVATION

If you have never taken that step of accepting Jesus Christ, the Son of God, as your personal Savior and leader, then this prayer is for you. It's important to remember the scripture Romans 10:8-10 that we just looked at a few pages earlier.

It simply says that you must believe in your heart and confess with your mouth that Jesus is who he says he is—the Son of God who died on a cross for the sins of all humankind, and was resurrected both physically and spiritually from the dead. You must believe that He lived a life free from sin so he could qualify to die for the sins of others, because he had no sin of his own to die for. You must accept, (usually with great joy) that he died for your sin too.

Here are two questions for you.

(1) **Do you believe these things in your heart?** Can you hear that voice inside you saying these things about Jesus are genuine and true? Do you know inside yourself that Jesus is the truth?

PERSONAL REVIVAL

(2) Are you ready to confess that you believe these things?

If you are, you can read this prayer aloud, and you will have confessed with your mouth what you believe in your heart, and you will be saved. You will have eternal life with Jesus in heaven. You will receive the Holy Spirit in you. Your conscience, which feels the weight of your sin, will be washed clean. You will be born again spiritually, receive a new heart that is open to God, and you will be a new creation spiritually as a child of God.

Jesus, I believe in you and I say so right now. In my heart I know that you are the Son of God and you died for my sin. Be my Savior from this day forward. I devote myself to following you.

I receive the Holy Spirit within me, and I realize that I am made new spiritually. Help me Jesus to grow ever closer to you throughout the days of my life here, and rest me in the assurance of my salvation into eternal life with you.

Thank you, Jesus. For the rest of my life I will say, Thank You Jesus.

SALVATION POEM

Take my heart, O Jesus, tender. All my life to thee surrenders.
Take my body, mind, and soul, Mold me into someone whole.
May each step I take be yours, You love unlocking all the doors.
My strength will be my courage, And devotion be my drive,
And love will keep me open, And make me be alive.
And if I gain one ounce of love For every time I fall,
Then Lord, it won't be long 'Til I'll have love to share with all
So take me, break me... make me yours
Forever and always dear Lord, I am Yours

Now, friend, if this is your initial salvation, then be sure to find a life-giving church with patient and challenging teachers. Learn about Jesus, prayer, and the Bible. A good church will be constantly teaching all three. Don't go on alone, or you'll get picked off. The enemy of Christians is ultimately the devil. He will often attempt to discourage you, so get going in a fellowship near you. They should help you and protect you.

PART 3
MAINTAINING YOUR REVIVAL
"IT'S A RELATIONSHIP"

God sometimes warns me not to develop a big romantic idea about how a revival/awakening will be a panacea of wonderfulness. He's telling me not to think that this next big revival/awakening is going to solve every problem and bring the Church and the nations back into the Garden of Eden where there will be no more death, or sickness, or tears, or division between people. I get that. But I do tend to think how great it will be.

> **REVIVAL MAKES GOOD THINGS POSSIBLE.**

So what God will often say to me is, "Revival doesn't make everything good, revival makes every good thing possible."

Your personal revival has established a flow of the things of God into your heart from the Holy Spirit. It's filling you up, but that flow is based on your renewed relationship with God. We humans are notoriously bad at maintaining strong relationships. Here are some ideas on how to keep on fanning the flame of your relationship with God.

It's no coincidence that roughly half of all marriages end in divorce, and roughly half of all people who get saved and join a church fade out and stop attending. We come into the Christian Faith often the same way we come into a marriage;

- with high hopes,
- lots of love,
- stars in our eyes,
- thinking about how good life will be now.

There's a famous phrase about newlyweds. "The honeymoon is over." It describes that time in every marriage when the husband and wife realize that this marriage is going to be a lot of work. This same thing happens to new believers, and newly revived believers, when we realize that our relationship with God is going to take time, effort, and commitment. But knowing God, knowing Jesus, and knowing the Holy Spirit is so worth it. And one thing you have going for you is how much God wants to maintain this relationship with you. Here are some thoughts about maintaining your relationship with God.

When I write a book, I am most interested in what my wife thinks about it more than anyone else. So, since the Church is the bride of Christ, read His book, and tell him what you think about it.

Converse with God in prayer, have a talk. Share your heart, and let Him share his. You can learn to hear Jesus in your heart.

> *My **sheep** listen to my **voice**; I know them, and they follow me.*
> *(John 10:27, emphasis added)*

Get closer to your faith. Do you save your faith for the BIG needs of your life, but carry the little worries on your own? Don't you know that all the little things are practice for the big things? Have faith in God for all things. Without faith it is impossible to please Him.

> *And without **faith** it is **impossible** to please God, because anyone who comes to him must believe that he exists and that he rewards those who earnestly seek him.   (Hebrews 11:16, emphasis added)*

Honor God by doing some good deeds in his Name.

> *Live such **good** lives among the pagans that, though they accuse you of doing wrong, they may see your **good deeds** and glorify God on the day he visits us.   (1 Peter 2:12, emphasis added)*

Declare your love for God often, in prayer, in worship, in writing, and by loving others.

> *He answered, "'Love the Lord your God with all your **heart** and with all your **soul** and with all your strength and with all your **mind**'; and, 'Love your neighbor as yourself.'"*
> *(Luke 10:27, emphasis added)*

WHEN GOD TURNS

My prayer is that you have now experienced the beginning of your own personal revival. And that now, with all of that flow you are experiencing in your heart, you too will pray for God to turn from the direction he has allowed things to go. That He will turn from wrath to mercy, revive his Church, and bring and awakening to this generation of truth and light and love, which will win the lost and sow them into His family.

CHAPTER 3

THE ELEMENTS OF AN AWAKENING/REVIVAL

PART 1
RECENT HISTORY WHEN GOD TURNED

Is revival a good word? Is it still a vital contemporary word, or does it have a "back in the day" connotation to it? Does it conjure up the "Bible belt tent meetings" of the last century, and harken back to the golden age of denominationalism? If we live in a post-denomination age, (and I'm not convinced that we do), did the idea of revival die with it?

Or does the word revival still engender hope for a future moment when wave after wave of salvation would again sweep across continents and invigorate the Church.

Certainly history has seen great awakenings. In fact, they have come in all sizes and rather regularly from the beginning of the protestant reformation until the middle of the 20th century. Now a generation has grown up not knowing a revival or an awakening in western civilization.

We hear that the Church is spreading underground in China, and that it continues to grow, despite persecution in many parts of Africa. But the last great revival to hit North America was 110 years ago.

Here is a quote from the front page of the *Denver Post*. The date is Friday, January 20, 1905. And the headline reads:

**"ENTIRE CITY PAUSES FOR PRAYER
EVEN AT THE HIGH-TIDE OF BUSINESS
AS THE SOUL RISES ABOVE SORTED THOUGHTS"**

Here's how the article begins:

> For two hours at mid-day, all Denver was held in a spell. The marts of trade were deserted between noon and two o'clock this afternoon and all worldly affairs were forgotten.
>
> And the entire city was given over to meditation on higher things. The Spirit of the Almighty pervaded every nook. Going to and coming from the great meetings, the thousands of men and women radiated this Spirit which filled them.
>
> And the clear, Colorado sunshine was made brighter by the reflected glow of the light of God shining from happy faces. Seldom has such a remarkable sight been witnessed," (and the article continues,) "an entire great city in the middle of a busy weekday bowing before the throne of heaven and asking and receiving the blessing of the King of the Universe.

A few months earlier, in 1904, Atlanta newspapers reported the same revival sweeping through their city. On November 2, Atlanta also saw stores, factories, offices, saloons, and even the Supreme Court of Georgia, close their doors so people could attend noon prayer meetings.

Following this great revival, virtually the entire population of Atlantic City, New Jersey became practicing Christians.

CAN IT HAPPEN NOW?

What about today, here, now? Can revival happen? Well, with God, all things are possible. But what's the likelihood that God will bring revival?

A study of the revivals of the past 300 years indicates that they don't occur in response to any particular set of circumstances. They have happened in times of peace and prosperity, and in times of war. They have happened around missionaries in regions of China, and they have jumped from town to town in South Africa. They often launch in one place, and

THE ELEMENTS OF AN AWAKENING/REVIVAL

then spread. But sometimes they stay put. Revivals never seem to have grown out of a church's careful planning, efforts, and investment.

There is, however one thing that does precede revival – fervent, expectant prayer. Every awakening's beginning can be traced to at least one person who believed that God was ready to move, or turn, and they began to pray for it. These prayers are often all consuming prayers that go far beyond the believer's normal prayer life, and persist until the expected event occurs.

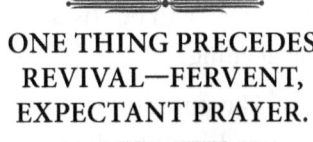

ONE THING PRECEDES REVIVAL—FERVENT, EXPECTANT PRAYER.

In a world of sound-bite media, instant gratification, and the technology of immediacy, the real question is—will anyone pray like this. We need people who know God's heart, people who can be certain of what they pray for.

> *I looked for someone among them who would build up the wall and stand before me in the **gap** on behalf of the land so I would not have to destroy it, but I found no one.*
> *(Ezekiel 22:30, emphasis added)*

I believe there are still those in our land who will stand in the gap and pray for revival from a position of assurance. Elijah was such a man. He had prayed for the rain to stop and it had stopped for three years. It was a draught that paralleled Israel's spiritual draught. When the foreign gods had been defeated, He knew the rain was coming even though there wasn't a cloud in the sky. The Bible says that he "heard the sound of heavy rain." So Elijah began to pray for what he knew was coming.

My purpose in writing is to stir up the hope and the prayers of God's people for revival in His Church, and an awakening in this generation. We must refocus our thoughts toward seeking God for an outpouring of conviction and connection with him, so that vast numbers of people living in darkness can again see a great light and enter into a saving relationship with Jesus and his Church. And, so that the Church itself will come alive and be the loving, committed, powerful servants we are called to be.

GOD'S PURPOSE

But when God brings revival to his Church and an awakening to the lost, what will be His purpose for doing so? Why does God want a revival/awakening?

The purpose of a great awakening speaks to the very purpose of all human life. Why did God create the universe and place humankind in it? What is God's primary purpose for us? What is His end game?

Fortunately, God has told us what will ultimately be achieved.

> *And I heard a loud voice from the throne saying, "Look! God's dwelling place is now among the people, and he will dwell with them. They will be his people, and God himself will be with them and be their God. He will wipe every tear from their eyes. There will be no more death or mourning or crying or pain, for the old order of things has passed away.* (Revelation 21:3-4)

Can we see in this passage that God's ultimate goal is a family of people whom He loves, and who love Him? But this is not any random group of people who happen to be hanging around at the time. This is God's Church, the bride of Christ. These are the people who, while living in God's creation, believed in God. These are the people who fell in love with Jesus.

The whole story goes like this:

- ◆ God wanted to live in love and closeness with people (Adam & Eve).
- ◆ God created everything to be perfect for this relationship.
- ◆ Instead, people chose to sin, and all creation became corrupted.
- ◆ God still wants a family, but he cannot lower his perfect standard to accommodate sinful humans.
- ◆ God's creation is now filled with all kinds of attractive temptations that entice people away from God.

THE ELEMENTS OF AN AWAKENING/REVIVAL

- God gives humankind his law, and they struggle mightily trying to follow it.
- God knows that those few people who choose to love Him, from all the other distractions in creation, will not be perfect.
- So God sends his Son to pay the price for the sins of those who choose to love Him.
- People who believe in Jesus are set free from their sin by Him, and God's family grows greatly under this new arrangement.
- At some time in the future, God will get rid of the corrupted creation, and make a new heaven and earth, and there He will live in harmony with the people from throughout all time who put their faith in him.

If God's purpose is to have a family of people who choose to love Him and believe in Him, then God's purpose for an awakening must be to draw people to himself and add to that family.

One thing more, God doesn't want to wait until the end of time to enjoy His family. He wants the closeness now! He doesn't even want to wait until we die and go to be with him. He wants the closeness now!

*And hope does not put us to shame, because God's **love** has been poured out into our **hearts** through the Holy Spirit, who has been given to us.* (Romans 5:5, emphasis added)

So, not only does God add new members to his family in dramatic fashion during an awakening, but he also inspires and draws deeper into his love, the members of his Church who are not nearly as close as He wants.

If awakenings were just conviction and repentance, then we might think that their purpose is our obedience. But conviction and repentance are just a way of quieting our worldly selves down so we can focus on the things of God.

We were created to love God, and to love His Son, and join their family, and be filled with their Spirit. And in doing all this, we get to be transformed into His likeness.

*And we all... are being **transformed** into his image with ever-increasing **glory**, which comes from the Lord, who is the Spirit.*
(2 Corinthians 3:18, emphasis added)

The fact is, God really loves all people, and he never wants anyone to be kept away from him by their sin. God wants a loving and saving relationship with all people. He says so often in his word.

BACK IN THE DAY

When I was young, social media consisted of:
- Paper and pencil (for the mailman or note passing).
- A telephone attached to the wall of our kitchen which shared a line with other households who could listen in if they dared. (Hillcrest 3-3376).
- A black and white TV with 3 channels ABC, CBS, & NBC.
- An AM radio – people could call-in and request songs.
- And, my Dad had a friend with a HAM radio. He could talk to people around the country and send telegraph messages.
- Boomers were united worldwide by the common experience of watching the exact same TV shows and listening to the same top 40 tunes.

Millennials are united by real-time communication—but only with the people they choose to connect to. In a larger sense, the common experience of the technology itself unites them. Millennials play many different video games, and use many different forms of social media, but they all know the controllers, the phones, the pads and lap-tops, the apps, the sites—the whole tech-media apparatus.

THE ELEMENTS OF AN AWAKENING/REVIVAL

Today, social media is overwhelming to me. Here are the few things I can do. If you don't see it on my list, then you can assume that I can't do it, and I may have never heard of it.

I can:

- Call on the cell phone.
- Receive and send texts.
- Word process on the computer.
- Send and receive emails.
- Draft and operate a fantasy football team (ESPN).
- Search the internet.
- Operate Bible Gateway's website.
- Use the "around me" app and play "Angry Birds."
- Play solitaire on both computer and phone.

That's about it. Your list is probably too long to be worth making, but my point is, when the entire concept is just too big to take in, it helps to break it down into small pieces. Revival is a broad concept, and each revival has it's own unique flavor and purpose, but there are certain elements that revivals have in common. Let's look at them, understand them, and apply them to ourselves, our churches, and our world.

PART 2
ELEMENTS OF REVIVAL

LIFE FROM DEATH

The actual word "revival" means life returning to something that has died or is dying. This is the wonderful hope we have, because this is what God does. And this is such a great hope because it applies to our weakest circumstances, and our "worst-case" scenarios. We can't "earn" revival, in fact, it seems to come when we most need it and least deserve it—when we are dead and dying inside.

WHEN GOD TURNS

Example:

In the mid 1800s the South African Church was dead. Churches were declining in attendance, lacking in commitment, and failing to connect and relate to the communities they were supposed to be serving. They had lost the ability to influence their culture.

On May 27th 1860, Andrew Murray, a young pastor just starting out, attended an inter-church conference held in Worcester, South Africa. By all accounts, Murray's prayer at that event immediately launched a revival that swept the country, filling churches as it went, forcing them to offer multiple services, and reenergizing the members, inspiring them to new heights of service. Obviously, Murray was simply a vessel of what God was prepared to do.

Later, Murray wrote this about revival. "Most would prefer to have a revival as the result of their programs and efforts. God's way is the opposite. Out of death, acknowledged as the wage of sin, and confession of utter helplessness, God revives."

I have served in some large churches that grew even larger because they offered a better product than the churches around them. They had the best music, children's ministry, small groups, facility, etc. They challenge every church to do better, but their growth is not revival. They mostly grow by drawing in the saved from other churches.

> **REVIVAL HAPPENS WHEN THE CHURCH, THE INDIVIDUAL, OR THE NATION IS BROKEN.**

Revival happens when the Church, or the individual, or the nation, is broken and they cry out.

I live in a high and holy place, but also with the one who is contrite and lowly in spirit, revive the spirit of the lowly and to revive the heart of the contrite. (Isaiah 57:15b)

Here is the heart of revival in the church. This is the awakening I believe in, the one I pray for. And I believe this is what God will bring. This is what you need. This is what the world needs. But what does it look like when God revives a person's spirit and heart? We've talked

THE ELEMENTS OF AN AWAKENING/REVIVAL

about it in "Your Personal Revival", but now let's apply it to the Church, while adding the other elements that are necessary for non-believers.

ELEMENT 1: CONVICTION

In virtually every addiction recovery program, the first step is for the addict to admit they have a problem. Evidently denial is our most basic human reaction to wrong-doing and the criticism that comes with it. It's a faulty, and a clumsy coping mechanism, but it's always our first line of defense, because no one wants change pushed upon them.

There are reality shows devoted to filming "interventions" where the family and friends of an addict confront them and try to persuade them to stop the denial and get help. It doesn't always work, but without the addict's genuine conviction and admission that a definite problem exists, change never even starts.

All mankind has a sin condition, and Jesus is the cure. First, however, we have to be convinced of our sinful nature, and then we must know that God will judge sin harshly, and therefore we begin to desperately need a Savior.

Unfortunately, we Christians often make the mistake of thinking it's our job to convince people that they are sinners. Cartoonists draw pictures of us in holocaust cloaks holding signs that say "sinner, repent", or, "Repent! The end is near". Nobody wants to listen to some mean old man pointing his finger in their face and yelling, "You're going to hell if you don't stop sinning".

Let's remember that God wanted Adam and Eve to eat from the tree of life, not the tree of the knowledge of good and evil. But since Adam and Eve just had to know, all mankind knows what sin is, and we tend to beat each other over the head with it. We love to point the finger and expose sin. We should oppose sin strongly in our own lives, but the Bible says to gently correct another.

The offer of salvation should be a life-giving presentation, and we can speak from the tree of life if we will stop doing God's job and just do ours.

WHEN GOD TURNS

It is God's job, or more accurately the Holy Spirit's job, to do the convicting. Jesus made this clear.

> *When the Helper (the Holy Spirit) comes, he will prove to (convict) the people of the world the truth about sin, about being right with God, and about judgment. He will prove to them about sin, because they don't believe in me. He will prove to them that I am right with God, because I am going to the Father. You will not see me anymore. And the Helper will prove to them the truth about judgment, because the ruler of this world is already judged.*
> (John 16:8-11, ICB, parenthesis added)

No one intervenes better than God. He orchestrates our lives in ways that leave us face to face with our need for a Savior. We who believe, have all felt the conviction and the weight of our sin upon us, and the great release of it as Jesus entered our lives.

The conviction of the Holy Spirit is the first evidence of revival. It explains what has happened in our hearts, and it explains how thousands can become convicted in a single meeting. Peter preached the first sermon of the Church age, and 3,000 came to Jesus. Was Peter that good, or was the Holy Spirit just doing what Jesus said he would do. I heard a pastor say once that Billy Graham could sneeze and ten thousand people would come to the Lord. How much is it Billy Graham, or any other preacher, and how much is it the Holy Spirit?

The New Testament Church saw the Holy Spirit convict people wherever they went with the life-giving message of the gospel. In the Old Testament, we look at the great revival when Elijah was God's prophet. Here too the people were convicted, of their sin of worshiping the false god Baal, by God's power, not Elijah's.

> *Then the fire of the LORD fell and burned up the sacrifice, the wood, the stones and the soil, and also licked up the water in the trench. When all the people saw this, they fell prostrate and cried, "The LORD—he is God! The LORD—he is God!"* (1 Kings 18:38-39)

THE ELEMENTS OF AN AWAKENING/REVIVAL

Whenever we pray for revival, we must pray for the Spirit of God to convince and convict. Only when this happens can true revival come to the hearts of people everywhere. District Attorneys sometimes brag about their conviction rate, referring the percentage of cases they try and win. The Holy Spirit has the best conviction rate in the world. But He doesn't convict people so they can be found guilty. He convicts people so they will find a Savior who will take away their guilt and make them innocent again.

The Holy Spirit is moved by prayer. We need to ask for the Spirit of conviction to fall on the lost in our towns and neighborhoods until they are drawn to the truth of Jesus Christ. This is what the beginning of revival will look like.

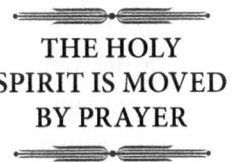

THE HOLY SPIRIT IS MOVED BY PRAYER

ELEMENT 2: REPENTANCE

During political campaigns, inevitably one candidate will try to paint his opponent as being a flip-flopper. The inference is that the opponent is weak on the key issues, and that they change their stance simply to gain votes and get elected. They can't be trusted.

People who don't understand Christianity sometimes see repentance the same way. They see Christians battling sin and they think we are weak and we are trying to appease God and get him to like us by changing who we really are. They think that being strong is to be man or woman enough to tell God, "This is who I am, Take it or leave it."

Christian repentance is really the opposite. We don't change to get God to like us better. He already loves us completely. His love is unmerited, and un-earnable, and this separates him from other religions of the world. We don't attempt to change and repent so God will love us, we repent in response to his love for us.

> *Or do you show contempt for the riches of his kindness, forbearance and patience, not realizing that God's kindness is intended to lead you to repentance?*   *(Romans 2:4)*

WHEN GOD TURNS

What exactly does it mean to repent?

Repentance usually follows conviction. First is the asking of forgiveness for wrongs we now realize we have committed, or things that we should have done and didn't. And next is the turning away from that sin and toward God and his path for our lives.

Many Christians ask for forgiveness, "forgive us our debts", but we don't turn away from sin. We dance back and forth, again and again, between sin and forgiveness, without taking on the challenge of pulling away from that sin with God's help. God is good to forgive a sincere believer who asks, but he also gives power to turn away from it. "Lead us not into temptation but deliver us from evil", this is the next line Jesus taught us to pray and it points us toward the completion of repentance, breaking free from sin and its influence. This line also makes it clear that God has the power to do it in us. This opens the door to true spiritual growth. Jesus is our Savior <u>and</u> our deliverer. We must walk with God to connect with this power to turn from sin, and Paul makes it clear that turning from sin is turning toward God.

> *I preached that they should **repent** and turn to God and demonstrate their repentance by their deeds.*
> *(Acts 26:20, emphasis added)*

It's this turning to God with appreciation for the freedom from sin that we have found in him and the new stronger relationship we now have with him, that fuels revival.

Many believers experience a measure of repentance at the moment of their salvation, when they first embrace a life with Jesus. But there are many more moments of repentance in our lives as we walk progressively into our sanctification.

I am aware that I have entered into an area where Christians disagree. Some Christians believe that there is no salvation without repentance, others disagree and think that adding repentance as a prerequisite to salvation represents a "works" mentality where salvation must be earned. Some believe that sanctification is a one-time event, and not progressive.

THE ELEMENTS OF AN AWAKENING/REVIVAL

Others believe sanctification is a life-long process that begins at salvation. Some believe that once we are saved, we are always saved, while others believe we need to repent each time we sin so we won't lose our salvation.

I don't want to enter into those debates. The scholars can make their cases, but not here. I simply wish we could all agree that repentance is a wonderful gift from God. Repentance is the mechanism that we Christians use to leave sin behind and return to God's path for our lives. I know of no Christian who doesn't feel guilt, shame, or disgrace from time to time. Repentance put's people back in touch with God's forgiveness and power, and gives us permission to push the reset button.

> *Let us draw near to God with a sincere heart and with the full assurance that faith brings, having our hearts sprinkled to cleanse us from a **guilty conscience** and having our bodies washed with pure water.   (Hebrews 10:22a, emphasis added)*

Repentance helps us to apply what Christ has done for us, to the specific things in our lives that we regret. It flushes that paralyzing junk out of us so we can still serve the God we love.

Peyton Manning, a famous NFL quarterback for the Colts and the Broncos—I guess he likes horses—talks about how he recovers from making a bad play that hurts his team. He calls it, "getting back to Zero." If the last play was terrible, he may feel like a minus eight, or if it was great, he might feel like a plus nine. But by the time he starts the next play, he wants to forget what is behind him and get back to even zero. Repentance is so good for us that way. We too can get back to zero in our hearts with God, and get back in the game.

Most non-believers who are in the process of salvation, will find themselves turning their backs on some of their bad habits without realizing that they are repenting. It's just a natural effect of grace to move away from things in our lives that now make us uncomfortable. This is conviction and repentance at work. Not all of our sins leave us this easily. Some are stronger in us and they require more conviction and more grace.

One last thought on repentance. Those who struggle mightily with a lingering sin, or an addiction that can be both physical and psychological, sometimes give up on repenting. We can get to feeling like God is tired of hearing us come back over and over again for the same thing. We desperately want his power for change, but the grip of some sins can be overwhelming. To you I say, don't give up. Instead, find a Christian who is in recovery from the same thing you struggle with. Someone willing to help you walk where they have walked. You may be embarrassed or uncomfortable sharing, but there is greater power in believers who share a common goal. A small support group of two or more can help greatly to support a repentant heart. That's why the Bible says;

> *And let us consider how we may spur one another on toward love and good deeds, not giving up meeting together, as some are in the habit of doing, but encouraging one another. (Hebrews 10:24-25a)*

ELEMENT 2.5: REPENTING FOR THE SINS OF A NATION

While personal repentance is central to an individual experiencing revival, what we see in the great revivals, of both the Bible and the last three hundred years, is one person or group of people who repent for the sins of their nation, or the sins of the Church in their nation, or both, while asking God to turn.

It's an awkward thing to repent for the sins of someone else. In most cases, the people praying these prayers were a part of the group they were praying for, so they were part of the sin problem. More importantly, they felt a burden for the country they were praying for. It seems that God inspires people to repent for their nation, or the Church. Here are some examples.

Daniel knew from reading the book of Jeremiah, that the 70 years of captivity and punishment of Israel were coming to an end, but he also knew that they had not learned their lesson, and they continued in their sin as a nation. So he fasted, put on sackcloth and ashes, and went to God to repent for the sins of Israel.

THE ELEMENTS OF AN AWAKENING/REVIVAL

So I turned to the Lord God and pleaded with him in prayer and petition, in fasting, and in sackcloth and ashes. (Daniel 9:3)

Daniel was specific in the way he listed those sins before God.

We have sinned and done wrong. We have been wicked and have rebelled; we have turned away from your commands and laws. We have not listened to your servants the prophets, who spoke in your name to our kings, our princes and our ancestors, and to all the people of the land. (Daniel 9:5-6)

Daniel begged God to keep his promise to allow Israel to return to their homeland and rebuild.

Lord, listen! Lord, forgive! Lord, hear and act! For your sake, my God, do not delay, because your city and your people bear your Name. (Daniel 9:19)

Nehemiah also prayed and repented for the sins of Israel not long after Daniel. God turned, and Nehemiah would end up leading the rebuilding effort. His prayer included turning back to God, and he reminded God of a promise in his word.

Let your ear be attentive and your eyes open to hear the prayer your servant is praying before you day and night for your servants, the people of Israel. I confess the sins we Israelites, including myself and my father's family, have committed against you. We have acted very wickedly toward you. We have not obeyed the commands, decrees and laws you gave your servant Moses.

Remember the instruction you gave your servant Moses, saying, 'If you are unfaithful, I will scatter you among the nations, but if you return to me and obey my commands, then even if your exiled people are at the farthest horizon, I will gather them from there and bring them to the place I have chosen as a dwelling for my Name. (Nehemiah 1:6-9)

Elijah also prayed in his day for the children of Israel to repent and turn their hearts back to God.

WHEN GOD TURNS

> *At the time of sacrifice, the prophet Elijah stepped forward and prayed: "L*ORD*, the God of Abraham, Isaac and Israel, let it be known today that you are God in Israel and that I am your servant and have done all these things at your command. Answer me, L*ORD*, answer me, so these people will know that you, L*ORD*, are God, and that you are turning their hearts back again."*
>
> (1 Kings 18:36-37)

In the great revival of the New Testament, as the Church began to expand rapidly, it is clear that repentance was a theme which was celebrated and taught in every setting.

> *When they heard this, they had no further objections and praised God, saying, "So then, even to Gentiles God has granted repentance that leads to life." (Acts 11:18)*
>
> *In the past God overlooked such ignorance, but now he commands all people everywhere to* **repent**. *(Acts 17:30, emphasis added)*

Paul even reports the bringing of repentance for sin to the people of two nations or people groups.

> *I have declared to both Jews and Greeks that they must turn to God in repentance and have faith in our Lord Jesus. (Acts 20:21)*

In more recent times, Andrew Murray saw a revival in the churches of South Africa, which coincided with a similar revival in parts of Europe in the 1800s. Murray believed in praying for revival by repenting for the sins of the Church.

> "Every true revival among God's people must have at it's root a deep sense and confession of sin. Until those who would lead the Church in the path of revival bear faithful testimony against the sins of the Church, it is likely that it will find people unprepared."

It's easy to list the sins of the Church today, but hard to apply them to ourselves.

- ◆ Pride.
- ◆ Compromise.
- ◆ Unfamiliarity with God's word.

THE ELEMENTS OF AN AWAKENING/REVIVAL

- Luke-warmness.
- Lack of commitment.
- Insensitivity to the plight of others.
- Quenching and grieving the Holy Spirit.
- Legalism.

Add your own to the list, but the revivals of the last few centuries were Church-centered and tended to start when Christians prayed about the terrible state of the Church in their region, and the need for the Church to impact the plight of underprivileged people.

These are prayers that changed things. These prayers brought repentance and revival. You and I can pray them!

I will admit here that I went to Home Depot, bought some burlap, and made myself a sackcloth outfit. It looks like some kind of a lame Halloween costume. Every year at a "National Day of Prayer" event, I put on sackcloth and ashes and repent for the sins of America and the sins of the Church in America. I don't think the outfit is necessary, but I like to identify with Daniel when he used it. It's my way of humbling myself and taking seriously the remorse that comes with the genuine confession of sin.

Shame is not as big a deal in American culture, as it is in some other cultures. Sometimes I think we're shameless! Drugs, divorce, cheating and DUIs only seem to add to a celebrity's fame. But if you and I are going to repent for what we know is wrong with Church and country, we should accept the burden of shame long enough to confess with that broken and contrite heart mentioned earlier. Emotions should be part of the driving force behind our prayers.

> **EMOTIONS SHOULD BE PART OF THE DRIVING FORCE BEHIND OUR PRAYERS.**

Are you ashamed when you see policemen beating an unarmed man to death? Are you ashamed when you hear about a policeman being shot in the head from behind while he was putting gas in his car? Are you ashamed when scientists proclaim that there is life on Mars because they see signs of water there, but science insists that a fetus in the womb is not a life, so we harvest half a million a year, carve them up, and sell their parts to fund more harvesting? Are you ashamed when the Church is weak, compromised, and unattractive? Are you ashamed that America is sending fewer missionaries into the field with each decade? Are you ashamed that you live your life more for yourself than for God? Are you ashamed when politicians lie, corporations cheat, priests molest, and pastors betray? Are you ashamed when babies are born addicted to meth? Are you ashamed that America doesn't seem to be "good" and the Church doesn't seem to be relevant?

Are you ashamed that all of this and so much more is going on today and you're not doing one blessed thing to change it? Yes? Good.

You might be ready to repent for the sins of Church and country. You might be ready to pray for an awakening.

Element 3: Tearing down Strongholds

I'm not sure how much American Christians know about the spiritual realm. The Bible gives us many pictures of it in both testaments. We are familiar with God's angels. We see them greeting the shepherds at the birth of Christ, and then they are joined by what the Bible calls "heavenly hosts"—nondescript inhabitants of heaven. What are they? We may never know until we get there.

There is a great and telling scene during Elisha's time, when the servant he was traveling with had become distraught because they were surrounded by thousands of their enemies.

> *"Don't be afraid," the prophet answered. "Those who are with us are more than those who are with them."*
>
> *And Elisha prayed, "Open his eyes, Lord, so that he may see." Then the Lord opened the servant's eyes, and he looked and saw the hills full of horses and chariots of fire all around Elisha.*
>
> *(2 Kings 6:16-17)*

Clearly the indication is that there is a spirit realm around us that we seldom, if ever, see. The scriptures also make it clear that there are "bad guys" in this spirit realm too.

THE ELEMENTS OF AN AWAKENING/REVIVAL

My concern in America today, and even in the Church, is that we don't recognize the reality of the Devil and his demons. Many Christians don't realize that approximately one third of Jesus' public ministry in the four gospels was spent dealing with the devil and his demons. Americans see the devil as an imaginative character that represents our sin nature. Many of us don't believe that he exists.

Paul talks about our spiritual enemy in vivid terms, and about our need to fend off this enemy and attack him as he attempts to control our thoughts and actions, and all of this world in general.

The weapons we fight with are not the weapons of the world. On the contrary, they have divine power to demolish strongholds.
(2 Corinthians 10:4)

Put on the full armor of God, so that you can take your stand against the devil's schemes. For our struggle is not against flesh and blood, but against the rulers, against the authorities, against the powers of this dark world and against the spiritual forces of evil in the heavenly realms. *(Ephesians 6:11-12)*

Many Bible scholars see in this language a hierarchy of evil organization. Rulers, authorities, and powers, in the original language, are political/military terms of position and rank, and we are equipped to tear them down.

The Amplified Bible, which uses additional language in order to better define the words in the text, renders the passage like this.

Put on the full armor of God [for His precepts are like the splendid armor of a heavily-armed soldier], so that you may be able to [successfully] stand up against all the schemes and the strategies and the deceits of the devil. For our struggle is not against flesh and blood [contending only with physical opponents], but against the rulers, against the powers, against the world forces of this [present] darkness, against the spiritual forces of wickedness in the heavenly (supernatural) places. *(Ephesians 6:11-12, AMP)*

I bring all this up because one of the elements of revival is the defeat (demolishing or tearing down) of a stronghold of our enemy. Here is the evidence.

In the time of Elijah, the stronghold was Baal worship. Queen Jezebel had intimidated Israel into abandoning God and worshipping this false god. Right after Elijah faced off with the prophets and priest of this idol, and the fire of God fell, the people returned to Jehovah and Killed 450 of the priests of this evil god. And the spiritual stronghold which had supported this false god, and had pulled the people away from God, was destroyed. This spiritual stronghold was torn down.

The revival of the New Testament, the spread of Christianity, was fiercely opposed by the very faith system out of which Christianity was launched—namely Judaism. Christianity went up against these strongholds:

- Most Jews who could not make the leap to faith in Jesus.
- Prideful Greek philosophy in the gentile world.
- Roman military and political power – Caesar was thought to be god.
- Starting with Jewish opposition, this revival eventually pulled down all three of these great obstacles.

Judaism still thrives today, but Jews in today's world are most often the allies of Christians. However, in the early decades of the Church, Jews famously persecuted Christians as heretics. In response, once Christianity was established as a world religion, we often persecuted Jews in retaliation. Thank God we seem to have gotten past those ugly chapters.

The Greeks highly influenced public thought for centuries leading up to the early days of the Church. John appears to have written his gospel after it became clear that the faith would be presented to these Greek-affected gentile cultures. He wrote in ways that would speak to these prevailing Greek philosophies and show how the Christian faith had many

THE ELEMENTS OF AN AWAKENING/REVIVAL

compatible understandings with them. Christianity definitely grew strong in gentile cultures.

Of course, Christianity eventually became the religion of Rome and the Roman Catholic Church was born.

These strongholds looked impossible to defeat. They were politically and militarily much stronger than the Church, but the Church had God, and that trumped everything.

The Wales revival in the early 1900s that swept through parts of Europe and North America pulled down strongholds of social injustice.

Wealthy business owners and Corporations were replacing the ruling nobility in Europe, and they grew even stronger in America where they had no opposition from any ruling class. These corporations were notorious for unspeakable working conditions, 12 hour shifts for small children, and no benefits for any workers. Women had no part in the political process, and no direct voice in their future. Alcoholism and gambling were ruining families. Minorities were heavily discriminated against.

On the heels of this revival we saw:
- Labor unions formed.
- Women received the right to vote and hold office.
- Child labor laws were passed.
- Alcohol and gambling were outlawed.
- The seeds of the civil rights movement were sown.

The Azuza street revival of 1906 was a revival of the Holy Spirit and it demolished the stronghold of dispensationalism, which is the theory that the great miracles and gifts of the Holy Spirit mentioned in the Bible were only dispensed for the first generation of the church, and ceased to occur after that time.

Speaking in tongues was considered by mainstream Christianity to be extinct. Yet the Azuza Street mission saw an outbreak of the Holy Spirit that led to the establishment of several Pentecostal denominations, and the expressions of the Holy Spirit spread from there around the world, and eventually into most of the other denominations and many nondenominational churches today.

> **REVIVALS BRING MORAL CHANGE.**

The evidence indicates that when a revival takes place, strongholds are demolished. Whatever it is that keeps people from pursuing God is removed. I believe that behind every evil in this world, be it a false god, an insane dictator, social injustice, or a terrible ideology, there is, in the spiritual realm, a stronghold propping it up. Revivals bring with them moral change on earth, as spiritual change happens where we cannot often see.

When we see a revival today, what stronghold will be pulled down? What's in the way? What problem plagues God's people? What exists in our culture that opposes the knowledge of God? After all, if there is a mind-set or a popularly held set of ideas that sets itself up against the gospel message, we have a duty to get rid of it.

> *We demolish arguments and every pretension that sets itself up against the knowledge of God, and we take captive every thought to make it obedient to Christ.* (2 Corinthians 10:5)

But how exactly do we go about demolishing these things?

Here is a picture from the Book of Acts where Paul does this very thing. A woman is telling people's fortunes using demonic power. This would be confusing to the people Paul is trying to reach with a message of divine power, so he simply demolishes this pretention.

> *Once when we were going to the place of prayer, we were met by a female slave who had a spirit by which she predicted the future. She earned a great deal of money for her owners by fortune-telling. She followed Paul and the rest of us, shouting, "These men are servants of the Most High God, who are telling you the way to be saved." She kept this up for many days. Finally Paul became so annoyed that he turned around and said to the spirit, "In the name of Jesus Christ I command you to come out of her!" At that moment the spirit left her.*

THE ELEMENTS OF AN AWAKENING/REVIVAL

> *When her owners realized that their hope of making money was gone, they seized Paul and Silas and dragged them into the marketplace to face the authorities.*   *(Acts 16:16-19)*

Again, Jesus did things like this all the time, but Jesus and Paul lived in a time when the existence of evil spirits was widely accepted. What was new then, to those people, was the idea of God's people having authority over evil spirits, or demons. Jesus gave believers this authority even before his death and resurrection, first to his disciples.

> *As you go, proclaim this message: 'The kingdom of heaven has come near. Heal the sick, raise the dead, cleanse those who have leprosy, drive out demons. Freely you have received; freely give.*
>   *(Matthew 10:7-8)*

Then, Jesus clarified this authority and gave it to all believers, but not until he would finish his work of salvation.

> *I will give you the keys of the kingdom of heaven; whatever you **bind** on earth will be bound in heaven, and whatever you **loose** on earth will be **loosed** in heaven."*
>   *(Matthew 16:19, emphasis added)*

Today we don't recognize evils spirits. We think that everyone who hears voices telling them to do terrible things is schizophrenic. No doubt some are. A study of the many types of evil spirits mentioned in the Bible could bring a much wiser approach to these kinds of problems.

If I have gotten you to rethink spiritual power, and if you're wondering about your God-given authority in this arena, then the next question is, "What stronghold today sets itself up against God – against his gospel message of salvation?"

People today have lives that are more comfortable than at any time in human history. The average person in America today lives better than the wealthiest person in the world did 150 years ago.

- ◆ We can fly anywhere in the world in a matter of hours.
- ◆ We have access to all forms of entertainment.

- Food from around the world is frozen in our refrigerator.
- Worldwide communications and media –
- We can write and perform symphonies on a computer.
- Drive at 75 mph –
- Prescription Medicine/cat scans/laser surgery –
- Gaming –
- HVAC –
- I phones / I everything –
- Robots –
- Nuclear energy –

What do people need God for? Maybe the stronghold is our comfort, coupled with the thought that we don't need God. We're doing just fine without him in our lives.

In the chapter on Hurdles Facing a Great Revival /Awakening, I have outlined several trends in current thought that often oppose the knowledge of God. As believers, we have the power to take out any strongholds that oppose Him. The Church should be vigilant in praying against these things and loosing them off of people until these strongholds are broken. In an awakening, we can see these ideologies being pulled down by God and his people.

Use your God-given power to pave the way for an awakening.

ELEMENT 4: TRANSFORMATION

*Now the Lord is the Spirit, and where the Spirit of the Lord is, there is **freedom**. And we all, who with unveiled faces contemplate the Lord's glory, are being **transformed** into his image with ever-increasing glory, which comes from the Lord, who is the Spirit.*
(2 Corinthians 3:17-18)

The central observable action of every awakening is the transformation of people from their worldly selves toward the likeness and the image of Christ. Some awakenings are focused on nothing else but increased obedience to God through conviction and repentance. Charles Finney writes about revivals of obedience in his book, *Lectures on Revivals of*

THE ELEMENTS OF AN AWAKENING/REVIVAL

Religion (1868). "Backslidden Christians will be brought to repentance. A revival is nothing else than a new beginning of obedience to God."

I believe that revival is so much more than repentance and obedience. God's goal for us is much greater than obedience, it is transformation into the likeness of Jesus. The whole Sermon on the Mount in Matthew, is Jesus teaching us how to act less like selfish humans and more like him. We talked about personally losing selfishness in the Personal Revival chapter of this book. Now we apply the same thing to large scale awakenings.

> **REVIVAL IS MORE THAN REPENTANCE AND OBEDIENCE ... IT IS TRANSFORMATION INTO THE LIKENESS OF JESUS.**

I know. It's not easy to imagine a wave of people acting like Jesus all of a sudden. It's not easy to see it, but it happens. I see things lining up in this generation that could come together when God turns. Let's consider some of them.

Jesus was generous and he taught others to be generous too. He wasn't very interested in gaining wealth. One of the characteristics of millennials is to live a minimalist lifestyle. This generation doesn't collect things, and doesn't want to inherit their parents stuff. They buy micro homes and stay in tiny hotel/closets. They avoid paper and paperwork. They minimalize their eco-footprint. They seek tech alternatives to avoid participating in old institutions. Their children may never set foot inside a bank. And, millennials are quick to give to worthy online individuals who need that help. While they are not adverse to money, they want to see it shared. I think this is a match with the teachings of the Rabbi Jesus.

Jesus questioned the status quo of his day. Every generation I know has done this, but it's the way that Jesus dealt with the institutions of his time that should appeal today. Jesus used intellect and words to disarm what he opposed. His arguments were pointed, incisive, and harsh where necessary. Then he had the courage to live an alternative lifestyle and offer it to those who would follow. He persuaded anyone who would listen, but he never sought to impose this new faith on anyone. Jesus lived what he believed. Gandhi, the famous non-violent leader of India once said, "If

Christians would really live according to the teachings of Christ, as found in the Bible, all of India would be Christian today." Although Christians will always be flawed, Jesus was and is the real thing. His genuine style should resonate with the intellect and sincerity of millennials and all the older members of this generation.

Jesus taught to sacrifice for others. This is His definition of love. Jesus died loving others, including the ones who were killing him. He was more than just an idealist, Jesus was God—living, loving, and sacrificing for the people he created. He was accountable. Millennials who seek to see the world come together and stop the hate (which was also a big theme for boomers) should respond to this message of Christ's. Jesus was God, and he still is God. No other religious or political system offers loving sacrifice to this hurting world like Jesus does. He has a track record of delivering this love to the world wherever he is believed and followed.

These are just a few themes that I see coming together around an awakening. The transformation in the hearts of individuals will come together in beautiful ways. This world will still have it's ugly side, but a transforming awakening will give wings to the drive of this generation. And this generation has Boomers, GenX, Millennials, and their children, who have yet to find their identity. My vision is a coming together of the noblest themes of our time under the banner of Jesus who makes us one, who planted in the human heart the need to connect to something finer than ourselves, and who has the authority and power and love to carry us through to a realization of sacrificial love being manifest in the people of a great awakening.

Still, transformation is more than obedience and more than seeing how it will impact this generation. Christians know what transformation is. It is moving from darkness into the Kingdom of Light. It is changing our citizenship from the place where we were born, to the Kingdom of Heaven, where we were reborn.

> *And giving joyful thanks to the Father, who has qualified you to share in the inheritance of his holy people in the kingdom of light.*
> *(Colossians 1:12)*

THE ELEMENTS OF AN AWAKENING/REVIVAL

> *But our **citizen**ship is in **heaven**. And we eagerly await a Savior from there, the Lord Jesus Christ.*   *(Philippians 3:20)*
>
> *Jesus replied, "Very truly I tell you, no one can see the kingdom of God unless they are **born again**."*   *(John 3:3)*

Most of all, transformation is pictured as the new creation that we become spiritually, a new person on the inside who has an intimate relationship with our Savior Jesus. This is the life-giving, life-changing reality of the transformed Christian life, and we are never the same. And thank God for that.

> *Therefore, if anyone is in Christ, the **new creation** has come: The old has gone, the **new** is here! (2 Corinthians 5:17, emphasis added)*

What will this look like in a great awakening that reaches vast numbers of new believers? We can only imagine and look with spiritual eyes at the vision- the glimpses of the future- that God gives us to pull us forward in prayer for it.

Can you see it? It's important that you can see a movement of people, awakened in their hearts, washed clean and born again, moving in their new-found salvation to live lives of spiritual significance. When God turns, this is what happens. This becomes the norm. I pray you can see it.

> *Where there is no vision, the people perish.*   *(Proverbs 29:18, KJV)*

But where there is vision, from God, the people awaken and thrive.

This is my dream, but I am not alone in dreaming it. I am joined by countless others who believe in this same hope, because God has called us to pray for it, and He has let us see it. I believe you too will see it when you look.

> *'In the last days, God says, I will pour out my Spirit on all people. Your sons and daughters will prophesy, your young men will see visions, your old men will dream dreams. Even on my servants, both men and women, I will pour out my Spirit in those days, and they will prophesy.*   *(Acts 2:17-18)*

We live in these last days. Humankind has been living in them ever since the Holy Spirit was poured out at Pentecost almost 2,000 years ago.

Vision from God is one of the greatest tools of leadership. It motivates us purely, and gives direction, but it is a difficult thing to wait for.

When God's people share His vision it transforms them. The early church ran with God's vision and achieved miraculous gains for the Kingdom of God. Now it's our turn. Let's run with it, first in prayer, and then as the vision manifests itself in our time.

ELEMENT 5: PASSION FOR GOD

We understand that, from a spiritual standpoint, our hearts are where we feel love. Please let me recap a few points that we developed in Chapter 2. We love others from our hearts, and we feel it in our hearts when others love us. God knows this. He made us this way. Passion is a burning love that demands our attention and our actions. When we are passionate about something, we are consumed with it.

In the Bible, the Pharisees were consumed with following God's Law. They once asked Jesus what was the most important commandment in the Law. Jesus said:

> **Love** the Lord your **God** with all your heart and with all your soul and with all your mind and with all your strength.
> (Mark 12:30), emphasis added)

This is how we love when we are passionate. We love with everything we have. In Christianity, love trumps everything else. So when God revives the heart, He must surely fill it with love and passion. Here is a picture of it.

> And hope does not put us to shame, because **God's love** has been poured out into our **heart**s through the Holy Spirit, who has been given to us. (Romans 5:5, emphasis added)

These are hearts being revived with an injection of God's love, not just so we can feel loved by God, but also so we will have His passion to love others. So why not start by loving God back?

THE ELEMENTS OF AN AWAKENING/REVIVAL

*We love because he **first loved** us. (1 John 4:19, emphasis added)*

Where is your passion for God? Are you consumed with loving Him? Passionate, sold-out, self-sacrificing love "bears all things, believes all things, hopes all things, endures all things." (1 Corinthians 13:7-8, NASB) It's time that your love for God starts to hope and believe with great passion for a revival/awakening, and that your love for God endures the ups and downs of life without wavering.

A revived heart is a broken heart that has been healed. Is your heart broken? Did you lose a loved one? Did someone betray your love? Has the unfairness of life overwhelmed you and caused you to hide your heart? Are you holding God to blame for something? The entire world is broken hearted, and they know not where to turn to get it healed. People turn to one vice after another trying to heal that brokenness.

> **A REVIVED HEART IS A BROKEN HEART THAT HAS BEEN HEALED.**

If any of this is true for you, (and many Christians are disappointed and hurt) then consider what King David figured out about God.

> *You do not delight in sacrifice, or I would bring it; you do not take pleasure in burnt offerings. My sacrifice, O God, is a broken spirit; a broken and contrite heart you, God, will not despise.*
> *(Psalm 51:16-17)*

David learned that God is much more interested in a person's heart condition than He is in seeing them simply follow the rules! This is radical. God has a righteous standard of perfection, He has the Ten Commandments and the Law, and He has a system of sacrifices for those who always fall short. But David tells us a greater truth. He knows God's heart, and he realizes that God sets aside His entire system in favor of the person who shares their broken heart with Him. This heart sharing is the sacrifice that is most meaningful to God.

Here is the first step in anyone's revival—to share their heart with God.

WHEN GOD TURNS

Tell Him where you're at. Let Him know how you've been hurting. You can write Him a letter, draw Him a picture, sing Him a song about it, or just talk to Him. You know He's listening. And then feel Him slowly mend your heart. Feel the hope come back, and the forgiveness flow. Feel his love pouring into your heart. Feel Him revive your heart, and as you live this way, pray for the brokenhearted in the world around you.

Keep in mind, God is in the heart repair business, and so is His Son.

> *The LORD is **close to the brokenhearted** and saves those who are crushed in spirit.* (Psalm 34:18, emphasis added)
>
> *He **heals the brokenhearted** and binds up their wounds.* (Psalm 147:3, emphasis added)
>
> *And He (Jesus) was handed the book of the prophet Isaiah. And when He had opened the book, He found the place where it was written, "The Spirit of the Lord is upon Me, Because He has anointed Me To preach the gospel to the poor; He has sent Me to **heal the brokenhearted**, To proclaim liberty to the captives And recovery of sight to the blind, To set at liberty those who are oppressed.* (Luke 4:17-18, NKJV, parenthesis and emphasis added)

These are just a few of the great promises we have from God regarding the health of our hearts in Him. And, a heart that has been healed, is passionate for the healer.

> **PASSION IS MORE THAN A MENDED HEART—IT IS MOTIVATION.**

But passion is more than a mended heart—it is motivation, it's what drives us.

After they had received the Holy Spirit, the men and women of the early church worked their way throughout much of the known world to spread the good news about Jesus and salvation. They risked their lives and many died martyr's deaths. The passion they had for Jesus drove them. Does it drive us today, or does the church need a revival of passion?

> *Not that I have already obtained all this, or have already arrived at my goal, but I press on to take hold of that for which Christ Jesus*

THE ELEMENTS OF AN AWAKENING/REVIVAL

took hold of me. Brothers and sisters, I do not consider myself yet to have taken hold of it. But one thing I do: Forgetting what is behind and straining toward what is ahead, I press on toward the goal to win the prize for which God has called me heavenward in Christ Jesus.   (Philippians 3:12-14)

This is passion! This is a man who will go all out to serve Christ. There is no thought here for the other parts of this man's life. Christ is all to him and he lives to serve. Don't we all want this motivation? Isn't this the way we should feel? We have Christ, but we don't give him his proper place. We fit Him into comfortable places in our lives instead of letting Him be all to us.

It is fair to say that not all Christians are meant to make their living in service to God. Even Paul, who wrote this passage, made tents for a living. But here in America, and in many other countries around the world, we are prosperous and we spend considerable time enjoying life. Our service to God is squeezed in around our jobs, and all the other things we like to do. Our passion is "lukewarm".

We are hard pressed on every side, but not crushed; perplexed, but not in despair;persecuted, but not abandoned; struck down, but not destroyed. We always carry around in our body the death of Jesus, so that the life of Jesus may also be revealed in our body. For we who are alive are always being given over to death for Jesus' sake, so that his life may also be revealed in our mortal body.
(2 Corinthians 4:8-11)

This is the life I want to live. Is it wrong to pray for this level of Christian experience? Is it wrong to want to live all-out for something greater than ourselves?

How many days each week do we spend as much time serving God as we do sleeping? My Bible says that we should work at our jobs as if we were doing it for Jesus. This is one great step toward a life of passionate meaningful service, and we don't need to change what we are doing in order to begin. We just need to change how we do it. Our bosses, our customers, and our fellow workers should feel pretty good when we start treating them like we would Jesus.

> *Whatever you do, work at it with all your heart, as working for the Lord, not for human masters.* *(Colossians 3:23)*

Okay, so you're taking a new approach to work, but maybe you're thinking about making a change toward something more meaningful. Perhaps it will be a better use of your spare time, or maybe even a job change. This quote I want to share with you isn't scripture, but it is all about passion. And if we take it along with the context of godly wisdom, it allows passion to drive our decisions.

> Don't ask what the world needs. Ask what makes you come alive, and go do it. Because what the world needs is people who have come alive, —Harold Thurman

What do you have passion for already? God designed you to be distinctly different from every other human being. It's possible that He built it into you to get excited about something that He has for you to do for Him.

But you say, "The things I'm really passionate about don't have much to do with God."

Okay, so what do you like to do? What are you really passionate about?

You say…

- Smoking & drinking.
- NASCAR.
- Baking.
- Fashion.
- Travel.

If one of these is really your great passion in life, here's how it works.

A Church in Denver has a small group (or community group) that meets in a smoking lounge where they pray, study the Bible and fellowship around pipe smoking. They also have a beer brewing small group that does

THE ELEMENTS OF AN AWAKENING/REVIVAL

the same. I know, you probably don't go to that kind of a church. So how does your church connect with smokers and drinkers who need salvation?

I know three men who are NASCAR Chaplains.

Our church serves a lot of meals. We are grateful for the good cooks, and so are the hungry.

During an outreach event to African communities in our city, we staged an ethnic fashion show. Fashion shows can also be great fund-raisers.

Like travel? Organize mission trips.

You get the idea. If God has given you the passion for something, then go to him and ask for the wisdom to know how to serve. God is obligated to give you that wisdom.

*If any of you **lacks wisdom**, you should ask God, who gives generously to all without finding fault, and it will be given to you.*
(James 1:5, emphasis added)

Also, it's not a sin to be creative. I believe that one of the ways we are created in God's likeness is that we are creative like him. Some of mankind's creations have done great damage, others have blessed us. Trust God to show you how to serve him with passion and wisdom. Partner with Him in creating your path.

I'm mentioning these things because part of a great awakening that would sweep across the world, will have to be a revival of God's church. Too many of us have lost passion because we aren't doing what He made us to do, or, we aren't doing these things with the right attitude in our hearts. *(Since you know personal revival, you have to step into all that God has for you.)* In order for the Church to find revival, we need to do the things that God built us to do, the things we're good at, and we need to do them with the right heart condition. Personal revival becomes church-wide revival when we all come to this place of service.

One more thing about passion – it's risky, because sometimes, what we are good at is tied to the greatest trials of our life.

WHEN GOD TURNS

Your Pain is tied to your Passion. Your Curse is tied to your Call.

Often, in the lives of believers, God will take a negative in our lives, and once we have submitted that negative to God and found victory over it, it becomes a positive for us and becomes central to how we serve Him.

- Many who counsel people with addictions used to have those addictions.
- Those who overcome disabilities become therapists.
- Atheists become evangelists.
- Poor students become teachers in alternative schools.
- The kid who gets picked on becomes the Karate Kid.

We've seen stories like this in our society and we admire them. But you may have a story like this too. The Bible is full of these stories. Perhaps the most dramatic one is the story of the Levites.

It starts with Levi's mother, Leah. She was not the wife that Jacob wanted, but he was tricked into marrying her. Jacob wanted Rachel and finally got her, but he still had children by Leah. Simeon and Levi were two of Leah's sons. Jacob loved Rachel's son Joseph, but he didn't value his other children nearly as much, and they felt it. How many of us were born to mothers that our fathers didn't want?

Leah also had a daughter named Dinah. She was date-raped by the son of a King in a city where Jacob's people were camping. Instead of being outraged, Jacob sought to set up a marriage between Dinah and her rapist. First however, the entire city would have to be circumcised because Jacob's family could not marry outside of the faith. The King agreed and all the men of the city were circumcised. Before they could recover, Simeon and Levi put them all to the sword in revenge for their sister. They felt like their father should have done it. Jacob was disgusted with them, and he never forgot this betrayal.

Years later, when Jacob was near death, his favored son Joseph asked Jacob to pass on his blessing to his sons. Jacob did, but when he came to Simeon and Levi, he cursed them!

THE ELEMENTS OF AN AWAKENING/REVIVAL

"Simeon and Levi are brothers— their swords are weapons of violence. Let me not enter their council, let me not join their assembly, for they have killed men in their anger and hamstrung oxen as they pleased. Cursed be their anger, so fierce, and their fury, so cruel! I will scatter them in Jacob and disperse them in Israel. (Genesis 49:5-7)

The Book of Genesis ends shortly after this scene, and as we turn the page to Exodus, we can see that the families of all of Jacob's sons have grown into huge tribes still living in Egypt, but now they are all slaves. Are the Levites still cursed with anger and violence? (Maybe the Egyptians enslaved the children of Israel because the Simeonites and the Levites had turned into street gangs.) It doesn't take long in Exodus for us to learn about the curse, because the main character, Moses, a Levite, kills a guy and buries him in the sand. Even though Moses was raised with privilege and respect, the curse still gets him.

Eventually, the Levites break this curse when Moses comes down from the mountain with the Ten Commandments and all the people are sinning and Moses calls out to see if any of them would come to the Lord, and only the Levites came across to Moses. They broke the curse, and God would make them the priests for the whole nation, but first God asked the Levites to do something hard to understand. God told Moses to have the Levites take their swords, and go through the camp and kill all of the ringleaders of this rebellion! Why would God call them to use the very swords and violence that had cursed them?

Because they had been the bad guys, they knew who had to die. The Levites were the perfect tool for God. He had threatened to wipe out all of Israel, but because God now had Moses and the Levites, they could perform a surgical strike and save hundreds of thousands of lives.

Their curse was tied to their call.

What about you? Have you struggled with something that could turn into a call on your life? Is there something that has consistently caused pain in your life that now might be a ministry of helping others in that same situation? It happened to Peter and Paul and Matthew. I have noticed that people who experience this kind of redemption usually have great passion for ministry. We need you, and we need your passion. If you are still stuck in the pain/curse part of your life, submit to God. Come across to Him. The blood of Jesus breaks the curse. Faith in Him is your only shield. You can use your own "Levitical sword" to protect others from what once hurt you. It's noble, it's good, and it's typical of God to build passion in the hearts of his people this way.

> But God chose the foolish **things** of the world to shame the wise;
> God chose the **weak things** of the world to shame the strong.
> (1 Corinthians 1:27, emphasis added)

ELEMENT 6: PRAYER
THE FIRST AND THE FINAL ELEMENT OF REVIVAL

The Oxford Dictionary defines a catalyst as: 1) A substance that… increases the rate of a chemical reaction. 2) A person or thing that precipitates or causes a change.

We need a catalyst. We need a person or thing that will cause a change. We need someone who will pray with faith. A catalytic converter in a car takes pollutant gases and converts them into harmless products. We need someone who will pray for the spiritually polluted condition of our nation, and see it converted by the power of God. We need revival.

PRAYER IS THE COMMON THREAD IN ALL REVIVALS.

Obviously, prayer is the most common thread in all known revivals. It's just plain praying for God to move – to orchestrate all the elements of revival and do what only he can do. The good news is, it appears that great numbers in prayer are not necessarily required. Often, in revivals past, it has been such a small handful of people who prayed the prayers that brought revival.

Fellow believers, we are the ones who can pray these revival prayers because we see the sins of our churches and our nation, and we have the great heart's desire to see a turning to God. We want to see our nation step

THE ELEMENTS OF AN AWAKENING/REVIVAL

into God's purpose and blessings. We need to see our churches making a difference for Jesus in our neighborhoods and cities. We want to see the lost added to God's family in spectacular ways. And we need it to happen in our hearts too.

> *"I looked for someone among them who would build up the wall and stand before me in the **gap** on behalf of the land so I would not have to destroy it, but I found no one.*
>
> *(Ezekiel 22:30, emphasis added)*

I mentioned this scripture in the introduction because it is the essential convicting verse for those whom God calls to for prayer—prayer for something bigger than ourselves—prayers that impact the church, and the nation.

When Ezekiel penned this verse, God was bitter toward Israel. He bemoaned the corruption of the rulers and the priests, and how they destroyed people for selfish gain. Even the common people had turned to extortion and robbery, and away from God. These were a people that couldn't produce a single soul to intercede with God for their nation. I guess they all thought that someone else would do it. But no one got around to it. So God determined to bring his wrath upon them.

This scriptural call to stand in the gap for our nation reminds me of one of my favorite movies, "The Three Hundred Spartans". I like the version made in the '60s better than the 2007 remake, but both movies tell the powerful story of three hundred men who stood against the vast Medo-Persian army lead by Xerxes. (It's a true story.)

The Persian army had to enter Greece through a narrow pass at Thermopylae. The Spartans were the greatest warriors of Greece and their king sought to unite the city states of Greece against this foe, but that union was not coming together, and his own Sparta denied him their army, so he took his personal body guard of 300 men and marched against the greatest army the world had ever seen at that time. They held the pass for many days against impossible odds. They never allowed their lines to break. They kept filling the gaps. Only when they were eventually surrounded were they finally defeated. They literally stood in the gap for their nation, and their example inspired their fellow county men to unite and defend their country.

This is exactly what I'm writing about. Who will stand in the gap, against overwhelming attitudes of selfishness and greed, and an increasingly godless society and government, and repent of the sins of our nation, and beseech God for revival?

Oddly, William Shakespeare spoke of this idea in Henry V.

> "Once more unto the breach, dear friends, once more;
> Or close the wall up with our English dead!
> In peace there's nothing so becomes a man
> As modest stillness and humility:
> But when the blast of war blows in our ears,
> Then imitate the action of the tiger."

We have admired similar people in history who stood up to defend their nation in crucial times. It happened at the Alamo. It happened to Revolutionary war hero Nathan Hale, who said just before he was hanged by the British, "I regret that I have but one life to give for my country." It happened when the depleted Royal Air Force of England took off in planes held together by bailing wire and glue to defend their country against the overwhelming German Luftwaffe which was determined to bomb England into surrender. Prime Minister Winston Churchill would say, **"Never was so much owed by so many to so few"**

Our war is a spiritual war of prayer for the souls of people we may never know in this life, but it is still the unselfish humble prayer of people who have been made righteous by Jesus, and who sense a pressing call to the noble life's work of men and women on their knees. We don't lose our lives in a glorious physical battle. Instead, we pour our lives out daily, hourly, in faith of a coming victory.

Many believers know that God has already mapped out history, and therefore they question whether we should ask God to do something he may not be planning to do. My answer to that is – while it's true that God

THE ELEMENTS OF AN AWAKENING/REVIVAL

knows what he will and won't do, we don't always know. And it is clear from Old Testament and New, that we are to ask, to make supplication, and to intercede for others. Further, it is clear that when God plans to move, he inspires people to pray for it. Paul constantly prayed for the churches he planted, and the ones he intended to plant. It's obvious from his letters that he considered his prayers for them, and their prayers for him, to be of vital importance.

> *This is the confidence we have in approaching God: that if we ask anything according to his will, he hears us. And if we know that he hears us—whatever we ask—we know that we have what we asked of him.* (1 John 5:14-15)

So the only question left is; does God want us to pray for the resurgence of his church, and the mass salvation of millions of lost people?

> *I urge, then, first of all, that petitions, prayers, intercession and thanksgiving be made for all people... This is good, and pleases God our Savior,*
>
> *Who wants all people to be saved and to come to a knowledge of the truth.* (1 Timothy 2:1; 4)

"We have the privilege offering ourselves to God to labor in prayer for the blessings He has in store for the church. Shouldn't we beseech God to make this truth live in us? And implore Him that we will not rest until we count the practice of intercession our highest privilege. It is the only certain means of obtaining blessing for the church, the world, and our own lives."

—Andrew Murray

Again, the people of Murray's time found revival through prayers. I want to see one in my time, or at least I want to leave a revival for my children.

"A TRUE REVIVAL MEANS
NOTHING LESS THAN
A REVOLUTION,
CASTING OUT THE SPIRIT OF
WORLDLINESS AND SELFISHNESS,
AND
MAKING GOD AND HIS LOVE
TRIUMPH
IN THE HEART AND LIFE."

—ANDREW MURRAY

CHAPTER 4

WAKING UP THE LUKEWARM CHURCH

I love the Church. I first got saved because, at a time in my life when my parents were breaking up, the Church was my positive family away from home. I wanted in, and it wasn't hard for me to believe in Jesus because these people were a family that was joyful, reverent, encouraging, and fun.

Jesus is the head of the Church.

> For the husband is the **head** of the wife as Christ is the **head** of the **church**, his body, of which he is the Savior.
> *(Ephesians 5:23, emphasis added)*

There are other verses which prove that Jesus is the head of the Church, but I chose this one because Jesus' relationship is not CEO, it is husband, and the Church is his wife. The Bible uses this imagery constantly because CEO's, and Generals, and Presidents, don't have to love those that they command, but Jesus must rule with love because it's a marriage. (If you don't like that the husband is the head of the wife, I'll try to write another book someday, but for now, try to get over it. The analogy simply forces Jesus to love the Church as its leader.)

This makes my chapter on the lukewarm Church a bit awkward because if I write critically about the Church, then I am also criticizing the head of the Church who makes all the decisions. I'm not about to criticize Jesus.

So I write this chapter with the same respectful arguing way that Moses used to get God to turn. I know that Jesus doesn't like lukewarm in His churches, and I'm just trying to get Him to turn from the direction the Church is taking, and lead us into a revival. I think He wants you and me to pray for it. And also, it's not really critical of Jesus if I am simply pointing out where the Church is disobeying Him.

AN OPEN DOOR

If you read the seven letters to the churches in the book of Revelation, you may be struck by the stark contrast between the letter to the church at Philadelphia and the letter to the church at Laodicea. Jesus has only good things to say about the Philadelphian church—they are faithful, they keep his word, they persevere, and he will make their enemies fall at their feet. Meanwhile, the Laodicean church is wealthy, and compromised, and lukewarm toward God's agenda, and God is ready to "spit them out"

Everyone likes to believe that their church is like the Philadelphia church. There is a bit of a mystery in the letter to the church at Philadelphia. Jesus says that he has placed an open door before this church that no one can shut. Later on in the letter, Jesus tells them to hold on to what they have so no one can take away their crown. The question is, "What is the open door. And what is it that they need to hold on to?"

Some say the open door is a door to heaven, and this church has great communion with God through it. However, we also believe that all of God's children have communion with him, if we will draw near, pray, and know him. So I'm not sure that this interpretation works.

I think the open door is something else. (And I am not alone) I believe that the open door is the opportunity to reach the world with the message of the Gospel. In Paul's day, we read about many who traveled from one country to the next planting churches and visiting groups of believers. They were missionaries. But shortly after those days of Paul and the disciples, the Church slowly changed that activity. By the time that Rome accepted the Christian faith, and the Church became the official religion of State, Paul's good old practice of sending out missionaries to unreached people had faded, and Christianity began to be spread by political and military power. Some tragic things were done with this crusading power in the name of Christianity.

WAKING UP THE LUKEWARM CHURCH

About 200 years ago, America sent out our first missionaries – Ann and Adoniram Judson. They joined a missionary couple from England in India, and then went on to Burma. The Missions door, that had been shut for so long, was now open again, and so far, no one has been able to shut it. Today thousands of missionaries are working around the world sharing the Gospel. Those churches that embrace this open door, are doing all they can to fund it, and they need to hold on to it. But others are lukewarm to all this. It's just not a big theme in their Christian lives.

Lukewarm is a difficult and offensive term to knowledgeable believers. It only appears twice in the Bible and it's used to describe a Christian church where Jesus is on the outside looking in, and God is ready to expel them.

> *I know your deeds, that you are neither cold nor hot. I wish you were either one or the other! So, because you are lukewarm—neither hot nor cold—I am about to spit you out of my mouth.*
> *(Revelation 3:15-16)*

This is Jesus talking, and later in this letter to the church at Laodicea, he talks about being outside.

Revelation 3:19-20

> *Those whom I love I rebuke and discipline. So be earnest and repent. Here I am! I stand at the door and knock. If anyone hears my voice and opens the door, I will come in and eat with that person, and they with me.   (Revelation 3:19-20)*

Most churches have a mix of lukewarm members and on-fire members. The outreach programs of each church, whether local, regional, or international, are usually driven by the few who are sold out for it, and the rest of the church is pleased that it's happening, but they don't get very involved. If this is an accurate observation that fits your experience in the Church of America, the question remains, how do we awaken the lukewarm Church?

The next question is,

"What motivates some Christians to be on fire for the lost?"

For many highly motivated Christians, the circumstances of their own salvation drives them to reach others. These are believers whose transformation was more radical than others, and often it came after they were adults. They are aware that they were delivered out of darkness, and they remember how that darkness felt, and how it had them bound up. When the message of Christ first found their hearts, the piercing light of his love and truth made such a wonderful transformation in them, and they carry that memory around with them close to the surface of their faith-walk. Therefore they are driven to reach others who are stuck in that same darkness, and they know how to speak the language of that reality.

Another Christian may have grown up in a Christian home where faith was a "given", and coming to Jesus was a natural expected step to be taken. Their salvation may have come around age 10 to 15, and since they have really known nothing but Jesus, their experience is much less radical because they weren't experiencing all that much darkness in their lives, praise God. But they can be lukewarm to the plight of the lost because they don't relate to where the lost are.

The early Church that we see in the book of Acts and the letters of Paul had a unique drive to it, because ALL of it's members were radically transformed and had that memory of being lost and finding Jesus. Paul calls upon those newly transformed Christians to step up and take hold of all they have in Christ.

> *So I tell you this, and insist on it in the Lord, that you must no longer live as the Gentiles do, in the futility of their thinking. They are darkened in their understanding and separated from the life of God because of the ignorance that is in them due to the hardening of their hearts. Having lost all sensitivity, they have given themselves over to sensuality so as to indulge in every kind of impurity, and they are full of greed.*
>
> *That, however, is not the way of life you learned when you heard about Christ and were taught in him in accordance with the truth that is in Jesus. You were taught, with regard to your former way of life, to put off your old self, which is being corrupted by its deceitful*

> *desires; to be made new in the attitude of your minds; and to put on the new self, created to be like God in true righteousness and holiness.* *(Ephesians 4:17-24)*

Missionary churches often have this same zeal on the mission field.

Let's be honest. It is much easier for the truth of Christ to break through the Chains of poverty, than to break through the bondage of affluence.

REACHING THE "COMFORTABLE" CHRISTIAN

Question: What radicalizes the comfortable Christians and gets them to burn with passion for the lost? What instills in us a heart for those living in this darkness? What transforms us into the dynamos that drove the early Church?

Answer: Two things we already have – The Word of God and the Spirit of God.

The Word — *Romans 12:2*

> *Be transformed by the renewing of your mind. Then you will be able to approve what God's will is.*

Nothing renews the mind like God's word. It is both intellectual and spiritual. It is alive and it always achieves the purpose for which God spoke it.

The Spirit — *2 Corinthians 3:18*

> *And we all, who with unveiled faces contemplate the Lord's glory, are being transformed into his image with ever-increasing glory, which comes from the Lord, who is the Spirit.*

God's Spirit is the agent of our transformation.

So, how do we apply and cooperate with God's word and Spirit in such a way as to achieve a heart for the lost that will drive us powerfully and effectively to reach them?

We use God's word, and the convicting power of His Spirit, to gain in ourselves Jesus' broken heart for the lost. Let's begin.

> *Fixing our eyes on Jesus, the pioneer and perfecter of faith. For the **joy set before him** he endured the cross,*
>
> *(Hebrews 12:2a, emphasis added)*

What was that joy set before Jesus? It was our salvation, friend. His joy was to see you and I united for all time with him. That was a goal he was ready to die for, and he did. And his joy is not just for you and I, it is also for every other human being on the planet. We know from his prayer in the garden that Jesus did not want to die. He spoke frankly with the Father to see if there might some other way to achieve salvation for the world. But there was no plan B. So, for the sheer joy of knowing all the good he would do for all those who would come to believe in him, and driven by the love he has for all of us, Jesus submitted to the cross.

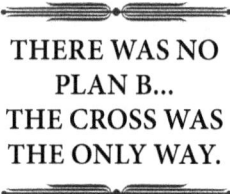

THERE WAS NO PLAN B... THE CROSS WAS THE ONLY WAY.

What does it do to Jesus when the majority of the people he died for turn their backs on him? And what does it do to his joy when those who are saved fail to reach out? I think it breaks his heart.

If we are to truly care passionately for the lost, we must share his broken heart. If we are to know the joy of the salvation of another, we must share in Christ's suffering for them. This was so central to Paul's walk, and it must be for ours too.

> *Now if we are children, then we are heirs—heirs of God and co-heirs with Christ, if indeed we **share** in his **suffering**s in order that we may also **share** in his glory. (Romans 8:17, emphasis added)*

Now let's look at our Lord's broken heart. We all know what it is to be close to the brokenhearted. We share their brokenness, and so does Jesus.

> *The LORD is close to the **brokenhear**ted and saves those who are crushed in spirit. (Psalm 34:18, emphasis added)*

Jesus' call and commission is to minister to the broken hearted.

WAKING UP THE LUKEWARM CHURCH

> *The Spirit of the Lord is upon Me, Because He has anointed Me to preach the gospel to the poor; He has sent Me to heal the brokenhearted, to proclaim liberty to the captives And recovery of sight to the blind, to set at liberty those who are oppressed.*
> *(Luke 4:18)*

And we too are called to this same ministry, the same suffering for the lost, and with the same empowerment from God.

> *To this you were called, because **Christ suffered** for you, leaving you an example, that you should follow in his steps.*
> *(1 Peter 2:21, emphasis added)*

> *I want to know **Christ**—yes, to know the power of his resurrection and participation in his **sufferings**, becoming like him in his death.* *(Philippians 3:10, emphasis added)*

I agree that many Christians suffer in other parts of the world just because they are Christians. But how do affluent, comfortable Christians share in Christ's suffering? We must choose to suffer, just like he chose to suffer for us. This is the core for revival of the Church. Wealth breeds selfishness, but we can make the better choice. We are driven to it as we see His overriding passion to provide for the lost. Jesus has made us to be the children of God, and we are called, and compelled, to join the family business. Certainly he was urging us toward these things when he told us to pick up our own crosses each day and follow him. Wasn't he talking about more than death to sin? Didn't he also mean the choice to suffer alongside him for the lost with the same broken heart as his?

> *I pray that out of his glorious riches he may strengthen you with power through his Spirit in your inner being, ¹⁷ so that Christ may dwell in your hearts through faith.* *(Ephesians 3:16-17)*

But Jesus urged us one other time to pick something up. It was an exchange – our burdens for his.

Come to me, all you who are weary and burdened, and I will give you rest. Take my yoke upon you and learn from me, for I am gentle and humble in heart, and you will find rest for your souls. For my yoke is easy and my burden is light. (Matthew 11:28-30)

And what is this burden which is so light and this yoke so easy? Most Bible scholars say that the hard burden which had been laid upon the Jews that Jesus was speaking about, was the burden of trying to keep the demands of God's law in order to achieve and maintain a righteous relationship with God. And, Jesus was saying to lay that burden down and take up his light burden, which is a righteousness that comes by the grace of God because they now believe in him to keep the law for them with his sacrifice on the cross. But there's also a yoke. He calls it His yoke. We will be yoked to him for the task of sharing this new light burden with the world. And why is it easy? It's easy because, we are yoked to the greatest love and power and broken heart in heaven and earth – Jesus.

WANT TO BE CLOSER TO JESUS? MAKE HIS CAUSE YOUR OWN.

Want to be closer to Jesus? Join him in the harvest fields. Be yoked to him in the effort to share the faith. Allow him to download into your heart his great love and passion for the lost. Choose to suffer and share his broken heart for all those living in darkness. Enter into the family business. Make his cause your own. Be transformed into his likeness with ever increasing glory which is from the Lord who is the Spirit. Pick up his burden.

PICK IT UP

Sharing the heart of Jesus for the lost – and being convicted by God's Spirit that we must join him in this cause – are not the only ways to awaken the lukewarm Church. Another motivator is purpose. To live a meaningful life, and the drive to make a difference, is strong motivation in every generation.

Can there be any greater purpose on earth than to reach people living in darkness with a message of hope and eternal salvation?

Let's consider how powerfully and miraculously Jesus can use our very human efforts to achieve this great purpose.

> *[The Crucifixion of Jesus] A certain man from Cyrene, Simon, the father of Alexander and Rufus, was passing by on his way in from the country ... and they forced him to carry the cross [behind Jesus.]* (Mark 15:21 and Luke 23:26, brackets added)

It sounds like Simon was in the wrong place at the wrong time. He's running late for Passover events that day. He wasn't able to secure lodging inside the city walls, and now here he comes hurrying to get inside the gate, when he comes across an execution procession. And of all things, they force him to carry the cross for a condemned man who is so beaten and bloodied that he can no longer carry it himself.

It doesn't sound like Simon did this as an act of kindness. He was forced. He was probably scared to death that he would somehow end up being executed himself. What do the executioners care if an innocent bystander gets hurt? There is no record that Simon said anything to Jesus, or that he knew Jesus.

The cross itself was probably slippery with Christ's blood. Simon's blood stained clothes would make him unclean and disqualify him from participating in Passover activities. There is no record that he stayed once he was finished carrying the cross. Most likely he got out of there fast, before he was mixed up with the three condemned prisoners.

This is a curious little side bar of a story taking place alongside the greatest event in all history. Why is it there? It runs counter to the rest of the crucifixion story in that Jesus was isolated from all help and support during his trial and crucifixion. No one helped him. He had to do it on his own because only He was without sin. Only he could be the perfect sacrifice. No one could do this for him. And yet, there is Simon, carrying the cross that would hold the Son of God and the sins of the world on it.

Simon probably had no idea that he was helping to complete the ministry of Jesus Christ to the lost people of the world!

I believe that the story of Simon shows us one crucial strategy of God's that He will always employ. God will share his ministry with his people, no matter how unlikely it may seem. God will always reach the lost in a way that requires our action too.

But don't be misled. Jesus did the hard part, by far. Simon's contribution was tiny, and not of his own choice. At the time, Simon probably didn't have any idea what he had done.

We read in the book of Acts that Men from Cyrene were instrumental in establishing and leading the church at Antioch. I wonder if a few years after the crucifixion, the gospel message reached Cyrene, and Simon heard it, and maybe realized for the first time what he had done. And Simon thought to himself, "That was me! I carried the cross. Jesus chose not to make it to Golgotha without my help. I helped to complete the greatest ministry the world has ever known!"

I believe Jesus is saying the same thing today. He will reach the world with a life-giving, life-changing message, but not without you and me.

We are all like Simon of Cyrene. We are all asked to PICK IT UP. This is our yoke with Jesus, and He chooses not to reach the world without us. This is the purpose of a lifetime.

Unlike Simon, we live under a new covenant, and we have a Bible with a New Testament, and we are filled with the Holy Spirit, so we have an understanding of what we are being asked to do. And we know Jesus personally. I don't believe that any member of the Church can remain lukewarm once they realize that Jesus is personally and intimately asking them to PICK IT UP.

Jesus will always do the hard part. He will:
- Send the Holy Spirit to convict.
- Place believers in their path.
- Open their spiritual eyes and ears.
- Send angels to orchestrate their lives so they will have to face their need for a Savior.
- Draw them in and touch their hearts.

And, once he has done most of the heavy lifting, he will ask each of us to PICK IT UP.

The discovery that YOU are part of God's plan to save the world can be both wonderful and a bit startling. Jesus does have a plan, and like Simon, you must become the hands and feet of Jesus Christ.

Here is a poem about such a discovery. I pray it will bless you and encourage you.

My Savior's Hands

I searched the fertile Valley floor
Across the mountain range, and more
I searched the swamp and the desert sands
For one touch from my Savior's hands

I traveled light, and seldom paused
So driven by a single cause
My purpose clear, my vision clean
I strained to realize the dream
To know my maker more than most
And draw so near, and press in close
I pushed through all the countermands
To touch the scars on both his hands

The quest consumed me, as I might
Take time in watches of the night
To dream of hands that broke the bread
And healed the sick, and raised the dead
Then break of day – again I'm going
Seeking Him, but not quite knowing
How a pilgrim might proceed
To where His Spirit meets the need
Of broken hearts in foreign lands
Who found revival in His hands

WHEN GOD TURNS

One time I had come close, I thought
A market place and I had bought
A bit of food to save for later…
Then I saw emaciated
Children begging for some bread
And I thought Jesus, in their stead
Would fill their bellies and their hearts

And I'd be there and play a part;
But Jesus didn't show that day
And sadly, I went on my way
But not before I fed each one
And made sure something good was done
And strangely, I had just enough
I never did run out of stuff
to give. But t'would have been so grand
If they'd been fed by Jesus' hands

Just then my world stopped revolving
The Holy Spirit, problem-solving
And yes, my eyes could finally see
The truth placed right in front of me
I can't believe I couldn't see it
Jesus said, "Don't search it – Be it!"
And I looked down and realized,
I'm looking at the hands of Christ!

The hands I'd searched for, far and wide
Were right here, one on either side
It's such a strange theocracy
But Christ does live inside of me
And His, the only vote that counts
And so each day the pressure mounts
To walk in this extravagance
These are his fingers and his hands

WAKING UP THE LUKEWARM CHURCH

They may not have the nail holes
But they have scars that hurt my soul
When I reached out in Jesus' name
And bore the brunt of someone's pain
And then I'd bleed a little while
And after that, a tiny smile
Would creep across my countenance
A joy to suffer such offense
Indeed, He suffered so much more
And now I stand here at the door

My quest to find my Savior's hands
Ended up where it began
The hands that open my front door
Must do just what His did before
Reaching, working, sometimes healing
Always loving, Christ revealing
His hands – how I used to chase them
Now I just don't want to waste them

Maybe I should calm a storm
Or maybe I'll just keep them warm
O they can heal with a touch
But maybe that's a bit too much…?
No! That's what they have to be
His hands aren't less attached to me
In fact His hands can now do more
They're not just mine. They're also yours!

If this gets out, 'bout what we've got
The Church goes from lukewarm to hot
What will God do with all these hands?
Could this have always been his plan?

Now this is really quite stupendous
Who knows where our God might send us
Every nation will befriend us…
Okay, some try to offend us
But every time we're hurt, He'll mend us
And we can trust God to defend us
So Holy Spirit recommend us
To each soul that needs salvation
For we will suffer every nation
To bring hope – the revelation
Of His loving subjugation
Winning our sanctification
Making us all one Holy Nation

And now my journey starts anew
O, what Jesus' hands will do.

The Selfishness of Unconcern

I pray that the scriptures are moving you to share Jesus' burden for the lost. This concern to reach people in darkness begins as a heart condition of great empathy for the majority of people on earth who have not experienced the light, hope, and freedom of salvation by grace through faith in Jesus.

Here are yet two more scriptures that spoke directly to the lukewarm of God's people in Jesus' day, and still speak loud and clear to us today. Let them convict us anew and with ever greater impact so that we can learn directly from Jesus and avoid the selfishness of unconcern.

> *In reply Jesus said: "A man was going down from Jerusalem to Jericho, when he was attacked by robbers. They stripped him of his clothes, beat him and went away, leaving him half dead. A priest happened to be going down the same road, and when he saw the man, he passed by on the other side. So too, a Levite, when he*

> *came to the place and saw him, passed by on the other side. But a Samaritan, as he traveled, came where the man was; and when he saw him, he took pity on him. He went to him and bandaged his wounds, pouring on oil and wine. Then he put the man on his own donkey, brought him to an inn and took care of him. The next day he took out two denarii and gave them to the innkeeper. 'Look after him,' he said, 'and when I return, I will reimburse you for any extra expense you may have.'"* (Luke 10:30-35)

Jesus' initial teaching here was to explain to a Pharisee that "loving his neighbor" included anyone in need that he might meet. And this story demonstrated something worse than just a lukewarm nature, it showed people with calloused hearts that were totally insensitive to the plight of others.

Consider for a moment, what if the traveler was under spiritual attack, robbed of eternal life, and stripped of any relationship he might have with the Father, because of his naked sin life? Be honest. There are those in our churches who don't want to see it. They don't want to deal with it. They have their eternal life secured and they prefer to stay comfortable within the fellowship. They may help with a family member, or a close friend, but they are not about to take on the burdens of the world around them.

The hero here is someone from outside the Jewish faith, a Samaritan. Samaritans had a copycat version of Judaism, which bugged the leaders of the Jewish faith. This wounded man, who was helped by the Samaritan and not the Jews, and whose faith is unknown in the story – is he more likely to become a Jew or a Samaritan? Exactly.

The same is true whenever the Church allows calloused hearts to walk us past opportunity after opportunity to demonstrate the love of Jesus, and testify to all he has done in our lives. Jesus' use of the Samaritan Hero was an insult to the Jewish leaders to whom he was then speaking. And a calloused heart must begin to resonate inside us as an insult to the very name of Jesus.

I know that there are many in the Church who are not calloused. But I speak of the Church as a whole with this problem, because we are members of one body, and if part of the body has a sickness, the whole body feels it and suffers. Let every member who is convicted, minister to those in need until we stand as one with a heart for the lost.

The parable of "The Prodigal Son" is a poor name for this parable. It should probably be called the parable of "The Two Ridiculous Sons".

Many of us have heard it. The younger son takes his inheritance from his father (God), and throws it away on worldly junk. When he finally decides to return to his father, his dad throws a great party for him. We traditionally see this part of the story as people in the world whom God created and loves, who finally come to believe in him and get saved. For our purposes, it's the second son who again shows a calloused heart, and even a disdain for his returning brother.

> *"Meanwhile, the older son was in the field. When he came near the house, he heard music and dancing. So he called one of the servants and asked him what was going on. 'Your brother has come,' he replied, 'and your father has killed the fattened calf because he has him back safe and sound.'*
>
> *The older brother became angry and refused to go in. So his father went out and pleaded with him. But he answered his father, 'Look! All these years I've been slaving for you and never disobeyed your orders. Yet you never gave me even a young goat so I could celebrate with my friends. But when this son of yours who has squandered your property with prostitutes comes home, you kill the fattened calf for him!'*
>
> *'My son,' the father said, 'you are always with me, and everything I have is yours. But we had to celebrate and be glad, because this brother of yours was dead and is alive again; he was lost and is found.'"* (Luke 15:25-32)

And this is the "good son?" In verse 28 he gets angry and refuses to go in to the party for his long lost brother. He comes off as spoiled, selfish, and jealous. Still, he is the one who stayed and was with the father all this time. Is he a picture of the Church? Certainly we are with God all the time. Do we enjoy the unmerited grace and favor of God in such a way that we are jealous to keep it to ourselves? Perhaps this older brother felt like his little brother had gotten what he deserved when he was destitute. After all, the younger brother took the money and ran. He didn't stay to work for the father. He wasn't responsible. Why celebrate that? The father answers him.

> *'You are always with me, and everything I have is yours. But we had to celebrate and be glad, because this brother of yours was dead and is alive again; he was lost and is found.'*

We, the Church, are with God and we do have everything He has.

> *And God is able to bless you abundantly, so that in **all** **things** at **all** times, having **all** that you need, you will abound in every good work.   (2 Corinthians 9:8, emphasis added)*

Do we allow ourselves this feeling about the unsaved world around us – that people are getting what they deserve?

I spoke to an older man once who was near retirement. He was upset, and when I asked why, he told me this story.

He had worked alongside several other men in the same business for all his work life. Many of the other men had stayed in this business for their entire work lives too. Their paychecks were about the same as his and it was a descent middle-class wage. Many of the man's peers had taken their money and bought expensive cars and the nicest homes they could finance.

This man, however, preferred to save his money. He bought a modest home, and he often drove clunkers over the years to avoid car payments. Instead, he was able to save one out of every 7 dollars he made. When his nest egg got big enough, he invested conservatively for minimal risk and small but dependable gains. His coworkers made fun of his cars. Some figured he wasn't making as much as the rest. Others called him a skinflint and a penny-pincher. They liked to say that he squeezed a nickel so hard that you could see the Indian riding the buffalo! (Of course the days of buffalo nickels are long past)

This man had his retirement all planned out. He had hundreds of thousands in his investment account, and he would have a reasonable Social Security check. He could gain a small but steady income from his investments without touching the principal amount, so it would never drain out, and that plus the social security and a home that was paid for, would allow him to live well. Now he would finally get that shiny new car.

Then, a Senator from his home state proposed that Social Security be cut for people who had hundreds of thousands of dollars saved up, so they could raise the amount to be given to the poor people who hadn't saved enough! His coworkers thought it was the best idea ever. He didn't know what to say. He should have spent it all, he thought. All of his efforts for total security would be slowly stripped away and given to those who had not been so responsible. "Responsibility is being punished", he cried out, "and recklessness is rewarded."

This, I think, is how the older brother of the Prodigal Son felt. It wasn't fair. But wait, there's a difference. Social Security only has so much money to go around, but God's resources are infinite. He can offer salvation to others and not take a thing away from those who are already saved. The father told the older brother that all that the father owned was his. The father wasn't rewarding the prodigal for being foolish and irresponsible, he was rewarding him for swallowing his pride and finally making a good choice. The father was cementing a relationship that had been lost. The older son should have been the first in line to greet his brother.

Every saved person has a fortune in heaven of things that money can never buy. We must not apply worldly thinking to spiritual truths. When we get to heaven, we will have it all, in fact we do now. And we will want the satisfaction that we did all we could to share our good fortune in Christ with this poor world.

If you still feel that people in the world are getting what they deserve, technically you are right. Our Bible says that the wages of sin is death –

eternal damnation. Keep in mind that we who are saved do not get what we deserve. Because of our choice for Jesus, we are spared the fate that our sin would have earned for us. We didn't earn Heaven, God just gives it to us because we believe in his Son. In light of this truth, can we possibly afford to brush off the unsaved this way? Are we really OK with people going to Hell? Even in ambivalence, we cannot possibly wish it on our worst enemy. Come alive Church, and wear the heart of Jesus on your sleeve. Find in ourselves the hope of Jesus for his lost family. Love the world with the love of Christ.

> **WE DON'T EARN HEAVEN, GOD GIVES IT BECAUSE WE BELIEVE IN HIS SON.**

> *And hope does not put us to shame, because God's love has been poured out into our hearts through the Holy Spirit, who has been given to us.* (Romans 5:5)

Yes, Christianity is under attack from parts of our media and government. Our culture is pushing back on us. But let us not take on the attitude of the older brother who could care less about the salvation of the younger. After all, one of the most powerful elements of this parable is the fact that they are BROTHERS. They have a bond, they share a father.

Jesus is telling us something here. All humankind is his family, and he leads his Church to the waterhole of evangelism, but we don't always drink.

- We must be the hands and feet of Christ. You've heard the phrase before, but we must now embrace it.
- We must share Jesus' heart for the lost.
- We must pick up the cross of completing this ministry in our day.
- We must pick up His burden, and the yoke we have to Jesus.
- We must deny a calloused heart, and selfish unconcern.
- Our heart's desire must be to see revival.

And we must celebrate the salvation of one soul as if it were our favorite brother or sister who has come home from a long absence.

We are transformed into the likeness of Jesus as we dwell in the word, and as the Holy Spirit brings it alive inside us.

God is in the business of changing hearts. We can all use a tune up when it comes to caring about the dark condition of lost souls. Oh how we need to bleed for them. They are facing such an ugly truth in eternity and we hold the keys to the Kingdom. Pray until your heart breaks. Don't settle for anything less than taking up the yoke, carrying the cross, and reaching out to the lost.

... Pick it up.

CHAPTER 5

HURDLES FACING A GREAT AWAKENING/REVIVAL

(Author's Note: In this chapter, I write about some socio-economic, political, and cultural issues. I don't personally have many political aspirations anymore. I did when I was younger. I grew up in a liberal setting but I always leaned conservative in politics, and evangelical in my faith. I have been in churches where being conservative was expected, and in churches where liberal politics were almost a requirement for membership. I work hard now to be as non-political as possible because I just want to reach all people with this message. I eventually realized that God rarely works politically to achieve salvation for the lost. Certainly God presides over all things on earth and he uses the nations and their leaders as he pleases. But God works spiritually for the saving of souls, not through legislation. If he did work politically, then Jesus would have been born in Rome. He would have become Caesar and would have imposed Christianity on the known world. Instead, Jesus was born in a backwater of the Roman Empire. He lived out his life without traveling more than a few miles in any direction. He had just a handful of committed followers, and he died having written nothing, owning nothing, and was a disappointment to most of the people to whom he preached. He was a socio-political disaster. But spiritually, he achieved everything!

Certainly when God turns, one of the many side effects can be a sharp change in the culture and politics of that time and place, but God works things out spiritually before we ever see the impact on our physical world.

So my purpose for writing about these issues, that separate and divide us as a nation and as a Church, is because these trends have tainted people's ideas about God. I have no desire to persuade anyone to be prolife, or progressive, or conservative, or Republican, or independent, or Democrat, or communist, socialist, tea party, 99%, marijuana smoking, anti-government, gun toting, pacifist, anarchist, left-leaning, right wing, or moderate. I only bring these things up to show how they can keep people from God, and how they divide the Church.

When we can recognize how contemporary thought impacts the way that people see God, then we can begin to appreciate what must be overcome, pray with wisdom, and be prepared to share God in today's confusing atmosphere.

Please don't be chased away by my observations. We need to talk about these things so we can reach the lost. I now resist political labels for myself. I am a believer in Jesus Christ, and I am tired of seeing culture, economics, and politics divide God's church and keep people from knowing Jesus. That's all.)

HURDLES FACING A GREAT AWAKENING/REVIVAL

Today's Christians have challenges unlike any generation before us. Some trends in social thinking seem to be lining up against the Christian Faith. At the same time, there seems to be a new hunger to understand the Christian Faith through media events and frank even-handed discussions. While people don't always want "God" deciding what's right and wrong for them, they still seem to want opportunities to cautiously learn about Him.

People have always wanted to decide what's right and wrong for themselves. That's what happened with Adam and Eve. And whether you believe that it's just a made up story, or that the Garden of Eden is historically and scientifically accurate, isn't important here, because either way, the lesson it teaches is the same. Humankind has always had a drive to be godlike and decide what is right and wrong, and God will always ultimately reserve that right for himself. This wrestling match over who determines the values by which we live, is usually at the core of socio-political movements and cultural trends. It gets difficult when these philosophies oppose God's perfect understanding.

HURDLES FACING A GREAT AWAKENING/REVIVAL

We can argue over how to interpret the Bible, but we can't wipe away the ink. The Bible says what it says. We can argue over how much weight we should give to the Bible. Is it God's inspired authoritative word to us, or, (to steal a line from the movie *Pirates of the Caribbean*,) "It's more like guidelines than actual rules?" Or worse, some would call the Bible a second rate history book that's out-of-touch with today's society. I could point out that the Bible has proven time and again to be accurate archeologically, that it forms the foundation of the laws and governing documents of western civilization, and that it has yet to miss on hundreds of prophetic predictions. But that would just be showing my bias as a Bible student since 1985.

Seriously, many people don't like God's opinions on some of the social issues of the day, and they openly wonder whether these opinions are really from God, or just positions that the Church, for some reason, has traditionally held. God's word has always been radical, and it has divided "father against son, and mother against daughter" (Luke 12:53). People in every generation have stumbled over God's word and his stated moral values. Some have found them to be hateful and unacceptable, while others have found beauty, wisdom, and eternal life. Our generation is no different. I would so love to reach this world with the realization that the overwhelming love and wisdom behind the statutes and the commands of God are so pure and powerful that they form the only true strong basis for successful human relationships, and justice, and mercy.

Still, folks are perplexed and filled with questions like, "If God is love, then how can the world be like this? How can He allow non-believers to go to hell?" For many in our time, God can seem, at best, irresponsible. Few people seem to understand that God is serious about giving us free will. People choose to make the world this way, and they choose whether or not they will go to hell. God allows humankind to make these choices, but he also provides a way to heaven – Jesus. But people have to choose to follow him. Choosing Jesus can redeem a lifetime of bad choices. That's why it's so important for

> **PEOPLE HAVE TO CHOOSE TO FOLLOW JESUS.**

people to actually connect with God, and not allow the biases of the world to decide for them what they will choose.

> This entire section is devoted to considering the ways that current public opinion paints God as different from how he truly is, and clouds the air with false notions and misunderstandings that drive people away from His love.

On a hopeful note, some cultural trends show that there is a new curiosity about the Christian faith. People want to know the basics about what Christians believe, but not in a pressure packed "come-to-Jesus" meeting. They want to get their questions answered in an open discussion where differing points of view can be shared. Bible-based movies and television events gather large audiences. Occasionally popular songs with Christian messages are big hits in secular markets. Curiosity about Christianity has grown from the Gen X days when Christianity wasn't even good for a punchline in a sitcom. If only the God portrayed in so-called Christian movies and on TV specials today was an accurate representation of Him. Too often screen writers decide that the Biblical God needs to be made more interesting and dynamic. I guess creator of the universe, ultimate moral authority, savior of humankind, and worker of various earth-shaking miracles, is not enough for Hollywood.

GETTING SPECIFIC

The very nature of God is often misunderstood? Non-believers have sometimes seen God as condemning or distant, because they don't understand how He loves us and provides for us. Christian believers are often the cause of this misunderstanding, because we come across as condemning, defensive, intolerant and inflexible. Too often the Church is not the life-giving, loving, and courageous group of people we are called to be. Don't let that stop you as you consider the Christian faith. Once you know God, you'll understand Christians much better.

Also, because God has a righteous standard, and He is jealous and unwilling to share heaven with all the other gods that people around the world like to believe in, He comes off as aloof and elitist, and distant, and not in-sync with modern society. It seems that some people have decided what God needs to be like, they think he needs to share, and they will only run in those circles that present the version of God that they like. If God is not going to cooperate with their idea of what He needs to be like, then he can forget it.

The God I believe in decides what people are going to be like, not the other way around.

TINKERBELL SYNDROME

In the stage play, *Peter Pan,* there is a scene in which Tinkerbell, the little pixie portrayed by a tiny but bright spotlight, is dying. Tink has gone into a glass dome, about the size of a cake, to die. Her little light is about to fade all the way out. Peter tries to talk Tinkerbell out of it, but it's not her fault. It turns out that she is dying because nobody believes in her anymore. So Peter turns to the audience and exhorts them to clap and cheer if they believe in Tink. The audience is slow at first, but Peter keeps urging them on until the people are cheering for Tinkerbell to show that they believe in her. (When I was 5, I screamed my "guts" out!) The light flickers and then gets brighter and brighter until Tink is all the way back, and Peter opens the dome so Tinkerbell can fly around the stage again – saved by the faith of those who believe in her.

Maybe people think that if enough of them just stop believing in God, then like Tinkerbell, He will go away and cease to exist. Some people get comfortable ignoring or denying God. Some even like to crusade against Him. They don't want anybody to, "clap" for God. They would just as soon see His light go out, so they can live in a world free from Him. If only they could understand that our faith in God doesn't save God, it saves us! Whenever humankind has grown away from God, He has done remarkable things to reestablish himself with us, and rekindle the relationship of love and respect. It is just this phenomenon of seeing God turn and awaken our generation that drives me.

It's one of the great purposes of an awakening – to see the God we love connect with people on a massive scale. The hurdle that must be

overcome, is the idea that people can choose whether or not God exists. The realization of God goes back to the beginning of mankind. No generation will ever be able to wish Him away, or imagine Him away, or philosophy Him away, or ignore Him away. He was here before time began, he created time and he operates it, and he will be here when time no longer exists.

Today there are a few ideas growing in popularity that are threatening to put out the light of western civilization's relationship with God. Here are the main trends that tend to separate people from knowing God.

THE ATTACK ON AUTHORITY

Our culture is slowly mounting and assault on authority.

Political Authority: Often, neither the congress nor the President of the United States has positive approval ratings. Leading political candidates for President of the United States are often people who never held public office before. Evidently we Americans are so fed-up with politicians that we'll vote for anyone who isn't one.

- **Law Enforcement Authority**: Our police are being shot and killed because of a perceived racial bias and use of excessive force. At the same time, black men are being killed on the streets, and in lock-up, at rates far beyond that of other racial groups.

- **Military Authority**: Our military, once a proud projection of America's determination to remain free, is shrinking for lack of funding. They are being downsized dramatically, in part, by those who don't trust them.

- **Classroom Authority**: Teachers are being stripped of their ability to maintain discipline in their classrooms by the ever-increasing rules resulting from lawsuits. We don't want authorities to hold us, or our children, accountable. More and more, we Americans see ourselves as victims who deserve special consideration.

- **Church Authority**: Disappointing Priests and Pastors form a sad parade on the nightly news.

HURDLES FACING A GREAT AWAKENING/REVIVAL

- **Legal Authority:** We've also seen District Attorneys and judges shot.
- **Parental Authority:** is under attack. Each year brings legislation telling parents how not to discipline children.
- **Workplace Authority:** Some feel that big greedy corporations are the problem.
- **Governmental Authority:** Some feel that big power-hungry government is the problem
- **Legal Representation:** Does anybody like lawyers? (I think one of the reasons why Judge Judy is such a popular TV show is because people secretly long for someone who is not afraid to say, "this is wrong and this is right".)

In this anti-authority atmosphere, God is a big target. Let's face it, He's an authority figure who is completely immutable - He will never change. He thinks he's right all the time, and He is. (For instance, he totally opposes evil, and he gets to decide what is evil.) He has some rules that are "set in stone" and his word and his Spirit constantly tell people what they should and shouldn't do. God acts like he's the boss of the world. He is absolute truth. Wow!

Therefore, another purpose of a great awakening, is for God to establish his creative and moral authority with people who don't know him. The hurdle that must be overcome is convincing people, who resent and mistrust most authority, to set it aside long enough to connect with the most trustworthy, incorruptible authority the world has ever known – the Judeo-Christian God.

TOLERANCE

A second movement, one of tolerance, is also gaining ground. What used to be a bumper sticker, "Tolerate Diversity", is now an anthem for many. In this growing philosophy, people are willing to compromise their beliefs and downplay their feelings, in order to accommodate and avoid inconveniencing or offending others. Being firm is being mean.

Standing on principal is being inflexible. Promoting your point-of-view uncompromisingly is uncomfortably pushy, a turn-off, and may be seen as evidence of a low I.Q. or brainwashing. In school, children are taught to be tolerant of those around them who have a different viewpoint, a different appearance, a different faith, a different background, or a different racial heritage. This is good, but they are not taught about how to defend their Christian beliefs, nor are they taught the courage of taking a stand against persecution of the Christian faith. The public schools have zero tolerance for; bullies, weapons, illegal drugs and all forms of child abuse, and Christianity. Apparently, those who promote tolerance are also those who determine what is and isn't tolerable. They reserve for themselves the right to be intolerant toward anything that opposes their world view.

The Bible remains the bestselling book ever banned from public schools by a U.S. District Court (in Denver). The lawsuit came from a Jewish family. Their son noticed a Bible on his teacher's desk during a silent reading period in a public school. They complained that, even though the teacher seldom read the Bible during the reading time, the very presence of that Bible represented an unfair influence over the students. The teacher also had a book on Native American Customs and Beliefs, but it wasn't complained about. The judge ruled against the Bible, and it was upheld in District Court. It can feel to Christians that the tolerance movement is intolerant of them.

On the surface, the philosophy of tolerance is founded on the noble desire to lead people away from self-centeredness and bigotry, and toward a more enlightened view of others. How badly has America struggled with civil rights and prejudice toward every ethnic group that reaches our shores? Our culture has demonized people for political beliefs, like communism and fascism, and for religious beliefs like Judaism and the Muslim faith. We struggle with sex biases against women, and folks with sexual orientations that may be uncomfortable to us. We have age discrimination, economic discrimination, and some look down on people who enter our country without our permission. We are woefully inad-

HURDLES FACING A GREAT AWAKENING/REVIVAL

equate at understanding people with disabilities, and providing for people with mental health problems. Every person in America with a heart wants to see us do so much better in all these areas, until everyone in our society has equal value, care, and opportunity.

I want all of these things fixed too, and I know how to do it. God loves and cares about all these people equally, and he calls every Christian to do the same! If everyone were Christian, and lived the way God calls us to live, the problem would be fixed. But not everybody is Christian, and not all Christians live up to God's standard.

However, telling people to be tolerant, without God, is unwise.

> **TOLERANCE ONLY WORKS WELL FROM A GODLY, BIBLICAL POINT OF REFERENCE.**

Tolerance looks caring and thoughtful, but underneath, in practice, it opposes absolute truth, and ushers in situational ethics. For example, tolerance dictates that we seek to understand what motivates others in the hope that we will be less judgmental – allowing others to deal with their reality in their way, and not condemning them for it. With this mindset, a tolerant person might endorse this axiom; "If you're starving, it's okay to steal some food." In this situation our ethics change to fit our needs, or to be more accepting of someone else's decision. But what if the food we steal causes two children to starve to death. Now the situation changes, and again we change the ethical value just a bit. "If you're starving, it's okay to steal some food from a wealthy man." Soon enough, human nature will start to take over. If the wealthy man has a lot and you don't, you may steal some of his wealth too. Soon we can rationalize doing whatever greed drives us to do.

On the other hand, with absolute truth, stealing is wrong. If you steal food, you go to God and repent and are forgiven. You join a church where people help you get on your feet. You eventually get a job and you go and payback the guy you stole from. As you grow, you start a food bank to take care of starving people and bring them into the church too. Agreed, this is an oversimplification, but I believe that the results wind up the same in more complex real-life settings. Tolerance presses toward situational ethics while Christianity believes in absolute truth. It's a moral conflict that plays out daily in our culture.

An ultimate example of this is the Christian understanding of salvation. We believe that faith in Jesus, as the Son of God, who died for our sins, is the only way for a person to gain eternal life in heaven with God. We can certainly be tolerant of other viewpoints, but we know that these other viewpoints lead people to eternal life in hell. Our tacit tolerance has eternal consequences that are unacceptable. We are obligated to "speak the truth in love" with wisdom and gentleness. We must not be silent, because our first duty is to God, and to love our neighbor. If you love your neighbor, do you let him go to hell? No. Instead, by being good neighbors, we try to earn the right to speak truth as we know it into their lives. <u>But we must not be silent!</u>

What if one of God's absolute truths says that people who live a certain lifestyle, or believe a certain faith, or follow a certain political belief, are wrong? Should Christians then be intolerant of people who are doing those wrong things? First of all, one of God's absolute truths is that everyone lives a lifestyle that is wrong.

> For ***all have sinned*** *and fall short of the glory of God.*
> *(Romans 3:23, emphasis added)*

God sent his son to forgive those sins so that people would be free to approach Him. Few ask for this forgiveness. Those of us who do, believe in Jesus, and become children of God. We are taught to be intolerant of sin, but to love sinners, and bless them and win them into the same freedom from sin that we have found. Again, we are human and not always good at being like our Savior, Jesus. My hope is that God will do again what he has done throughout history, and bring upon our generation a great awakening that will supernaturally win people into his family.

The bottom line is that the cultural value of tolerance ends up ultimately branding God as intolerant. It's unfortunate, because God completely loves all people. The Bible is clear on this. He is also holy and perfect and does not tolerate sin. Instead God provides forgiveness, so that sinful people can be with Him. I pray to see Him bust loose on this world with love and conviction and transformation, so His Church will be more like him, and those who know him not, will experience his love and move toward him.

That God's forgiveness might be experienced by more people, is another purpose of an awakening. The hurdle to be overcome is the fact that Jesus is the only way to eternal life in heaven, and tolerance of other viewpoints allows people to go to hell. The world must allow Christian truth back into the marketplace of ideas. At the same time, if God allows diversity, so should Christians.

POLITICAL CORRECTNESS

Political correctness is another good-sounding movement in our culture. It seeks to fix the gap between the "haves and the have-nots". Political correctness attaches value to those efforts which even out the inequities of society, and it devalues those efforts which appear to maintain or increase those inequities. Political correctness also seeks to save us from ourselves by getting people to change bad habits. For instance, bad nutrition from fast food restaurants is politically incorrect, so in New York City, they have tried to pass laws limiting the size of fountain drinks in an attempt to change people's habits. The media cooperates often by running stories on the ills of drinking too much soda.

Political Correctness has its roots in a few basic ideas with which you may or may not agree.

1. **Haves and Have-nots –**
   There are people who have advantages over other people. These advantages include wealth, appearance, education, fame, and positions of authority, influence, and control. For the most part, these people usually discriminate against disadvantaged people. They do this to maintain what they have, and to keep others from joining them.

2. **People don't know what's good for them.**
   Although we live in a democracy where many decisions in government are made by voting, people don't always make good decisions. People

tend to vote selfishly and live with short-sighted values that don't serve them well. Those few who see the bigger picture, can influence every day citizens into changing their bad habits, both in life and in voting, by constantly pointing out the many disasters that await people if they don't change now.

3. Government is the first Equalizer.

Governments must correct these imbalances in society by passing laws that require advantaged people to share with the disadvantaged, and by creating pathways for all people to gain advantages. The end goal is that everyone will have a similar piece of the pie, economically, socially, and legally. And, as much as possible, government must pass laws that require people to make better choices and change those bad habits.

4. The Media is the Second Equalizer.

The media's job is to expose the injustice that disadvantaged people suffer at the hands of the advantaged, and to tell the positive stories of the changes that result from the social engineering of political correctness. The media is also the key to creating fear in people who don't want to change, by broadcasting dire predictions of their future if people don't change, and scientific studies that substantiate what they are saying.

5. Public Education is the Third Equalizer.

Public Education, which is funded and run by the government, must teach about the need for equality in all things, and fill their curricula with the wisdom of politically correct causes.

It's not hard to list the current Agenda of political correctness. We see it in politics, the media, and in public schools. Again, these are a sample of the noble goals and causes that need to be addressed.

- ♦ Equal pay for people who hold the same position and do the same work.
- ♦ Taxing the wealthy to pay for various services for the disadvantaged

- Voting rights for legal citizens who were denied the vote.
- Hiring quotas for minorities, women, and disadvantaged workers.
- Raise the minimum wage.
- Corporations have unfair political influence and unfair economic advantages.

With regard to changing the bad habits of society so we will live more responsibly, political correctness supports things like;

- Fighting global warming by legislating energy consumption, recycling, etc.
- Fighting against our poor nutrition habits in fast food
- Legislation to permit more lawsuits against corporations
- School curricula that emphasizes the contributions made to America by people who belong to groups of all kinds that are discriminated against

So what's that got to do with God? Is God opposed to equality for all? No. In fact, God loves people equally and desires their salvation equally. On the other hand, He never promises that things will ever be equal or fair in this life. I think God knows human nature too well. The way that the PC movement ends up conflicting with God is when He gets in the way.

Perhaps the most classic of the many clashes between God and political correctness is abortion. One of the habits that the PC agenda wants to change is the birth rate in the world. They are worried that the world will become overpopulated. PC predictions when I was a boy claimed that humankind would outgrow the planet by the end of the century (That is—the last century). Therefore the PC push was to legalize abortion, and provide free abortions through the government. Schools got on board, but not by teaching abstinence. Instead they chose to promote methods of birth control. The media champions the cause of Planned Parenthood which provides abortions largely on Uncle Sam's dollar.

Christians generally believe that abortions go against the will of God, who is for life and involved in the creation process, and therefore we opposed the legalization of abortion. PC won the battle in 1969. Prior to this conflict, Christians battled for, and lost, school prayer. The politically correct movement often pushes for freedom from traditional Christian moral values that tended to be written into our laws by our forefathers, or supported by the common law practices of the first 150 years of our nation. This is just one of several big disconnects between God and our society.

Today, absolute truth and the Christian worldview have become politically incorrect. Most Christians will choose God over the laws of any nation, when those laws cause them to oppose God. A larger conflict looms.

Here are some examples of this clash in everyday life.

> When my son was in second grade, he and his friends were playing tag on the playground, and it was boys against girls. (Uh-oh, is that equal?) When the boys tagged the girls, the girls had to return to base. They proved the girls had been tagged by pulling out their shirt tails. This became inappropriate so the principal called them into the office. Then the principal called the police, and in the presence of an armed police officer she threatened them with sexual assault charges. (Did I mention that my son was seven years old and one of the smallest kids in his class?) Then she called the parents and suspended the boys from school. We grounded our son for the weekend, even though we disagreed totally with this overreaction, because we wanted our son to know that we support the authorities that he is placed under and he needs to follow the rules. But inside we were upset with the principal.

> This same principal, who was part Native American, brought in a special tree that native Americans believe has a spirit which would bring reconciliation to those who would sit under it, and when students had fights, she would have them sit under the tree while they settled the dispute. (I call this kind of thing Idol worship.) She was commended for her work.

HURDLES FACING A GREAT AWAKENING/REVIVAL

As the PC movement champions the cause of those in our society who have been discriminated against, like women and native Americans, they run roughshod over the people and institutions that they believe have done the discriminating.

Since Christianity has been the primary religious belief in America since our nation's inception, the Church is seen as an institution that has fostered the problem. In some cases they are right. Christians have occasionally done terrible things in the name of the Lord, but our overall track record has been to put more time, effort, sacrifice, and money into helping the downtrodden of this world than any other institution in the history of the world. Christians have built hospitals, schools, and orphanages in huge numbers, on every continent on earth except Antarctica. We were the champions of the needy long before the PC movement branded us as part of the problem. But because of this branding, this generation holds God at arms-length. They are slow to even investigate our faith. My heart breaks when I see them remain distant.

1. Everyone gets the same trophy at the soccer tournament even though one team won all their games and another team lost all of theirs. We just ignore the excellence of one team and the failure of the other. But when these children reach High School, and try out for the varsity team and most don't make it, they sue the coach and the school, because no one has the right to tell them they aren't good enough. God teaches us to speak the truth in love". He teaches us to be humble, and not all about ourselves and our trophy. Adolescence is too late to begin this training.

   We used to see the sad results of this, "nobody ever loses" approach to teaching, every year on the *American Idol* TV show. Some people have never been told they can't sing very well. They get furious and swear and throw things because the professional singers who judge them are telling them that they are terrible. They can't handle the truth. We are slowly beginning to think of ourselves as a nation of victims of unfair treatment, instead of a nation of people who hold ourselves responsible for our own success.

God teaches that we will have all kinds of struggles in this world, but He will be there to help us get through them. The PC movement doesn't want to hear that. They just want God to fix it, or else he must not exist.

The conflict is this simple. God instills self-worth and purpose in people. Political Correctness causes people to feel like victims who have been taken advantage of and now they deserve to be reimbursed somehow. Victims want justice and restitution. Christians want mercy and freedom from sin. Once people have been convinced that they've been wronged, it's hard to get them to focus on living a sacrificial lifestyle for the benefit of others. And, again, people miss out on connecting with God.

2. We sacrifice honesty in order to give the appearance of equality. I have been in too many teachers meeting when we were planning the year-end awards assembly, and I have seen them manipulate the scores of the top students in order to achieve the appearance of equality. When each teacher shares their top students, and they are all from the same race, or gender, or economic background, the teachers begin to make changes as if nothing were wrong with it. By the end of the negotiations, they had achieved a reasonable balance of honorees, but few of the awards went to the actual students with the highest scores.

The PC moral dilemma—is it unfair to give all the awards to the one student who is a genius and won them all? Or, is it unfair to manipulate the process in order to spread the awards around to achieve Political Correctness? This may seem like a small example, but it plays out on stages small and large. Who gets the ninth grade science award may be inconsequential, but who gets the government grants and contracts is serious business.

God teaches us not to seek worldly rewards, but to measure ourselves by how well we serve others and love them—to be Christ-like. With this as our goal, we don't have to lie. We just let God promote whom he will. But this doesn't sell in PC driven society. Recognition and promotion for people, programs, and causes which line up with the PC agenda, are vital to this movement, and they will bend rules and spin truth to

HURDLES FACING A GREAT AWAKENING/REVIVAL

make it happen. Therefore the knowledge of God is never understood or shared. When God gets marginalized by the PC agenda, people who don't know God are okay with that, and everyone loses.

3. Here's another PC staple. It's terrible when a society has super wealthy people and super poor people, therefore the wealthy people must be forced to give much of their money to the poor. I love when people give to charities, but when the government forces the wealthy, through taxation, to give more than they want to give, and then doles it out to other people, sometimes with political motives other than charity, then the rich people end up moving to a country that won't do that to them.

   What remains is a country that just lost some key employers who create jobs for the poor, and everyone else. I realize that this is an over-simplification of the problem. But it plays out in reality, which explains why so many American corporations have moved their headquarters to European countries with low tax rates.

   Again, God goes against the grain. He says that people who believe in his Son get to go to Heaven, and all the rest have to go to hell—(winners and losers.) He tells us all to be generous from our hearts. The wealthy should take care of the poor voluntarily out of the goodness of their hearts (because believers share God's heart), and everyone who can do something should work or go hungry. God says to honor your boss, especially when he's unfair, and work even harder than he asks, so you can be a good example as a Christian and bring glory to Christ. God says to be honest, and make sure you speak the truth with love. God says that it is wrong for the poor to love the idea of lots of money. God says it is wrong for the rich to love the idea of lots of money. God even says to pay taxes to the government! God drives the PC movement crazy! In the wake of this disconnect, people who might be saved never really consider God as a possibility.

4. When it comes to legislation, God sets this example. Laws should be written to apply to all people equally, not separate rules for different groups of people. i.e. "Thou shalt not steal." It's for everyone. Well intended laws written to help and/or protect specific groups of people

can force some change, but they don't change people's hearts. God knows that unless people's hearts change, the prejudice will always find a way to discriminate. God is in the business of changing hearts. He's not opposed to trying to improve the lot of disadvantaged people through legislation, but if our country would embrace God again, instead of pushing away, He could make the bigger changes which legislation cannot achieve.

5. Okay, here comes God's biggest current un-PC rule. Sex is only for married people. There can only be two people in a marriage, and they must be male and female. I'll be honest. It's really hard to find a Christian who hasn't broken this one in one way or another, hence the need for God's forgiveness. Much of the world just doesn't want an ancient moral authority telling them they can't do what they want to do. However, God isn't going anywhere. God has an opinion, and his is the only one that counts. Many people today are incredulous that I would even bother to bring this up. Can God be any more out of touch? And yet the divorce rate is so high because people bring so much baggage into marriage from their past physical relationships. Both of my sons voluntarily told me that they had waited with their wives for marriage. I never asked. I believe them. Their marriages seem strong so far.

Could this old idea of God's actually be the answer for divorce, unwed mothers, child welfare, unpaid child support, neglected children, etc? O how I wish that PC and God could get together. How many who now seek greater meaning in life, could find it in the life, death, and resurrection of a carpenter who is also the Son of God?

6. And now, the "Elephant in the Room"- LGBTQ!
LGBTQ is an acronym that stands for Lesbian, Gay, Bisexual, Transgender, and Queer or Questioning, and is used to designate a community of people whose sexual or gender identities can create shared political and social concerns. (google search)

  - Conservative Christians will tell you that, for the most part, LGBTQ lifestyles oppose God's moral code as defined in the Bible.

HURDLES FACING A GREAT AWAKENING/REVIVAL

   Those who practice these lifestyles are at risk of going to hell when they die.
- Liberal Christians are slowly embracing this community and some are beginning to allow them into leadership positions. They are starting to say that there is nothing especially wrong at all with this lifestyle more than any other.

So who is right? (Please stay with me until I complete this explanation.) Let's let God's word speak for Him.

> *Because of this,(human-kinds refusal to accept God) God gave them over to shameful lusts. Even their women exchanged natural sexual relations for unnatural ones. In the same way the men also abandoned natural relations with women and were inflamed with lust for one another. Men committed shameful acts with other men, and received in themselves the due penalty for their error.*
> *(Romans 1:26-27)*

Here, the author Paul is explaining that these kinds of activities take place because people refuse to accept God. It's a sin and a rejection of God. Okay, but the Word also says this.

> *For **all** have sinned and fall short of the glory of God.*
> *(Romans 3:23, emphasis added)*

So it appears that all people, including believers, have sinned and can't get to heaven without believing in Jesus

> *For God so loved the world that he gave his one and only Son, that whoever believes in him shall not perish but have eternal life.*
> *(John 3:16)*

It also appears that "whoever" believes in Jesus does go to heaven. This begs the question, "What if someone who is LGBTQ believes in Jesus as the Son of God who died on the cross for their sin and was raised on the third day?" Will they go to heaven? Yes.

What if they genuinely believe in Jesus, but they continue to live a LGBTQ lifestyle? Won't their insistence on that rebellious lifestyle knock them out of heaven? Let us look at one more scripture.

> *You have heard that it was said, "You shall not commit adultery." But I tell you that anyone who looks at a woman lustfully has already committed adultery with her in his heart.*
>
> *(Matthew 5:27-28)*

I am an American Baptist Pastor, and if this is the definition of adultery, and it is, then I am guilty of it—often. Yet, I consider myself saved. However, I don't defend this as the way I should be. I simply recognize that I desperately need a Savior, and I do work at denying lust in my life. Frankly, I'm getting old enough that it's just not as big a deal as it used to be. So if a LGBTQ person believes in Jesus and wants to change from their lifestyle, but they keep failing, they too are saved like me.

But what if they defend their rebellious lifestyle and say that they are not wrong to pursue it? A little further on, Paul writes this.

> *Although they know God's righteous decree that those who do such things deserve death, they not only continue to do these very things but also **approve of those who practice them**.*
>
> *(Romans 1:32, emphasis added)*

Now I am worried, and my heart breaks, because the insistence that nothing is wrong with LGBTQ lifestyles is clearly addressed here in God's word. It's wrong to say that it's OK.

I have close friends who smoke cigarettes. Most Christians agree that smoking hurts our bodies, and it's not what God wants for us to do. We would say that it is sinful to not take care of what God has given us.

I believe these believers who smoke are saved, and they have worked alongside me, sometimes for decades, to reach the lost, and serve in God's church. Like many smokers, they want to quit, but it is such a difficult addiction to break. I've always felt that they probably started as an act of defiance toward their parents or other elements of society that had somehow alienated them. Or maybe it was a cry for help that went unanswered. Either way, they chose an interesting act of rebellion—they chose to do something that would hurt themselves, in order to hurt the ones that were hurting them.

HURDLES FACING A GREAT AWAKENING/REVIVAL

Let's suppose for a moment that my smoker friends love Jesus and totally believe in him, but they also defend their smoking, and say, "I'm just not going to change. It's too hard to change, and Jesus loves me anyway. I'm going to heaven either way. If he wants to make me stop smoking, then He can take away the desire. Otherwise, I will continue to love and serve him, and I will continue to smoke." Wow! Still, the definition of salvation —belief in Jesus as Savior—is in place in their lives and they are saved.

I think we want to say to this statement, smoking isn't as big a deal to God as being LGBTQ. But is it? And, what about the sins that persist in every believers life, are they forgiven? The final question is, "Does the sacrifice of Jesus on the cross cover even the sins that we fail to recognize or accept as sin?' Does it cover even the sins we cling to and defend?

I know stubborn Christians who were prideful and who died in that pride, but they loved Jesus and believed in him. They never seemed to understand that the prideful opinions that they readily shared were sometimes totally inappropriate.

I know Christians who were alcoholics, and they died paying lip service to recovering, but never really trying. They worked hard to find enablers that would bring them booze even on their death beds. But they dearly loved the Lord and cried at their own plight.

Every Christian I know has blind spots when it comes to their own sin, and we continue to sin in certain areas of our lives unapologetically. But we love Jesus and follow Him. Sometimes he deals with our sin and we go through a painful trial and eventually repent and change for the better. But let's be honest, some of our sinful traits go undealt with.

EVERYONE HAS BLIND SPOTS... CHRISTIANS INCLUDED!.

I believe that all have sinned, and continue to sin, and fall short of the glory of God, but God's grace is totally undeserved and he gives it to all who believe in Jesus. Period!

WHEN GOD TURNS

> *For it is by **grace** you have been saved, through faith—and this is not from yourselves, it is the gift of God— not by works, so that no one can boast.   (Ephesians 2:8-9, emphasis added)*

I personally have come to the conclusion that LGBTQ folks need Jesus just like anyone else, and we need to pray for them to be part of the great awakening, and stop reviling them as having a sin that is somehow, "greater" than ours. We cannot say to them, "change first, and then you can be saved." It's always the other way around.

God wants "all people", and so should we. Let us share Christ with them, and let Him deal with their sin just as he deals with ours. They are not better or worse than the rest of humankind, because we are all sinners in need of a gracious God. Amen.

How much has our demonizing of LGBTQ types, chased them away from Jesus? We may resent their movement, but are we in part responsible for it?

What a stumbling block all this has been to this generation in their approach to God. No one wants a God that hates certain elements of society. Christians must not paint God as the great disapprover. He loves all people, even when we find it hard to do. Let's get over it and move on to reaching everyone with the Gospel message.

If only I could say this to the PC types who resent all these things about God. God's opinions and commandments are based in His love for all people. He understands the human heart better than anyone, and his rules are designed for our own good, just like speed limits on our highways. (Nobody follows those rules either) God is not a villain trying to get in the way of positive change in our culture. God is the positive change our culture needs. God is the only mass means of changing the hearts of people for the better. His process is not perfect, because he allows us to have our own free will. But the history of the Church, with all her human failings, is still a steady march toward freedom and love for all humankind. God's victory in the human heart eclipses anything the Political Correctness movement could ever want.

HURDLES FACING A GREAT AWAKENING/REVIVAL

I encourage every reader who is not a believer to withhold judgment on Christianity, until you have experienced God personally in your heart. This can be done by sincerely asking Him for a touch of His love, wisdom, and Spirit. These things he gives to those who ask, because he wants you to know him.

So another purpose of a revival/awakening is to reset our understanding about the absolute truth of God in Jesus Christ, especially as it applies to relationships and equality. The hurdle seems almost insurmountable. Can we get people to realize that God's really old-school answers are still the best answers? They aren't easy, but they have the wisdom and the heart changing power of God behind them.

THE NARRATIVE

Many of today's cultural norms are driven by public education and the mainstream media, something that most of us share in common. Both of these organizations have a strong democrat/progressive/liberal bias. Please set aside your conservative or liberal/progressive bias, and just consider the data.

Since the 1960's the numbers of media journalists voting for democrat presidential candidates has fluctuated between 81% and 93%. Most teacher surveys show that 45% to 50% of teachers are democrat, 25% to 30% are republican and most of the rest are independent, but liberal leaning. 95% of the NEA's campaign contributions go to Democrat candidates. This bias drives the PC movement and shapes our culture in ways that line up against God.

Mainstream media and public education have set the table for today's social trends too. These biases decide what is taught in our schools and what stories make the evening news. If we don't like a preacher we can go to another church, but for many parents, going to another school is impossible, and the NEA spends tens of millions of dollars annually to defeat voucher programs that would allow parents to take the money that their state will spend to educate their child, and give it to the school they want for their kids. Political correctness is winning.

The idea of "the narrative" is strong in this government/public school/media driven influence. The "narrative" is the culmination of all the societal issues that many people in these institutions wish to impact. If a news story doesn't fit the narrative, they don't report it. Out of all the murders that occur in America each year, there are a hand full that become national media stories. Some of those murders are just sensational or bizarre enough to make the news. Other murders make the national news because they fit the narrative—they illustrate a social problem on which the media types have decided to focus our attention.

Sometimes, if a scientist discovers that life begins at conception, or there is no man-made global warming, or if statistics show that teachers with guns save lives, these things don't fit the narrative, so they won't get government grants to study it, or make it into textbooks, or get broadcast on the evening news. Of course the same kind of bias exists in conservative corners too. They tend to dominate talk radio the way liberals dominate TV news. Conservatives have their own narrative, and are just as likely to screen out or spin those news stories that go against their world view.

The problem with all of this narrative business comes when God doesn't fit the narrative.

God does fit the narrative when it comes to charity. Christians are called to be humanitarians, and the media and government accept and encourage these efforts in the church. But on many moral issues, as I have previously documented, God's opinions fall against the narrative. When this happens, the government/public school/media types try to ignore Him and his church. When they can't ignore God, they discredit Him. It is easy to see this dance today with the media and the Pope. They broadcast when the Pope gets tough on past child abuse cases by coming down hard on offending priests. It fits the narrative that large corporations and institutions take advantage of people. But when the Pope opposes female priests, they either go quiet on those statements, or they use biased language like, "The Pope still hasn't budged on women priests." This makes clear where they expect him to go next, and what he must do to gain their approval and support. I'm not for or against women priests. I'm a Baptist.

HURDLES FACING A GREAT AWAKENING/REVIVAL

We have women pastors. But I hope we can see here how this idea of the narrative works through certain cultural and governmental institutions, to gradually manipulate people into opposing God on many of today's current issues, and this has the effect of blocking people from an experience of the living God.

Yet another hurdle of revival/awakening is for God to work around these institutions to demonstrate his love and wisdom directly to these people who have been influenced away from Him.

Things are changing.

- It is good news to me that many people are getting their news and information from their phones instead of ABC, NBC, and CBS.
- It is also good news that more and more parents are home-schooling their kids, in part, to avoid the bias and the social engineering of Public Education.

THE REEMERGENCE OF SOCIAL CONSCIENCE

Maybe the best news in social trends is the heightened sense of social conscience in America today. People give when they see a flood on TV or hear about a young girl with cancer. They give to refugees one day and tornado victims the next. People also show up to help in surprising numbers to search for the lost or to rebuild someone's home.

There was terrible flooding in Boulder, CO a few years ago, and the pastor of the 1st Baptist Church of Boulder was leading a team from his church to help clean the mud out of people's houses. One basement had taken much of their day and they were running out of strength when a large group of college students came down the street to help. Just before they started, the students wanted to make it very clear that they were not Christians, and they didn't want to be confused with any of the several church groups around. It was vitally important for them to make the statement that Christians aren't the only ones who help out in times of need. These students had a need to do "something good", without God, to prove it could be done. I can only guess why, but it saddened me to see people expressing brotherly love, but excluding the author of it.

Even in a time when social conscience is on the rise, God's name doesn't always receive glory. It's hard to imagine that any organization has done more in the last 2,000 years for the poor, the hungry, the orphans, the sick, and the imprisoned, than the church, and para-church organizations like the Red Cross, the Salvation Army, Compassion International, and their ilk. But somehow the Christian church sometimes gets painted as one more giant corporation out for itself. Or worse—we are a global force bent on ruling the world and imposing our faith system on the unwanting masses.

Wow, last time I read my Bible, Jesus didn't kill or enslave a single person! He didn't even try, nor did he teach others to do so. He tended to feed people and then he would send them out to love, teach, and offer eternal life, pretty much in that order.

In this time when many people who don't know God, and others don't like what they think they know about him, some would like to quietly bury him. However, the last time folks tried to bury him, revival happened. Out of death came new life. I would love to see today's new social conscience connected to all the scriptures that call for us to take care of those in need.

> *Religion that God our Father accepts as pure and faultless is this: to look after **orphans** and **widows** in their distress and to keep oneself from being polluted by the world.*
> *(James 1:27, emphasis added)*

Another great purpose of an awakening in this generation would be to be to see charity thrive to the benefit of all mankind as the wisdom and resources of God inhabit the great charitable drive of this new generation. The hurdle to be overcome is the brokering of a divine partnership. I do pray for it.

HURDLES FACING A GREAT AWAKENING/REVIVAL

WHY ALL THIS?

Okay, I've been whining and moaning about how unfair the socio-political landscape is, because it paints God and Christianity in a negative light, and it drags Christians into an unfortunately defensive stance where it's much more difficult to share faith than in an open and honest discussion.

The reason I have taken time to share my observations of today's society is not so I can try to start a socio-political movement to correct the ills of our culture. That's the last thing I would hope for. What I want is a move of God. I want God to reintroduce himself to my fellow citizens. I also want society to realize that there is a growing predisposition against God. Sometimes it's subtle, and sometimes it's obvious and even violent. If we are to pray and prepare for God to turn in this environment, we need to know what we're asking for, and the hurdles we must jump as we share our faith.

Many people know something about God, but few actually know God. This is yet another hurdle for an awakening/revival. People need to be cleared of the smokescreen in order to make a clean approach to God.

A DIVIDED CHURCH

Please let me point out one more sad fact that works against God in today's world. His Church is divided too!

(I'm going to be somewhat critical of the Church here, which goes against my training and beliefs. I have been taught that Christians should not criticize the Church, because Jesus is the head of the church. He runs the Church the way He wants to, and to criticize the church is to criticize Jesus.

I certainly do not mean to criticize my Lord and Savior. Nor do I question His leadership in any way. I just think we're not listening to His leadership. As my close friends have pointed out to me, there is nothing wrong with criticizing the Church where we are being disobedient to Jesus.

WHEN GOD TURNS

I have served in the largest church in Colorado, and also in the smallest. I've served in non-denominational churches and in denominational churches. I've been a member of eleven different churches over my lifetime, and I'm saying that we don't listen well enough to Jesus, our leader, and when we do hear him, we don't always commit to do what he says to do. So my criticism is aimed at me, along with the rest of his church in my country. We are a small shell of what he calls us to be, and so I beg Jesus to revive His Church. And, I criticize in the hopes of seeing change and growth in our unity and strength as his people.)

When I mention the divided Church, I'm not talking about the way that some denominations have differing opinions on how to interpret scripture. We may disagree on when to baptize, or how much to expect from the Holy Spirit, but what we have in common is much more than what separates us. The absolutes of the Christian faith unite all true Christians. These absolutes are the very things that must be believed in order for salvation to occur in a believer's heart. Namely, Jesus Christ is the Son of God who died on the cross for our sins, was buried in a tomb, and was resurrected on the third day. Believing these things in our hearts and confessing them with our mouths is salvation.

> **THE ABSOLUTES OF THE CHRISTIAN FAITH UNITE ALL CHRISTIANS.**

We should therefore be united, but we are not, because we are divided politically, and by how we respond to cultural pressure. We are divided into liberal and conservative, much like the nation in which we live. The National Council of Churches tends to be a liberal organization, and the National Association of Evangelicals is the conservative wing of Christianity. The truth is we don't work well together very often because we don't believe much in each other. The liberals accuse the conservatives of turning their backs on social justice and withholding support for oppressed people. Conservatives accuse the liberal churches of de-emphasizing scripture and misinterpreting God's word so as to eliminate the uncomfortable positions that God takes on current social issues.

HURDLES FACING A GREAT AWAKENING/REVIVAL

We are a divided church. I'm just touching the surface of how these socio-political ideologies separate us from each other. It's time for reconciliation. This includes the way we separate on Sunday morning along racial lines, too. More than half a century after segregation was made illegal we still have separate churches for whites, blacks, Koreans, Hispanics, Ethiopians, Kenyans, Burmese, etc. I realize that some of the immigrant churches are separate because they speak different languages, and people gather together for comfort and tradition which helps their worship. But what kind of a witness are we to the rest of the nation when they see immigrants and locals, blacks and whites, Hispanics, Africans, and Orientals, all playing together on the same basketball team, but not in the same church?

The answer is, we make the Kingdom of God look petty and trite!

We need a revival in the church. We need to be united under the head of the Church, Jesus Christ.

Here is a purpose for revival—so the Church will start to act like the united organization we are called to be. The hurdle is for Christians to focus on what unites us, and give up on what separates us.

I have noticed that when the Bible talks about the unity of the Church, it almost always mentions humility at the same time. It seems that unity cannot occur amongst people unless they are humble.

> *As a prisoner for the Lord, then, I urge you to live a life worthy of the calling you have received. Be completely humble and gentle; be patient, bearing with one another in love. Make every effort to keep the unity of the Spirit through the bond of peace.*
> *(Ephesians 4:1-3)*

This word from God through Paul describes the attitudes and mind-set of a church that has found unity and is trying to keep it. Two things jump out. One is the total absence of pride. And two, is the realization that God's Spirit has brought that unity. It is a spiritual unity.

> *So Christ himself gave the apostles, the prophets, the evangelists, the pastors and teachers, to equip his people for works of service, so that the body of Christ may be built up until we all reach unity in the faith and in the knowledge of the Son of God and become mature, attaining to the whole measure of the fullness of Christ...*
> *(Ephesians 4:11-13)*
>
> *... Instead, speaking the truth in love, we will grow to become in every respect the mature body of him who is the head, that is, Christ. (vs. 15)*

Now we see that Jesus puts people in leadership who must lead toward unity, which is a mature trait, and this unity takes the Church toward Jesus.

> *Therefore, as God's chosen people, holy and dearly loved, clothe yourselves with compassion, kindness, **humility**, gentleness and patience. Bear with each other and forgive one another if any of you has a grievance against someone. Forgive as the Lord forgave you. And over all those virtues put on love, which binds them all together in perfect **unity**.   (Colossians 3:12-14, emphasis added)*

(*Again we see these genuine traits of humility which bring love and unity to the Church.*) This is what the Church is called to be. This is what Jesus is saying. We shouldn't need great gifts of discernment, or encounters with a burning bush in order to know this. It's written right in God's word. Oh, how I pray for a revival of the Church.

Jesus is the head of the Church, and he must bring these things to fruition in His time and on his schedule. I'm not trying to tell Jesus what to do. He tells me what to do. I think that Jesus is leading us in this direction. If indeed the church comes up against greater persecution in the decades to come here in America, then His Church will surely grow closer together. I hope we won't need persecution to unite. I hope a great revival in the Church will pull us all together in Christ. In the meantime, I pray that our example to the lost will be stronger and more loving. I pray that our love and sacrifice for others will be the hallmarks of how Jesus is known through us.

HURDLES FACING A GREAT AWAKENING/REVIVAL

To see God's Church revived and being the humble, united, and spiritually strong Church that Jesus calls us to be is definitely a purpose for revival. Can we get over the hurdle of our own comfort levels, and instead risk joining each other?

BELIEVERS, BUT NOT CHRISTIANS

A new phenomenon is occurring in the Church, or perhaps I should say it's occurring away from the Church. Occasionally I have met or heard of people who believe in Jesus, but they refuse the tag of Christian. They believe in him completely, as far as I can tell. To them He is the Son of God who died on the cross for their sins and was resurrected back to life on the third day. It's not my call to make, but in every way the Bible defines salvation, these people are there. They love Jesus like I do.

At the same time, they want no part of the Church. To them, the Church is just another in the parade of greedy large corporations that destroy people's lives and crush whoever gets in the way of a healthy bottom line.

They can point to centuries ago when the Roman Catholic Church had its own armies and sought to extend the faith through brutal conquest. At the same time they extinguished and crushed any other form of Christianity but theirs.

They can point to the torture of Jews during the Spanish Inquisition, and the atrocities committed during the great Crusades to the Holy Land. They can point to the church's ridiculous stances <u>against</u> all kinds of ideas, for instance;

1. Believing that the world is round.

2. Opera.

3. The idea that all races of humankind have savable souls.

4. Allowing witches to live.

5. Women teaching men.

6. Organ music. (Yes, there was a time when church leaders considered it too seductive.)

They can point to the social issues of our day, as I have outlined above, and see how the Church is condemning, insensitive, and destructive toward the people and the lifestyles they oppose.

They can point to the Child abuse scandal and cover-up in the Catholic Church, or the tele-evangelist scandals of the 80's, or the Christian cults that led people to their deaths, or the too many pastors that have committed fraud, stolen money, cheated on their spouses, and were thrown in jail for breaking the law.

Because of all this and more, Jesus has a black eye, and the Church is permanently stained in the courts of public opinion.

And so, some of the newly saved in this generation call themselves believers, or followers of Jesus, but they reject the term Christian. Some of them have been hurt by Christians or know people who have. Others see hypocrisy in the Church, and still others see lethargy. Whatever they see in the Church, count them out.

I have a certain sympathy for these believers. I think most Christians have been put off by the Church, and hurt by other Christians from time to time. We know that the Church is seldom the unselfish, humble, and sacrificial organization that we are called to be. So, to these believers, I humbly offer these observations.

- It seems clear that Jesus wants believers to come together in His name to seek Him in prayer and song, and to learn about Him from each other. Jesus also likes to see his people take care of each other, and to reach out to unfortunate people in our society who need help.

And let us consider how we may spur one another on toward love and good deeds, not giving up meeting together, as some are in the habit of doing, but encouraging one another. (Hebrews 10:24-25a)

- Jesus prayed for us to love each other and he defines love as sacrificial in nature. Jesus seemed to understand that believers would always need to draw strength and comfort from Him and from each other.

HURDLES FACING A GREAT AWAKENING/REVIVAL

- Jesus also wanted us to take his message of eternal life to all the people of the world. Sometimes it takes a group of people to send a missionary couple to an unreached part of the world.
- Jesus was often concerned that the devil would attack believers so he prayed for us to stay safe, united together as one.

I will remain in the world no longer, but they are still in the world, and I am coming to you. Holy Father, protect them by the power of your name, the name you gave me, so that they may be one as we are one. (John 17:11)

- Jesus is the head of the Church, so believing in Him and following Him should include being in the organization He runs. It's easy to criticize the Church, but a very strong case can also be made that the Church has done more to help people in this world than any other organization in the history of the world. The truth is that the Christian Church collectively has;
    - Fed more people.
    - Raised more orphans.
    - Tended more wounded and sick.
    - Clothed more people.
    - Educated more people.
    - Built more hospitals and schools.
    - Stood against more social injustice.
    - Saved more women and children from sex trafficking.
    - And promoted the causes of more voiceless people around the world than any other organization ever.

The Christian Church has this history of being so many good and bad things in the world. If we would just follow Jesus, it would have been so much better. But imperfect people make the Church an imperfect organization.

There are some ways to choose a church that will control itself and largely avoid the big pitfalls. Nothing is a guarantee, but here is a list of what to look for in a church that has a strong likelihood of following Jesus accurately.

These ideas are based on the simple thought that Jesus may have never meant for the church to become a series of international corporations. Instead, it appears in scripture that all churches should be organized and operated at the local church level, and only loosely associated beyond that.

I agree that the early church had a group of Church leaders in Jerusalem who were making decisions for all of the brand new churches springing up around the known world. And further, I agree that Paul seemed to travel between the churches he had started almost as if they were his "denomination" as he corrected and directed them.

However, these two evidences of organization above the local church level only work because the counsel at Jerusalem was a group of people who were eyewitnesses of Jesus' ministry. People knew that they had seen and heard the Savior, and therefore they were trusted. Likewise, all of the churches that Paul coordinated knew him personally. They knew he had integrity. They knew his story.

Today no one in my church knows the leaders of our denomination at the national level personally, and here's why it is so important that we do know them.

> *Here is a trustworthy saying: Whoever aspires to be an overseer desires a noble task. Now the overseer is to be above reproach, faithful to his wife, temperate, self-controlled, respectable, hospitable, able to teach, not given to drunkenness, not violent but gentle, not quarrelsome, not a lover of money. He must manage his own family well and see that his children obey him, and he must do so in a manner worthy of full respect. (If anyone does not know how to manage his own family, how can he take care of God's church?)*
> *(1 Timothy 3:1-5)*

These are Paul's rules for church leaders. How can we tell if someone meets these requirements if we don't know them? In the local church, we do know them.

HURDLES FACING A GREAT AWAKENING/REVIVAL

We can see how the pastors treat their kids, and if they are temperate and self-controlled. We can tell if someone is qualified. But we cannot know these things at any higher level. I don't want leaders I hardly know deciding who will pastor my church, or how we should interpret scripture, or requiring money from us. Therefore, I firmly believe that the power for decision making must be at the local level where Paul's rules can be applied to the leaders. The church may then choose to participate voluntarily in joint efforts that are coordinated by regional or international leaders, but I believe in local church autonomy.

Therefore here are my recommendations for what you should look for in a church.

1. **Look for transparency.** The church should publish its financial statements and the minutes of all business meetings, which should include salaries and benefits of the pastor and staff members. You should be able to tell how all the money is handled and spent. Also, those who teach and preach should be transparent too. If they claim to be wonderful examples of how to live the Christian faith, can we tell if they are being honest? If they want to say how great they are, they must equally share their failures.

2. **Look for accountability.** If one or two people are making all the decisions, and no one can question those decisions and override them when necessary, then the decision makers (usually the pastors) are not held accountable.

3. **Look for in-house decision making.** Some churches are told what to do by larger corporations. They pay money to these larger interests and they are sometimes told who the pastor will be. When the decisions are made by the local church, you can know how and why they are made. When the decisions are made elsewhere, there is a bigger chance that they will be made by greed.

4. **Look for opportunities to participate.** Most churches are non-profit corporations, when they are not part of larger corporations that include many churches(as mentioned in #3). Chose a church that is its own

corporation, and chose one where you can be a voting member, hold office, and have influence. You know what you don't like about corporations, so don't let yours be like that. There are good corporations too, and the smaller ones are easier to keep on track if the members are allowed to participate.

5. Most people chose a church on how it feels when they first walk in. Of course I want you to find a life-giving church with great teaching and preaching that grows you closer to Jesus, and where you can find friends and support and community. If they have in place the things I've suggested, then you have a chance of seeing to it that your church will stay that way.

Finally, we should recognize the possibility that, as this phenomenon of anti-church sentiment grows, a great percentage of believers may not attend any conventional church. They may instead meet in coffee shops, homes, parks, and in the workplace—wherever they can find a space to use. These groups will grow organically wherever people already meet. There may be no formal pastor, or music, or sermon. They may not take up an offering or support missionaries. They may simply discuss what is on their hearts, pray for each other, and try to figure out how to apply the big ideas of the Bible to their lives. They may never support the traditional Church, or go near it.

This is often how the underground church survives in hostile environments, but it may become a voluntary choice for the next generation. It will be a set-back to organized religion. The schools, hospitals, missionaries, and parachurch organizations which are central to mainstream Christianity may fade out. The trend is already noticeable. I believe in Jesus as the head of the Church and I trust Him to do what's best.

Dear Believers,
I'm not too worried if you ever call yourself Christians, but please don't avoid the Church. Find one that works the way you know it must, and get involved. You may be just what the Church needs.

HURDLES FACING A GREAT AWAKENING/REVIVAL

> *Not giving up **meeting together**, as some are in the habit of doing, but encouraging one another—and all the more as you see the Day approaching.* (Hebrews 10:25)

We need the actions and the reputation of the Christian Church to be redeemed, healed, and made whole, so that future believers will not shy away from all that Jesus leads them to be.

HOW DO THESE HURDLES GET JUMPED?

Fortunately, we do not have to jump these hurdles alone. In fact, God is a master hurdler. When God turns, he overcomes these things with a wave of his hand. This is why prayer always precedes a revival, so we can put in some time outlining all that we are asking Him to do. We must always pray for what we cannot do ourselves. It pleases God that we are always in situations where we need His help. It keeps us on our knees in relationship with Him.

I have pulled all of these hurdles together for quick reference whenever you and I have a moment to pray. As we see God jumping in on these things one after another, we will know what is coming. These are noble unselfish prayers that will mightily bless the Church, and win the lost.

RECOUNTING THE HURDLES

1. To see the God we love connect with people on a massive scale. The hurdle that must be overcome, is the idea that people can choose whether or not God exists. The realization of God goes back to the beginning of mankind. No generation will ever be able to wish Him away, or imagine Him away, or philosophy Him away, or ignore Him away. He was here before time began, he created time and he operates it, and he will be here when time no longer exists. May nonbelievers understand this.

2. For God to establish his creative and moral authority with people who don't know him. The hurdle that must be overcome is convincing people, who resent and mistrust most authority, to set mistrust

aside long enough to connect with the most trustworthy, incorruptible authority the world has ever known—the Judeo-Christian God.

3. That God's forgiveness might be experienced by more people, is another purpose of an awakening. The hurdle to be overcome is the fact that Jesus is the only way to eternal life in heaven, and tolerance of other viewpoints allows people to go to hell. The world must allow Christian truth back into the marketplace of ideas.

4. To reset our understanding about the absolute truth of God in Jesus Christ, especially as it applies to relationships and equality. The hurdle seems almost insurmountable. Can we get people to realize that God's really old-school answers are still the best answers? They aren't easy, but they have the wisdom and the heart changing power of God behind them.

5. For God to work around the institutions of Media, Government, and Public Education, to demonstrate his love and wisdom directly to these people who have been influenced away from Him.

6. To stir up the hope and the prayers of God's people for revival in His Church, and an awakening in this generation. We must refocus our thoughts toward seeking God for an outpouring of conviction and connection with him, so that vast numbers of people living in darkness can again see a great light and enter into a saving relationship with Jesus and his church.

7. Another great purpose of an awakening in this generation would be to be to see charity thrive to the benefit of all mankind as the wisdom and resources of God inhabit the great charitable drive of this new generation. The hurdle to be overcome is the brokering of a divine partnership. I do pray for it.

8. Many people know something about God, but few actually know God. This is yet another hurdle for an awakening/revival. People need to be cleared of the smokescreen of cultural bias in order to make a clean approach to God.

HURDLES FACING A GREAT AWAKENING/REVIVAL

9. So the Church will start to act like the united organization we are called to be. The hurdle is for Christians to focus on what unites us, and give up on what separates us.

10. To see God's Church revived and being the humble, united, and spiritually strong Church that Jesus calls us to be, is definitely a purpose for revival. Can we get over the hurdle of our own comfort levels, and instead risk joining each other?

11. We need the actions and the reputation of the Christian Church to be redeemed, healed, and made whole, so that future believers will not shy away from all that Jesus leads them to be.

12. The ultimate and final great purpose for a great awakening that would reach people in all walks of life, is so the love of God will be answered by the love of humankind, and the family of God will grow. All the other purposes for a revival of the church or an awakening in this generation are secondary to this purpose. And the hurdle is as old as the Christian faith, the sharing of the Gospel of Christ, with everything we've got, in Jesus.

THE BASIC TROUBLE WITH THE CHURCH TODAY IS HER UNWORTHY CONCEPT OF GOD… OUR RELIGION IS WEAK BECAUSE OUR GOD IS WEAK… CHRISTIANITY AT ANY GIVEN TIME IS STRONG OR WEAK DEPENDING ON HER CONCEPT OF GOD.

—A.W. TOZER

CHAPTER 6

PRAYING FOR REVIVAL

(In this section, we focus on praying for revival. Many of the scriptures already mentioned in earlier sections are also vital for prayer. There are many ways that the prophets and disciples asked God for revival, and we learn so much about how to pray when we look at their prayers.

I have organized this section into a number of prayer ideas. In the appendix, these ideas appear again, each as a one page devotional. You are free to reproduce them and share them with others anyway you see fit. Please use them to help to stir up prayer for a revival in ourselves, our churches, and our nation. You may also get these devotionals electronically on our church's website www.aurorashillschurch.com and look for "resources".)

PRAYING FOR REVIVAL

I prefer to let Reverend Charles Finney (1792-1875) introduce this chapter. He was one of America's greatest evangelists. 500,000 people were "soundly converted" as a result of his efforts in ministry. He believed in the power of revival and the great awakenings throughout the history of the Christian faith. And more, Finney believed in seeking God to bring us these outbreaks of salvation and devotion to our Lord. In his book, *Revivals of Religion*, Finney makes this challenge that I would like you to accept now from me.

> "Will you follow the instructions I shall give you from the word of God, and put them into practice in your own lives? Will you bring them to bare upon your families, your acquaintance, neighbors, and through the city? Or will you spend the time in learning <u>about</u> revivals, and do nothing <u>for</u> them? I want you, as fast as you learn anything on the subject of revivals, to put it in practice, and go to work and see if you cannot promote a revival among sinners here. If

you will not do this, I wish you to let me know at the beginning, so that I need not waste my strength. You ought to decide now whether you will do this or not. You know that we call sinners to decide on the spot whether they will obey the Gospel. And we have no more authority to let you take time to deliberate whether you will obey God, than we have to let sinners do so. We call on you to unite now in a solemn pledge to God, that you will do your duty as fast as you learn what it is, and to pray that He will pour out his Spirit upon this church and this city."

He wrote this in 1835. I am struck by the confidence of it, and I am moved by respect for this challenge. I have prayed for you, that you will join me in praying for God to turn, to revive His Church, and bring a great awakening to His Gospel in this generation. I too challenge you to wade into prayer and not stop until we see the hand of God move—until we see God turn!

Finney may have been America's greatest revivalist, but he had help, and so did most great and small revivals in the last 5,000 years. They had the support of tremendous intercession and prayer. Sometimes it came from vast numbers of people, and other times it came from just a small handful. Let us consider three who changed the world.

Daniel Nash (1775-1831)

Finney had a powerful man of prayer who went before him to the site of proposed revival meetings and prayed continuously—sometimes for days, sometimes for weeks—before and during Finney's meetings. By all reports, Nash, and his closest prayer warrior Abel Clary, would pray face down on the floor for days without eating. Their prayers were laborious and they were at times in agony with what Finney called, "a spirit of travail". Finney recognized that the remarkable power of the Holy Spirit which typified his revival meetings, was a direct result of his tiny prayer team. After working together for seven years, and seeing one out of every ten Americans come to salvation, Nash died. Finney never attempted another revival meeting, and instead he took a position as a pastor where he continued to build local congregations through preaching.

Evan Roberts (1878-1951)

I have mentioned more than once the Great Wales Revival which started in that English coal-mining town and spread to Europe and North America in 1904. What I haven't mentioned is that Evan Roberts, the man who led that revival in southern England, had prayed for revival for over ten years ahead of it. However, it was in the months leading up to 1904 when Roberts got an understanding in prayer that 100,000 souls might be saved. He then asked his pastor if he and a few of the younger adults might meet after church for prayer. Once the revival hit, the Wales newspapers got wind of his vision, and over a period of nine months, documented the names of the saved until they reached the 100,000 plateau.

Praying Hyde (1865-1912)

After years in India trying to master languages and largely failing, John Hyde had an encounter with the Holy Spirit. He experienced also what he called a "deliverance from sin" and he understood that what he could not do by speaking native languages, he could do through prayer. Praying Hyde would now give himself to prayer. During the great Sailkot revival, he prayed for one a day, then two, and then four. He got what he asked for. If on one night he would not see four saved, he would not eat or sleep until the next night would make up for the loss. A friend once wrote, *"I could see the flash of the electric light as he turned it on. I watched him do it at twelve, and at two and at four, and then at five. From that time the light stayed on until sunrise. By this I knew that in spite of his night watches and illness, he began his day at five."* (McGaw)

I share these brief glimpses of people who were devoted to praying for revival to inspire us with the thought that you and I may be enough! We may not need an army. We only need devotion, fervency, and wisdom.

WHEN GOD TURNS

Every day 152,000 people in the world die. On average, 31% of them identify as Christian. This means that every day, God watches over one hundred thousand people, who he loves desperately, slip through his fingers into hell. It feels like the devil is winning when he gets over two-thirds of those who die. My Bible says that God wants all people. I think God wants us to ask him for all people. I believe that God wants to revive his Church and bring a great awakening that will save the people he loves.

If you are finding in yourself the devotion and passion to pray, the rest of this chapter will give you many practical ways to approach God in prayer for the lost.

1. PRAYING WITH RIGHT MOTIVES

In 1985, the hit single *We Are the World* became the fastest selling song in US history. The record was written by Michael Jackson and Lionel Ritchie and was produced by Quincy Jones. It was all done for charity for Africa and on the album were an unbelievable number of top recording artists.

The song, *We Are the World* opens with Lionel Richie, Stevie Wonder, Paul Simon, Kenny Rogers, James Ingram, Tina Turner and Billy Joel singing the first verse. Michael Jackson and Diana Ross follow, completing the first chorus together. Dionne Warwick, Willie Nelson and Al Jarreau sing the second verse before Bruce Springsteen, Kenny Loggins, Steve Perry and Daryl Hall go through the second chorus. Co-writer Jackson, Huey Lewis, Cyndi Lauper and Kim Carnes follow with the song's bridge. This structuring of the song is said to "create a sense of continuous surprise and emotional buildup". *We Are the World* concludes with Bob Dylan and Ray Charles singing a full chorus, Stevie Wonder and Springsteen duetting, and ad libs from Charles and Ingram."(Wikipedia)

In a TV interview shortly after the release of this quadruple platinum blockbuster which won the Grammy for best new song, Jackson was asked how he was able to work with all the high-powered talent that had showed up for the recording session. Michael said he just told everyone to check their egos at the door with their coats.

As we begin to look at how to pray for a great awakening, I need to ask you to check your agenda at the door.

When I share with people about the hope of revival in Today's atmosphere, I can see people get excited about all the good things that could come from a great awakening in this country or in their church. But then their concerns begin to surface as they realize the many goals they have that a revival could fix.

Some think politically and they can see a great change in voting patterns following a revival.

They think of all these new Christians praying and voting their faith, and they begin to hope for political changes across the spectrum like:

- Changing the Supreme Court.
- Overturning Roe v. Wade.
- Election reform.
- Redistribution of wealth.
- More government run charitable programs.
- Less government run charitable programs.

Some people envision an influx of new passionate believers and they hope for changes like:

- Lowering the crime rate.
- Limiting addiction.
- Fewer divorces.
- Rethinking the legalization of marijuana.

Of course there are those who imagine the wonderful impact on the Church;

- Increased Church attendance.
- Greater acceptance and respect for Christianity in our nation.

- More support for para-church organizations like the Red Cross.
- More strong Christians in every part of society from schools to science labs.

I'm sure there are hundreds more of hopes and goals, that Christians might imagine, which a great revival would bless. The problem is, there are Christians of all persuasions in America and we no doubt have conflicting ideas about the good that might come from a great awakening. If we're not careful, we could wind up accidentally praying against each other!

All of this brings us to the first great understanding that we need if we are to pray for revival.

When you ask, you do not receive, because you ask with wrong motives, that you may spend what you get on your pleasures.

(James 4:3)

We must not pray for revival with selfish motives! We can't drag our agenda in and attach it to God's. Sure, we all want security and stability in our world, but the only security God promises is eternal security. Meanwhile, down here, we are supposed to be working for Him. Agreed, he does everything important and worthwhile for us, but God is not the great smorgasbord in the sky. Jesus paid a price for us and we belong to him. He is the head of the Church, and so, if you feel the call to pray for revival—if God has laid it on your heart that you should be on your knees for this—then let's adopt the correct motivation.

THE ONLY SECURITY GOD PROMISES IS ETERNAL SECURITY.

So let's consider what God wants out of revival. It's not really political, or cultural, economic, or even very social. It's relational. God wants a family of people who choose to love him (BOOM!). God wants a loving family so much that he died for it and he continues to live for it. He has orchestrated all time and space in order to lead the crowning achievement of his creation—humankind—to a point where they need only love his son and say so, and all of salvation is wonderfully given to them. We become his children. He tells us this desire of his, in so many places in his word.

> *This is good, and pleases God our Savior, who wants **all** people to be saved and to come to a knowledge of the truth.*
> *(1 Timothy 2:3-4, emphasis added)*
>
> *But the angel said to them, "Do not be afraid. I bring you good news that will cause great joy for **all** the **people**.*
> *(Luke 2:10, emphasis added)*
>
> *And **all people** will see God's salvation.'"*
> *(Luke 3:6, emphasis added)*
>
> *And the **people all** tried to touch him, because power was coming from him and healing them **all**.*   *(Luke 6:19, emphasis added)*
>
> *Therefore go and make disciples of **all nations**, baptizing them in the name of the Father and of the Son and of the Holy Spirit,*
> *(Matthew 28:19, emphasis added)*
>
> *"'In the last days, God says, I will pour out my Spirit on **all people**. Your sons and daughters will prophesy, your young men will see visions, your old men will dream dreams.*
> *(Acts 2:17, emphasis added)*
>
> *In the past God overlooked such ignorance, but now he commands **all people** everywhere to repent.*
> *(Acts 17:30, emphasis added)*
>
> *To the weak I became weak, to win the weak. I have become **all** things to **all people** so that by **all** possible means I might save some.*
> *(1 Corinthians 9:22, emphasis added)*
>
> *Consequently, just as one trespass resulted in condemnation for **all people**, so also one righteous act resulted in justification and life for **all people**. ¹⁹ For just as through the disobedience of the one man the many were made sinners, so also through the obedience of the one man the many will be made righteous.*
> *(Romans 5:18-19, emphasis added)*

This is such a small sampling of verses that prove the one great reason why God wants revival. He tells us over and over that he wants all people. His plans include all people. The goal He sets before us is to reach <u>All People</u>. This is how we learn that our God is a jealous God, because he loves all people and therefore he wants all people in his family. How broken is God's heart, because he never gets all people?

If we pray with any other motive than to see the God we love draw all people to himself, then we pray with wrong motives.

Why do you love God? There must be so many reasons, but you do love him. So do I. Our love for him is human and not perfect the way he loves us. But with all the human love we have for Him, let's just constantly ask him for the one thing he tells us over and over that he wants to do. Let's simply ask him to bring wave after wave of salvation to <u>all people</u>. Let us set aside every other motive that threatens to make our request impure, and let us pray with child-like innocence and persistence that God would add to his family in a mighty way by flooding our land with revival.

Let's Pray - 1

Father, as we come before you in prayer for a great turn that would revive your Church and awaken this generation, we first empty ourselves of lesser and selfish motives. We put aside thoughts of whatever personal gain we might derive from a great revival and we resist political, social, and economic reasons why we might hope for another great awakening.

Instead we pray for the lost, all of the lost, that they might be drawn to the light of Christ, and that in that light they would find meaning and salvation and a personal relationship with You, Lord.

Forgive us if we dream of seeing our churches full and our churches' needs funded by growing congregations. We have faith in you for that Lord, but we ask for this awakening only to fulfill your plan and to satisfy your love for all people. We want to see your family grow, and see your love answered by wave after wave of the lost and lonely coming to you for love and wisdom, strength and salvation.

Our one true goal is to see the sacrifice of Christ not wasted on a single soul, but that all would come to a saving knowledge of Jesus Christ, and rejoice in the gift of your grace through faith alone in Your Son.

Lord, in times past you have turned and made a great change in those generations that were drifting from you and rebelling against you. You must see our generation drifting too. You must feel the sting of our rebellion. Turn from wrath, God, so that all people would be caught up in the wonder of the one true God Almighty, as You demonstrate Yourself in power and love for all to see. Redirect the hearts of all people and open their eyes to your truth and love. Win them to yourself Father, and grow your family.

For God's sake, your sake, bring it.

2. PRAYING WITH DESPERATION

There is a teaching in God's word that our prayers should begin with thanksgiving and praise.

> *Enter his **gates** with **thanksgiving** and his courts with praise; give thanks to him and praise his name. (Psalm 100:4)*

In this scripture, entering into His gates and courts is tantamount to entering into his presence with thanks and praise. It's a good teaching and wise to follow on most occasions of prayer. But let us consider another Psalm that does not follow this pattern. It's a Psalm of desperation and it starts right in after the briefest of praises.

> *Lord, you are the God who saves me; day and night I cry out to you. May my prayer come before you;turn your ear to my cry.*
>
> *I am overwhelmed with troubles and my life draws near to death. I am counted among those who go down to the pit; I am like one without strength. (Psalm 88:1-7)*

We can feel the author's angst in each line. His life is on the line and he is desperate for an answer from God—NOW, before he dies. When conventional prayer is replaced by a prayer of great need, there's no time for usual practices, either God answers or this man dies! Most of us pray with this kind of urgency at some time in our lives.

Here are a few other desperate prayers.

The disciples went and woke him, saying, "Lord, save us! We're going to drown!" (Matthew 8:25)

Jesus did not answer with, "You forgot to praise me first". Instead he calmed the storm. This prayer got immediate results. This next prayer shows humble desperation.

But the tax collector stood at a distance. He would not even look up to heaven, but beat his breast and said, "God, have mercy on me, a sinner." (Luke 18:13)

Again we see a simple prayer that Jesus himself admired and praised to those he was teaching. It was well received by God. It got results, and it was a desperate plea, prayed by someone who no-doubt felt inferior and shamed by the man who's lengthy, impressive prayer was admired by the crowds that day.

And here is a prayer of positive desperation as Paul prays for tender new believers to gain the greatest possible understanding of the love of God so they will be able to survive.

And I pray that you, being rooted and established in love, may have power, together with all the Lord's holy people, to grasp how wide and long and high and deep is the love of Christ, and to know this love that surpasses knowledge—that you may be filled to the measure of all the fullness of God. (Ephesians 3:17b-19)

I believe that prayers of desperation hold a special place in God's heart. He made us human, and he knew that desperation would drive us to him with urgency and passion. It's part of his plan.

A few years ago, my wife had a check-up, and she was told that an expert would need to take a closer look at something they found in the routine exam. It's the kind of report that no one wants to hear. It could be nothing, or your lives may never be the same again. I prayed calmly with my wife so as not to alarm her any more than she already was. She knew what was at stake. But on my own I prayed with desperation. I besought God with everything I knew about prayer. I prayed my guts out! Of course it took way too long to get into the next appointment, and then they couldn't tell you anything right away. (There must be some bizarre medical administrator somewhere who writes rules about delaying test results as long as possible). Finally we got the news and it was good.

I realize that sometimes we don't get that good report, and then desperate prayers become a way of life. People in that situation can teach more than I can about praying with desperation.

What I'm asking now is that we stare straight at the truth in our churches, in our neighborhoods, and in our nation, until we become desperate for God to move and bring an awakening. The reality of our situation is desperate.

The Church is shrinking in every measurable way—in size, in influence, in funding, in our witness and testimony to the glory of God. Because we grow weaker, so does our nation. The darkness grows, and there are too few of us shining the light of Christ against it. If you're as old as I am, you can remember a time when Christianity was still the default belief system in America. I knew many people who didn't go to church very much, but I knew very few who didn't believe in the Judeo-Christian God.

> **AS THE CHURCH GROWS WEAKER, SO DOES THE NATION.**

Today, millennials who believe are a small minority of their generation, and there is no true single default faith. My overriding impression is that today's young believers have a greater commitment and capacity to share and defend their faith than believers in my day ever did because they've grown up having to do just that.

Desperation comes from life-threatening situations, and we can find our desperation in the notion that the vast majority of our fellow citizens are going to Hell. I used to work for a pastor whose slogan was, "Let's make it hard for people to go to Hell from our town!" Occasionally, he would send this slogan out to our staff along with the obituary column from our local paper. The message was loud and clear. Those who had died were our responsibility according to the pastor who hired us and wrote our job descriptions. Had we failed? I soon realized that I needed help if I was going to assume responsibility for my town. I needed God desperately.

Let us set aside convention and professionalism and pray with a desperate heart for the lost, beseeching God to hold back his justice, turn, and instead offer mercy to the lost.

> *Do not hold against us the sins of past generations; may your mercy come quickly to meet us, for we are in <u>desperate</u> need. (Psalm 79:8)*
>
> *Listen to my cry, for I am in <u>desperate</u> need; rescue me from those who pursue me, for they are too strong for me. (Psalm 142:6)*

Once again the psalmist captures our mood, our emotion. Don't let us be afraid to cry out. Don't let us be afraid to tap into the passion of seeing eternal life at risk. We must pray for the lost, and desperation is a powerful tool when it flows from the life-threatening reality of our day.

Let's Pray- 2

Father, hear our cry and listen to our plea. We are surrounded by people hurrying on their way to hell. We live in a land known for its freedom, and yet so few are free from sin. Your Church is losing influence, Lord, and your people are not strong in representing you. Our nation is slowly turning its back on you.

We are desperate to see you change the direction of our culture, and to see you return your Church to its rightful stance of strength through love and service to others. Late at night, prayers from your faithful ones come to you. Early in the morning, their prayers greet the sun's first rays. And yet, we have not seen you turn. We have not seen your Church revived in every corner of this land, and we have not seen your mighty hand move across the face of America declaring your glory as it goes, and requiring worship from those who previously did not know you.

How long, Lord? How long will you wait to revive your Church? How long must we wait to see your move? Forever?

No, not forever. You are a God who hears the prayers of your people. You long for the salvation of every soul, and love the people of your creation. You have moved heaven and earth to provide salvation under a new and better covenant, sealed by the blood of your own Son. Will you not declare his glory again among the nations? Will you not renew the offer of salvation in this generation?

Our God is a God who saves! We will see you turn your face toward the lost. We will see your Church humbly serving and powerfully witnessing. We will see an awakening that calls to the emptiness in every human heart and says, "I am here, walk with me. I am the God who loves you." Amen.

3. THE HOLY SPIRIT MUST CONVICT

If you have decided to pray and ask God for revival, what specifically do you want him to do? We have thoughts of people coming in droves for salvation, perhaps at great meetings where the gospel message is shared. We imagine the Church with all of her people working to assist the effort. But what exactly do we expect God to do?

Jesus tells us how revival works. Let's remember that there was tremendous revival in the early Church. People were coming daily into the ranks of the saved. It was happening in large meetings and small, inside the temple courts, and in everyday homes. Here's what Jesus said to them just before he was crucified.

> *And He (the Holy Spirit), when He comes, will convict the world about [the guilt of] sin[and the need for a Savior], and about righteousness, and about judgment: about sin [and the true nature of it], because they do not believe in Me [and My message]; about*

> *righteousness [personal integrity and godly character], because I am going to My Father and you will no longer see Me; about judgment [the certainty of it], because the ruler of this world (Satan) has been judged and condemned.* (John 16:8-11, AMP)

In this passage we see that the Holy Spirit is the one who convicts people. He proves to the lost that they are guilty of sin and in need of a Savior or they will be judged and condemned. For all of us who have trained to share our faith, who witness at every opportunity, and who study to defend our faith in the hopes of changing just one heart so they will come to salvation, this is the best news we can have. We don't have to convict people that they stand guilty of sin, and that they need Jesus. The Holy Spirit does that! All we need to do is love people and tell them the simple truth of Jesus and trust the Spirit to do the rest. The Holy Spirit also convicts people of coming Judgment. Jesus has already defeated the devil, and anyone who does not stand with Jesus stands with the devil, by default, in condemnation.

> *Whoever is not **with** me is **against** me.*
> (Matthew 12:30, emphasis added)

Hell is not a popular idea today. Millennials don't buy it. A God that sends people to Hell is a tough sell. No matter how well we teach about free will as the source of humankind's condemnation, people just don't want to hear about judgment and Hell. But Oh, can the Holy Spirit convict people about God's inevitable Judgment. The Spirit can give it a weight that will cause people to pause and reflect. He can and does convict people that one day God will judge this world and all who are in it. By the Spirit's power people can be made to feel it, and with this conviction comes the fear of God which is "the fear of the LORD is the **beginning** of **wisdom**" (Psalm 111:10, emphasis added).

> **WE DON'T CONVICT PEOPLE OF SIN... THE HOLY SPIRIT DOES.**

Because Jesus understood the importance of the Holy Spirit in the launching of his Church, he told them not to launch until they had received the Holy Spirit.

PRAYING FOR REVIVAL

> *Listen carefully: I am sending the Promise of My Father [the Holy Spirit] upon you; but you are to remain in the city [of Jerusalem] until you are clothed (fully equipped) with power from on high.* (Luke 24:49 AMP)

Jesus wanted them to be tapped in to the power, and fully equipped and supported from heaven through the Holy Spirit. A big part of that was the power to convict.

In Old Testament times, the Holy Spirit only filled prophets or an occasional high priest, or sometimes kings. But for the most part, the children of Israel were not filled with the Spirit. They did not have that intimacy with God, nor did they have that inner spirit-led conscience that testified to the truth so they could discern right from wrong. They had to rely on reading the Law. The Jews of Jesus' day were still unfamiliar with the companionship of the Holy Spirit, so it was a ground shaking idea when he said that they might actually be filled with it.

When the Spirit came at Pentecost, Peter got up, preached a sermon, and 3,000 came into the faith and believed in Jesus. We can read his sermon in the book of acts, and certainly what he said was strong. But was Peter just that persuasive, or was it the conviction of the Holy Spirit of God that fell on those people. I'm sure that Peter would agree that the Holy Spirit should receive most of the credit.

We have this same Holy Spirit today, and His job description still includes conviction. So let's pray for the Holy Spirit to bring a new wave of conviction across our land. Let's pray that people everywhere will suddenly recognize that their lives are too dominated by unhealthy appetites and wrong motives which drive them to be and do things they don't want to be and do. And let us pray that the Holy Spirit should point them to Jesus as an antidote for their sin condition.

After all, the Bible contains a nifty promise for people who ask for the Holy Spirit.

WHEN GOD TURNS

> *If you then, though you are evil, know **how** to give good gifts to your children, **how much more** will your Father in heaven give the Holy Spirit to those who ask him!* (Luke 11:13, emphasis added)

Can God resist this prayer for the Holy Spirit to convict? Why would he want to? We can surely pray with assurance that God will send the Holy Spirit as we ask for him. We have seen this kind of Holy Spirit mass conviction in modern times too.

The Billy Graham Crusades, and others, saw tens of thousands of people come forward under the conviction of the Holy Spirit in a single evening. More recently, Promise Keepers filled stadiums with men who were convicted to be better husbands and fathers.

I pray that it's time for the Spirit to leave the stadiums and spread through entire towns, counties, and states.

But let's remember yet one more thing about Pentecost. The believers, on that day of Pentecost, were not praying for revival. They were just waiting for the Holy Spirit that Jesus had promised. We have also been promised the Holy Spirit. Without him, who can be saved? Therefore, having prayed for the conviction of the Holy Spirit to fall, we ought to have that same faith in his coming that the believers at Pentecost had. We dare not take a step into the harvest fields until we have complete faith that the promised Holy Spirit is with us and actively doing what we have asked for him to do. He orchestrates and completes our efforts. It's a symbiosis of Spirit and flesh, redeemer and his redeemed, that God has always intended, and it's been going on like this for nearly 2,000 years.

It's time for this particular demonstration of the Holy Spirit's power to convict, to come to us in this generation. Everything is in place.

- We can easily demonstrate the need.
- We know that it is God's desire.
- We have the promise of the Spirit to claim.
- We know to ask, and we do (often).
- We have faith.

PRAYING FOR REVIVAL

As we move on the course of revival, the Spirit goes with us and before us. So when you find yourself in prayer again for revival, ask for the gift God cannot refuse to give. Ask for the Holy Spirit. Ask for the Spirit to come with conviction. And ask for him to start now.

Let's Pray-3

Jesus, in your word you said, "How much more will the Father give the Holy Spirit to those who ask". Well, we are asking now. Send your Holy Spirit God. Convict the lost ones of our generation that are weighed down by sin. Help them to see and sense what a burden they bare. Give them an understanding of how sin infects and undermines their more noble impulses.

You are Holy and pure God, and you do not tolerate sin. And yet, for those who love your Son, you forgive everything. How will non-believers ever know that they need this forgiveness unless you expose them to their own sin by the conviction of the Holy Spirit? And how will the lost know how to be rid of their sin unless you, Holy Spirit, convict them of their need for a Savior in Jesus?

Send the Holy Spirit Lord. Send him to fulfil his purpose - the conviction of this generation. Create those individual and global events that will resonate in the hearts of people everywhere and cause them to see the sin on themselves that you see every day.

Holy Spirit, hold up the sin mirror in our lands, so the unsaved people of our nations will see the stain of their sin upon them, and shudder with the desire to cleanse themselves. And Spirit, make it clear that their guilt is taken away and cleansed off of them by the blood of Jesus alone. O Father if the people can have this revelation again, if nations of people can be struck with this reality and forced to see it as they did in the days of Israel, and later in the days of the New Testament Church, then you will receive glory from every land as the people see you turn and change the course of their lives. Then we will gather as a Church united to praise your name every day of the week. Then your family will grow and the world will again be shaken by love.

Father we do not pray these things pridefully. We are not impressed by our righteousness, but we are impressed by the one who made us righteous—Jesus. Humbly we want all people to find what we have found in Christ. Let freedom from sin become the most sought after freedom in our land, and let the vessel of this freedom, Jesus, become the center of the hearts of those who are convicted of their need for him.

Father we will step out in your name. Send before us the Spirit to convict. We ask it all in Jesus' name, Amen

4 - SIGNS AND WONDERS

I've been a pastor of local churches since 1987. It's always fascinating when people share with me how they got saved. A surprising number of them recall miracles that happened to them. One woman, who was Jewish at the time, was near death during a difficult child-birth when she cried out in fear and pain. She saw a vision of Christ on the wall in front of her, comforting her and telling her that both she and her baby would live. They did. Needless to say, she got saved.

Some people feel that they were supernaturally led to a particular meeting or church where they heard just what they needed to hear. Others were in need and got miracles of provision or healing that convinced them to pursue Jesus. Sometimes people have miraculously survived crashes or other horrific events and they believed that God had saved them from harm so they could then "get saved".

If you were to conduct a similar survey of salvation, I'm sure you would find this to be true for a significant percentage of believers.

I never judge or question these accounts of the miraculous. I take them at face value, because it's not uncommon for God to support the effort to save the lost with supernatural signs that will resonate with that person who is not paying attention, or who is trying to understand. And there are always wonders designed to touch a person's soul.

> *So Paul and Barnabas spent considerable time there, speaking boldly for the Lord, who confirmed the message of his grace by enabling them to perform signs and wonders.* (Acts 14:3)

Perhaps the message of God's love and grace is so simple and available that it is hard to believe. Most people think they must have to earn it through study and sacrifice, and all kinds of prerequisite commitments. Saved by grace through faith alone is even offensive to some Christians who continue to try to add something to salvation. They don't want it to be that easy. To be sure, the Christian walk is not easy. But becoming a Christian is based on one thing only—belief in Jesus as Lord and Savior. I heard this phrase to describe it: "Jesus plus nothing equals salvation."

In light of the unbelievable simplicity of salvation, God sometimes proves it with wonders.

> *I will not venture to speak of anything except what Christ has accomplished through me in leading the Gentiles to obey God by what I have said and done—by the power of signs and wonders, through the power of the Spirit of God. So from Jerusalem all the way around to Illyricum, I have fully proclaimed the gospel of Christ.* (Romans 15:18-19)

A full on awakening will certainly bring with it a bevy of signs, wonders, and miracles. And, as we pray, we should realize from this scripture that the Holy Spirit is the author of these signs and wonders. However, if we are going to pray for miraculous support for a great awakening, let's consider what kinds of miracles we might need.

The greatest set of spectacular signs and wonders the world has ever seen occurred when God brought the Israelites up out of Egypt. The ministry of Moses was marked with the burning bush, pillars of fire, supernatural plagues of all kinds, the parting of the Red Sea, manna from heaven, water from the rock—it goes on and on. Still, when these children of Israel finally arrived at the foot of the mountain where they could worship God and follow his law, they shrank back from entering the promised land. They didn't trust God.

Jesus noted the same failure of miracles in His time on earth just prior to the cross

> Then Jesus began to denounce the towns in which most of his **miracles** had been performed, because they did not repent. "Woe to you, Chorazin! Woe to you, Bethsaida! For if the **miracles** that were performed in you had been performed in Tyre and Sidon, they would have repented long ago in sackcloth and ashes.
> (Matthew 11:20-21, emphasis added)

All the miracles had failed to grow faith in their hearts. I believe that change in the human heart is the greatest miracle of all, and the hardest to get. But heart-change is exactly what an awakening needs. These signs and wonders that touch the heart are the miracles—piling up one upon another—that fuel salvation.

Therefore pray for miracles in human hearts. Pray for signs and wonders to occur that will touch hearts and minds, and call the lost into saving relationships with Jesus.

Finally, let's ask ourselves this question, "What are the great miracles that God has done to demonstrate himself in our generation?" We share the joint experience of many disasters like, the "Teacher in Space" who died in the space shuttle explosion, 911, the Tsunami, and several mass shootings, but what are the miracles that God has done to unite this generation, call us to salvation, and present himself to us as the author of eternal life?

Definitely there have been countless miracles for individuals and groups of believers that are largely unknown except for those who experienced them, but have even these miracles been in short supply lately?

There was a time in Israel's past when the prophet Habakkuk realized that God's power and miracles were not known to a generation that was falling away from God. He also knew from God that his nation was soon to be conquered by a massive Babylonian Army, so he prayed this prayer that God might bring back his wonders to the remnant of people who would survive the devastation.

> *Lord, I have heard of your fame; I stand in awe of your deeds, Lord. Renew them in our day, in our time make them known; in wrath remember mercy.* (Habakkuk 3:2)

Here is a man who is about to see his nation dismantled by the wrath of God because they had turned away from God, and he's praying for mercy. He needs to know that God will move miraculously again in his time, so he prays, "Renew them in our day".

This phrase must be prayed by every generation, because each generation must have its own experience of God. It's not enough to read about the power and the love of God in our Bibles, or to read about great awakenings in Church history. We must experience it for ourselves or it will never drop into our hearts, and it will never happen to our generation.

I want so much for millennials, GenX-ers, baby-boomers, and the rest, to see a move of God that will confirm to them his matchless might and incomparable love. I live to see God once again shape our nations to do His good will. Most of all, my heart's desire is to see the hand of God bring a great awakening that will win the lost and revive his Church with such power and might that even the greatest of skeptics will be swept along with the current of His love and purpose. These things have all happened before, so let us pray with passion; "*Renew them in our day, in our time make them known.*" Support your call to the lost with the great miracles that unite us all, and the small unshared miracles that change the heart.

> **RENEW YOUR MIGHTY DEEDS IN OUR DAY, O LORD.**

And finally, here's one last idea about praying for miracles. Let's ask for the specific miracle we most need. We've already seen that miracles which change the hearts of the lost are the most needed, and the hardest to get, but how much harder is it to get heart-changing miracles in a prosperous nation? Jesus once recognized the difficulty of reaching prosperous people when he met the Rich Young Ruler.

WHEN GOD TURNS

The young man left Jesus, and walked away dejected, because Jesus had told him to get rid of his idol—wealth. Jesus could see that the man worshipped and trusted in his wealth, and it would always come in first place ahead of his faith in God. Here in America, we live in a prosperous country. Yes, we have poor people and homeless people. But in general, we are incredibly well off. It frightens me to wonder how many Americans, if given a choice between being saved by grace through faith in Jesus, and winning the lottery, would choose the money. With prosperity comes a false sense of safety. Our money says, "In God We Trust", but our hearts say, "In Money We Trust". Non-believers have this deception built deep into themselves, and the Christian faith is just another commodity they might purchase someday. This, I believe, is why Jesus said;

> *Then Jesus said to his disciples, "Truly I tell you, it is hard for someone who is rich to enter the kingdom of heaven. Again I tell you, it is easier for a camel to go through the eye of a needle than for someone who is rich to enter the kingdom of God."*
> *(Matthew 19:23-24)*

This is bad news for anyone praying for a great awakening in America. It looks impossible, but then Jesus continues.

> *Jesus looked at them and said, "With man this is impossible, but with God all things are possible." (vs. 26)*

This is the miracle we need, the miracle of the eye of the needle! This is the one we should ask for. When we ask God to renew the miracles in our day, the heart changing miracles we need are the impossible ones that only God can make possible—dragging our generation through the eye of the needle, so the love of God can take place in the hearts of the lost. Please pray with this vision. There is nothing wrong with asking for miracles, signs, and wonders, but let us ask specifically for the wealth-challenged of America to make the passage through that impossibly narrow path to salvation by the miraculous power of God's grace and love.

PRAYING FOR REVIVAL

Let's Pray-4

Holy Spirit, we pray now for your power. We ask to see your power bring signs and wonders to support revival in your Church, and an awakening in our nations. Because it is part of your glorious job description, we ask you to move in ways our generation has never known, and demonstrate the love, power, and salvation of the Gospel of Christ in such a strong and undeniable way that the hearts of the lost will be touched and moved, and the people will come to the Lord Jesus.

We have read, Holy Spirit, how you have done these things in the past. You were tremendous in the days of Moses, Elijah, John, and Paul. And throughout the history of your Church, miracles of healing, provision, and protection, have marched through the years. So we ask with great humility, not complaining, but imploring—"Renew them in our day, in our time make them known!"

Surely God, You have seen the condition of the lost, and the half-hearted efforts of your Church. Let us all see the move of your hand. Shake the earth where we pray. Cast a sign in the heavens. Calm the storm, feed the masses, raise the dead, and present your glory as much as we can endure. Do these things and a thousand new things that will declare your glory and support the Gospel message.

But this alone will not satisfy us Lord. The miracles we want most are the ones that will change the hearts of the lost ones in our generation. Only you God know the hearts of people and only you can present each one with the personalized sign that will confirm in their hearts the truth of Jesus Christ. Send the Holy Spirit to perform this task, so that the nations will swell with the ranks of new believers who have been individually touched by the one true God, through the sacrifice of His Son. Do these things, dear Lord, not because we deserve them or have earned them in any way. Do them because that's how much you love us. Renew them in our day, in our time make them known.

5. CONFESSING THE SINS OF OUR NATION

(This topic was covered as one of the "Elements of Revival" in Chapter 3. I will only add here some additional thoughts drawn from parts of the Bible not previously mentioned.)

Ezra was a great teacher and priest who led a remnant of exiled Israelites back to Jerusalem to rebuild the temple that had been destroyed 70 years earlier. Following their return, many of the men he led who had been slaves all their lives, had married outside the faith. This was something that Old Testament Jews were never supposed to do according to God's law. At that point, Ezra prayed so powerfully about the sins of his nation, that the people repented right there at his side, and they over-turned their mistakes. His prayer was clearly filled with accuracy, wisdom, and genuine emotion that cut his people to the quick.

> *While Ezra was praying and confessing, weeping and throwing himself down before the house of God, a large crowd of Israelites—men, women and children—gathered around him. They too wept bitterly.* (Ezra 10:1)

This is one prayer that got instant, tangible results. Let's look at some of the elements and make them our own.

> *I am too ashamed and disgraced, my God, to lift up my face to you, because our sins are higher than our heads and our guilt has reached to the heavens. From the days of our ancestors until now, our guilt has been great. Because of our sins, we and our kings and our priests have been subjected to the sword and captivity, to pillage and humiliation at the hand of foreign kings, as it is today.*
> (Ezra 9:6-7)

We are impressed at once with his honesty. He doesn't try to downplay anything. Instead, Ezra seems to empathize with God as he understands how this sin blemishes the holy, just, and perfect nature of God. He isn't just repenting for the current sins of his people. Ezra is going all the way back to the sins that got the temple destroyed, and the people exiled in the first place.

PRAYING FOR REVIVAL

Ezra even says that God went easy on them.

> *What has happened to us is a result of our evil deeds and our great guilt, and yet, our God, you have punished us less than our sins deserved and have given us a remnant like this.* (Ezra 9:13)

Can we, in our nation today, really say that God has gone easy on us? I think so. In fact, hasn't God gone much easier on America than he did on Israel? We have not yet been conquered and forced into labor in foreign lands because we turned from God and worshipped or pursued other things.

Christians in every nation need to pray like we are the remnant—the few who still place God above all else.

> *Lord, the God of Israel, you are righteous! We are left this day as a remnant. Here we are before you in our guilt, though because of it not one of us can stand in your presence.* (Ezra 9:15)

This is the end of Ezra's prayer. Unlike other Bible prayers for national sin, Ezra never gets around to asking for mercy or forgiveness. By this point in his prayer, Ezra had thrown himself against the house of God that they were all rebuilding, and he may have sensed that so many around him were joining him in his grief and suffering for their collective sin as a people.

O how I wish that we will pray like this, with the shame of our nation clinging to us like a death shroud which we will not take off until God himself lifts it off all of us. We may well need to put on sackcloth and ashes as a physical picture of this sin. Without this kind of prayer, we cannot clear the spiritual atmosphere for a nation, so their spiritual eyes can see truth. This kind of prayer can be gut wrenching and exhausting, but we must do it.

My Bible says that for the joy set before him, Jesus endured the cross. For those of us who are willing to shoulder the sins of our country in order to pave the way for a great awakening, there is a joy set before us too, and God makes it clear in his word.

WHEN GOD TURNS

> *And if that **nation** I <u>warned</u> repents of its evil, then I will relent and not inflict on it the disaster I had planned.*
> *(Jeremiah 18:8, underscore and emphasis added)*

This is yet another great verse that shows how God will turn from his stated plans. He will turn from his wrath of disaster for a sinful nation, and show mercy if that nation repents of its evil. It's always about God turning. Is God warning our nation?

In the time of Ezra, he spoke as the prophet to his nation. Today all Christians have the Holy Spirit and can hear from God his warning. I live in Colorado, which is now famous for skiing and recreational pot. Just today the local news reported that hospitals in Pueblo, Colorado are banding together to try to stop the sale of pot in their county because of the high rate of children being born with pot in their system. Nobody knows what marijuana will do to unborn babies, but it's legal. For the first time in the history of Colorado Public Schools, more than half of the children who are caught with illegal drugs in school say that their supplier is their parents. Are we sedating our children so we don't have to deal with them?

I don't need a mysterious prophetic communication from the Holy Spirit to hear God's warning. My heart is screaming inside me, "God will not tolerate this!"

If you're reading this now, you have probably felt God's warning in many ways at many times. You've sensed his warning against the evil. Well, now is the time to take this on. We are the people called by his name, and we need to pray, and confess, and repent for all that we know is sinfully wrong in our countries.

I believe we continue to see God relent, show mercy, and even bless us in part because of the prayers of his Church. My hope is that this targeted purposeful prayer we consider here, will do more than just forestall God's punishment. I seek God's next great awakening to rejuvenate this nation with the life of God, and renew his call on us to be the great missionary nation that sends food, education, medical help, and salvation around the world, and restore our strength so we can. America has done these things more than any other nation in the history of the world, but it is slowing down dramatically.

We need God to turn and heal our land. We need revival. We each need to be awakened. And we would so love to see respect for God, and his will reflected, in the nation we call our own. Let us carry the sins of our nations to God, and in doing so, prepare our nations, the way John the Baptist prepared his nation, in service to Jesus.

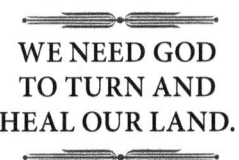

WE NEED GOD TO TURN AND HEAL OUR LAND.

> *Prepare the way for the Lord,* **make straight paths** *for him.*
> *(Mark 1:3b, emphasis added)*

(Author's note: I encourage you, for this prayer, to put on sackcloth and ashes, or some other covering, and mess up your face. I see the sackcloth and ashes of the Bible used in Old Testament and New. To me, the sackcloth represents being covered with the sins of your nation, and the ashes rubbed on your face represent your shame.

This prayer is for my country, America, but please substitute your own country's name.)

Let's Pray-5

Heavenly Father, the sins of our nation are so many that we can scarcely mention them all. We are overrun with greed. Money is certainly the root of all kinds of evil in America. Lust no longer brings shame to us. We celebrate multiple partners, publish child pornography, sell books about presidents who have affairs, and find all manner of sexual sin on our computers and devices.

We can never seem to avoid racist thoughts and actions. Is it getting better? I can't say that. I'm sure it's not getting better for everyone who feels the sting of racism, Lord. At the same time, the leading cause of death among blacks, whites, Hispanics, Asians, and all other ethnic groups in America is not racism, it's abortion. It's epidemic.

Self is everything in America, Father, and the Church is not immune. I have no statistics, but my observation is that acts of kindness are outnumbered by acts of selfishness by a ratio of at least 8 to 1.

Help us God. Come to us in this time of struggle and loss. We deserve your wrath. We have earned the loss of your protection. I sense the gradual withdrawal of you hand of protection over America, and it breaks my heart. I fear that you are, "trampling out the vintage, where the grapes of wrath are stored." And, that you are about to loose "the fateful lightening of your terrible swift sword". But this time, it will be aimed at all of America.

O God, turn from your great wrath! Spare my nation from your terrible justice. Turn toward mercy. Instead, destroy the plans of Satan, the enemy. Revive your Church, and bring an awakening to this generation so that wave after wave of salvation will pour across this country, and fill your family in heaven.

Have mercy on us Lord, because so many Americans don't realize what they are doing. They don't see or think spiritually. Their hearts are hardened and they are far from you. Do not destroy us Lord, but turn and restore us to faith, purpose, and direction in Christ.

Mercy, Lord, have mercy on America. We ask in Jesus' name, Amen

6. REVIVAL FOR THE SAKE OF GOD'S NAME

It seems that names are more important to God than they are to most people. I'm not saying that we think of names as unimportant, but God really puts a premium on a name. He chose His son's name, Jesus, and gave it to Joseph so he could get it just right. Also, God will often change someone's name after a significant event in their spiritual walk. The examples are several:

- ♦ Abram (exalted father)… to Abraham (father of many).

- ♦ Sarai (Chaldean for princess)… to Sarah (Hebrew for princess).

- Jacob (he deceives)… to Israel (wrestles with God).
- Simon (flat-nosed)… to Peter (rock).

In each case, the new name had a significant added meaning which spoke of the purpose that God was building into the lives of these saints.

God also gives himself several names in the Old Testament, and Jesus also carries many names or titles. A study of the names of God is an education in itself because we learn so much about His character and our relationship to Him. Jesus' name is so powerful that he encourages us to ask for things in prayer "in his name".

An interesting prayer tool that comes into play, when we see the great prayers of the Bible for revival, is asking God to move for the defense or the reestablishment of His name. Certainly scripture reveals that God does certain things for the sake of His name.

Perhaps you remember this famous line from the twenty-third Psalm, "He leadeth me in paths of righteousness for his name's sake." David flat out says here that God helps him to walk and act in a righteous manner so that God's name will receive honor and glory by those who see God's righteousness in David. This is an Old Testament picture of the "Breastplate of Righteousness" which Paul writes about. But what I want us to see here is that God does things so that His Name will not be tarnished among non-believers. This is not an egotistical thing on God's part, instead it is a practical matter. Who will come to God for salvation if his name is defamed, ridiculed, and dragged through the mud? No, the name of God is to be revered, respected, and held in honor. This moves God's people to defend Him, and to pray and call on him to take those actions which will reestablish him, and His name, in each generation.

Indeed the title of this book, as mentioned in Chapter 1, is based on a prayer as Moses beseeches God to turn from his intent to destroy all of Israel because they have sinned so greatly. In this great intercessory prayer,

Moses appears to convince God that if He follows through with His plan to destroy the people, the Egyptians will see the God of Israel as evil.

> *Why should the Egyptians say, "It was with evil intent that he brought them out, to kill them in the mountains and to wipe them off the face of the earth?" Turn from your fierce anger; relent and do not bring disaster on your people.* (Exodus 32:12)

After all, Israel means "wrestles with God". The Israelites were completely known as God's chosen people. They had his name on them. If God were to destroy them, he would also be destroying his name. Moses got what he prayed for, and he wasn't the only one to pray and ask God to move or turn for the sake of His Name.

Asaph, a contemporary of David's, also wrote Psalms, and he had no problem asking God to protect and defend His Name.

> *Do not hold against us the sins of past generations; may your mercy come quickly to meet us, for we are in desperate need.*
>
> *Help us, God our Savior, <u>for the glory of your name</u>; deliver us and forgive our sins <u>for your name's sake</u>. Why should the nations say,"Where is their God?"*
>
> *Before our eyes, make known among the nations that you avenge the outpoured blood of your servants. May the groans of the prisoners come before you; with your strong arm preserve those condemned to die. Pay back into the laps of our neighbors seven times the contempt they have hurled at you, Lord.*
> (Psalm 79:8-12, underscore added)

Asaph doesn't just want people to admire the Name of God, he wants them to fear it. He wants the nations around Israel to be paid back for insulting God. This kind of praying for vengeance was not uncommon in the Bible before the life-giving message of Jesus told us to pray for our enemies. Still, the tactic of asking things for the sake of God's Name is often modeled. Once again here's David.

PRAYING FOR REVIVAL

> *But you, Sovereign LORD, help me for your name's sake; out of the goodness of your love, deliver me.*   *(Psalm 109:21)*
>
> *For your name's sake, LORD, preserve my life; in your righteousness, bring me out of trouble.*   *(Psalm 143:11)*

David knows that he is closely associated with God. He was chosen by God and anointed by God's prophet to lead Israel. His successes in battle were known for how powerfully God orchestrated them. David's success was God's success and David knew it, so he prayed this way when he was in trouble.

Maybe no one used this kind of prayer as effectively as Daniel. He knew that God was ready to turn from punishing Israel, and allow them to return to their homeland after 70 years in captivity, so he begged God to let them go home to Jerusalem and rebuild the city and the temple, so that His name might once again be known. Look at how powerfully Daniel uses this idea in prayer.

> *Now, our God, hear the prayers and petitions of your servant. <u>For your sake, Lord</u>, look with favor on your desolate sanctuary. Give ear, our God, and hear; open your eyes and see the desolation of <u>the city that bears your Name. We do not make requests of you because we are righteous, but because of your great mercy.</u>-Lord, listen! Lord, forgive! Lord, hear and act! <u>For your sake, my God</u>, do not delay, because <u>your city and your people bear your Name.</u>*
>   *(Daniel 9:17-19, underline added)*

God did what Daniel asked. The rulers who enslaved Israel suddenly had compassion on them, and Ezra, Nehemiah, and others led the people back to rebuild, and to reestablish the name of God among the nations.

Here is what really excites me. Today, we also bear the Name of our God. We are Christians! We believe that Jesus Christ is Lord and Savior, and his name is all over us. Yes, we ask for things in his name, but might we also ask for God to turn in our day for the sake of His Name? Jesus defended the honor of God. He seldom defended himself. Jesus let the Father defend him. I'm asking in Jesus' name for God to reestablish his name in my nation and bring a revival, an awakening—that for the sake of His Name, he will turn and shake us into revival.

While there's nothing wrong with praying prayers for the sake of God's name, we also realize that He changed it up on us in the New Testament.

> *Therefore God exalted him to the highest place and gave him the name that is above every name, that at the name of Jesus every knee should bow, in heaven and on earth and under the earth, and every tongue acknowledge that Jesus Christ is Lord, to the glory of God the Father.* (Philippians 2:9-11)

Now we see this new reality that God the Father receives glory when His son Jesus is worshipped and acknowledged. Jesus knew that His name would become premier, and he told his disciples. Also, Jesus knew that soon the day would come when the Son would be the means of glorifying the Father.

> *Very truly I tell you, whoever believes in me will do the works I have been doing, and they will do even greater things than these, because I am going to the Father. And I will do whatever you ask in my name, so that the Father may be glorified in the Son. You may ask me for anything in my name, and I will do it.* (John 14:12-14)

> *Until now you have not asked for anything in my name. Ask and you will receive, and your joy will be complete.* (John 16:24)

So now our complete understanding is this. We sense the need for God to move for the sake of His name.

We also realize that God has given us a new standard that he wants to receive glory and honor now through his Son's name. So when we ask God to bring an awakening, we can also ask for the sake of Jesus' name. And finally, we can also ask in the Name of Jesus. It may sound a bit redundant, but it covers all the bases of His name.

LET'S PRAY-6

God, I feel shame for the way you are seen in my nation. Your opinions are belittled. Your word is called bigoted, hateful, out of touch, and just plain wrong. Jesus, the Son of God, is sometimes called a good teacher, but he is mocked and denied in many parts of our culture. Your Holy Spirit, and all that he does, is made fun of by comedians and in letters to editors, and even in your Church, He is misunderstood.

Where once we made laws in this country based on the wisdom of your word, now our lawmakers regret your influence and seek to overturn it with newer legislation that is more politically correct. More and more, our political candidates distance themselves from you God, because association with You might hurt their chances of being elected.

Whenever you and your opinions come up for a vote in this country, you get voted down, God. And your Church is so much a part of this culture that we are compromised and poor representatives of all you stand for. Even many who believe in you, Jesus, will not call themselves Christians, because they do not want to be associated with the history of your Church.

How long, Lord? How long will you let this continue? How long before you do something more? For 15 years I have personally seen and heard your people, who are called by your name, come together on National Days of Prayer, and beg you to move and bring change. Many of these people <u>do</u> live the life you have called them to. They pour out their hearts to you on behalf of this nation, beseeching you to bless us and to restore us and mold us into a nation more in tune with your call—one that will reflect your values and your love. But every year, we see the opposite happen. Your impact is shrinking, God, and your people are dwindling on the vine.

For the sake of your name, God, turn from the wrath that must be building in You toward this nation. Do not destroy us, and do not simply let us fade into meaninglessness, but instead, in your great mercy, come to us in power and glory, as only you can, God. Plant us again in the center of your will. Change the very direction of this

WHEN GOD TURNS

nation. For your name's sake, TURN. Change the course of human events. Don't allow this godlessness to go on. Your Church bares your name. Won't you breathe new life into us again, that we might reflect your glory into this land?

Father God, almost everything in America that bares your name looks weak—the churches, the charities, the political efforts, the attempts at godly laws, para-church organizations—all these things that represent you are not nearly strong enough.

Your name should inspire the masses. Your name should shine in the darkness. Your name should cause the nations to bow down. Your name should mean love for the broken-hearted, and hope for the lost.

But now in America, lottery tickets are the hope of the lost more than You, and the broken hearted turn to drugs, bars, and online dating before they will come to your Church.

My heart breaks because the people no longer know the power of your name.

Please God, my Savior and redeemer, my comfort and my hope, do not let your name go out, and don't let it be confined to a handful of wonderful and dynamic churches that now exist like a string of shiny diamonds in a sea of darkness.

Father you word says that at the name of Jesus every knee shall bow in heaven and on earth and under the earth, and every tongue shall confess that Jesus Christ is Lord, to the glory of God. How I long for that day. How I long to see your name as the banner headline over my nation. How I long to see my countrymen and women know your loving salvation. O God, will you not turn, and defeat this plan of the enemy, revive your Church, and bring an awakening to this present generation like the world has never seen before?

This is my hope and prayer, in the NAME OF JESUS, and for the SAKE OF HIS NAME. AMEN

7. TEARING DOWN A STRONGHOLD

(Again, I have already developed this theme under the "Elements of Revival" so I will only mention some additional thoughts here)

When God turns and authors a great awakening, He often destroys a supernatural stronghold that has wielded power over people and caused them to be blind to the truth of God. Here are some biblical examples.

1. In the Old Testament days of Moses, God humbled the greatest nation on earth, Egypt, because they had enslaved the children of Israel, and refused to let them go. Egypt was a powerful nation with a fearsome military that was propped up by a complex set of idols whom the Egyptian people worshipped. The Egyptians were very much bought into this hierarchy of gods, and the Pharaohs and other members of the ruling class clearly believed too. Their tombs and pyramids are full of superstitious objects that were there to help them in their journey through the afterlife. Of course behind all of this idol worship is demonic activity setting itself up against the knowledge of God. The Hebrews prayed, God turned, and the plagues God brought on Egypt demonstrated his authority over these idols. Then, in the sea, God also destroyed their army. Yes, we saw the physical destruction of the army, but we also saw the humiliation of the demonic stronghold that spiritually supported Egypt

2. Elijah came against another form of idol worship ushered in by Jezebel, who had married Ahab, Israel's King. She worshipped Baal, and she killed those priests and prophets who tried to continue Israel's faith in God. Jezebel was able to intimidate the nation of Israel, propped up by a stronghold in the spirit realm, a power she no doubt inherited from her father, Ethbaal king of the Sidonians. When this stronghold was torn down during the epic face-off between Jehovah and Baal on top of Mt. Carmel, the 450 prophets of Baal were put to death, and both the spiritual and actual droughts in Israel were broken.

3. Daniel prayed against the rebellion of the children of Israel which had caused God to send them into exile at the hands of the Babylonians.

The spiritual stronghold here was the unwillingness of the Israelites to follow God! God's word says this,

> *For rebellion is like the sin of divination, and arrogance like the evil of idolatry.* (1 Samuel 15:23a)

Even in captivity they remained so unfaithful that Daniel had to beg God's forgiveness. Not all Jews returned to Jerusalem to rebuild their temple, their city, and their faith, but the ones who did return were ready to follow God again. The stronghold of rebellion was finally broken off of them for a time.

4. The New Testament Church fought strongholds on three fronts.

- The Jewish faith which gave birth to Jesus and the Christian faith, considered Christianity to be heresy, and they tried to stamp it out.
- Greek philosophy wasn't completely in opposition to Christian doctrine, but prideful intellectuals were ready to debate it to death. Christianity had several hurdles to overcome in order to reach the Greeks and their disciples throughout the known world.
- Roman political and military might opposed any faith like Christianity that would set itself, and its God, above Caesar, whom Romans believed was a god. Rome killed and persecuted the early Church mercilessly.

Of course, we can see the Devil's plan in all of this to derail the Church before it could even get started. It's amazing that the early Church survived it, except that the hand of God was on His Church.

It took about three centuries for Christianity to triumph over these three strongholds, but that first revival which established the early Church could not be denied, and eventually Rome embraced the Christian faith, and the Roman Catholic Church was begun.

God defeats strongholds, when he turns, so that people will no longer stumble over lies or persecution, and instead they will be able to come to him by seeing His truth.

All of this begs the question, what strongholds exist today that inhibit people from seeing God's truth and entering into a saving relationship with Jesus?

Consider these next three scriptures.

> *For the time will come when people will not put up with sound doctrine. Instead, to suit their own desires, they will gather around them a great number of teachers to say what their **itching ears** want to hear.*   *(2 Timothy 4:3, emphasis added)*

> *For the secret power of lawlessness is already at work… and all the ways that wickedness deceives those who are perishing. They perish because they refused to love the truth and so be saved.*
>   *(2 Thessalonians 2:7, 10)*

> *Woe to those who **call evil good** and **good evil**.*
>   *(Isaiah 5:20a, emphasis added)*

I am aware that Christians who hold up moral standards in today's culture are under attack. We are a turn-off. We are not welcome in politics, and we are not welcome in the judicial system. The Supreme Court has hung a curtain over the Ten Commandments in their own chambers. Nobody wants to hear it.

But these are not just the ideas of Christian people, they are God's. Yes, we must be loving and life-giving—we must be gentle and wise—but whether our culture likes it or not, our God has an opinion, and we must fight so that He will be heard. However, let us consider fighting in prayer against the secret power of lawlessness that blinds people so that they call evil good and good evil. We have what we need to restrain lawlessness.

> *For the secret power of **lawless**ness is already at work; but the one who now holds it back will continue to do so till he is taken out of the way.*   *(2 Thessalonians 2:7, emphasis added)*

Who is the one who holds back lawlessness? Many Bible scholars say it is the Holy Spirit. Let's remember that the Church is a world-wide organization full of people who are filled with the Holy Spirit. There is a time when the Church will leave this world " in a flash, in the twinkling of an eye" (1 Corinthians 15:52).

Then this lawlessness will go unchecked. But for now, we stand in the way if we will pray against it with power and wisdom and giftings from the Holy Spirit in us.

> **CHRISTIANS ARE DRAFTED INTO A SPIRITUAL BATTLE AGAINST DEMONIC FORCES.**

The fact is, we are called to this spiritual fight, as surely as if we were drafted into the army, Christians are drafted into a spiritual battle against demonic forces. I know this sounds like some big romantic idea of mine, but it's not. Let me share with you a couple of spiritual battle scriptures. Please allow yourself to be convicted (or drafted) into this conflict.

For though we live in the world, we do not wage war as the world does. The weapons we fight with are not the weapons of the world. On the contrary, they have divine power to demolish strongholds. We demolish arguments and every pretension that sets itself up against the knowledge of God, and we take captive every thought to make it obedient to Christ. (2 Corinthians 10:3-5)

Ideas have spiritual powers behind them. The big ideas of the Bible have the force of God Almighty behind them. No one can stop Him from saving believers!

Some ideas go against God's knowledge, and they too have spiritual powers behind them. Anyone who has ever struggled with addiction knows this demonic power that is so hard to resist. Communism sounded so right, and destroyed the lives of millions in Russia alone. Jesus understood that ideas have power when he said, "But I tell you that anyone who looks at a woman lustfully has already committed adultery with her in his heart" (Matthew 5:28)

Thoughts steer the heart, and Jesus knows that, unless we take these thoughts and ideas captive and make them obedient to Christ, we will end up acting upon these thoughts. Therefore we must take charge. Not just of ourselves, but also in the marketplace of ideas. We can win the argument, but we must win the war by defeating the powers behind those counter-productive ideas from the enemy.

> *For our struggle is not against **flesh and blood**, but against the rulers, against the authorities, against the powers of this dark world and against the spiritual forces of evil in the heavenly realms.* *(Ephesians 6:12, emphasis added)*

Come on man. Come on woman. You've been called out! This is the word of God. He calls his Church to wage war in heavenly realms. I'm sure God's angels are on our side, but it's clear that God is sending us in. Heed the call. Take it seriously, and wade into the enemy. How do we fight?

> *I will give you the keys of the kingdom of heaven; whatever you **bind** on earth will be bound in heaven, and whatever you **loose** on earth will be **loosed** in heaven."* *(Matthew 16:19, emphasis added*

We can bind up the enemy, or we can loose him off of people. When we do, Jesus says that it will happen in heaven—in the spiritual realm. Paul practiced this very thing when he loosed a demonic spirit off of a woman.

> *She continued doing this for several days. Then Paul, being greatly annoyed and worn out, turned and said to the spirit [inside her], "I command you in the name of Jesus Christ [as His representative] to come out of her!" And it came out at that very moment.* *(Acts 16:18, AMP)*

In the name of Jesus, as His representatives, we have this authority. But Christians rarely use it. So if you accept that you are called to this spiritual war, don't leave your weapons behind. Wherever you see thoughts and arguments that set themselves up against the knowledge and the word of God, take them out. Loose them off of the people they are affecting. Fight this way against the devil.

Let's Pray-7

In the name of Jesus, and as one of His representatives here on earth, and as a member of His Church, I come against every pretension and argument that sets itself up against the knowledge of God in my country. I loose these things off of the people, and I bind these people to the truth of the living God.

I hold captive the selfish and self-serving thoughts that sometimes drive this generation, and in the name of Jesus, I make them obedient to Jesus.

Devil, get your filthy hands off of this generation. I forbid you from blinding people from God's truth, and I bind you from speaking lies into the hearts of the lost so they cannot hear the truth. I pray for a hedge of protection around the people of this world so they will live in an atmosphere clean of the schemes of the devil.

I know you have plans to interfere with the Gospel message, devil. And I know that you have hatched out great plans for the confusion of many so they will not come to a saving relationship with Jesus, but in His name which is above all names, I cancel your plans and I declare that no weapon formed against this generation shall succeed.

Jesus I bind your Church to all of the great things you have called her to be, and I ask that you would strengthen the angels of every church and every believer so that the plans of our enemy will not succeed, but instead, a great awakening will break across the land and nothing will inhibit the progress of salvation and intimacy with God. I pray all these things in the name of Jesus.

8. WILL YOU NOT REVIVE US?

Psalm 85 is the revival psalm, but it was not written by David or Asaph. It was written by the Sons of Korah. The fact that the sons of Korah have written anything in the Bible is remarkable considering that Korah, the father of their line was killed when he led many of the leaders of Israel against Moses and Aaron.

Like Moses and Aaron, Korah was a Levite and he longed to serve in the Tabernacle with Aaron and his sons, but Korah and his sons were assigned to carry the gold and silver items used inside the tabernacle whenever God told Israel to move. These items were always wrapped up before Korah's family could see them. What made it even more difficult was that most of the tabernacle and the items used in its construction and operation were carried in ox carts, but the heavy items that Korah's family carried were considered too sacred for the carts, so they had to be hand carried. Also, Aaron put his son in charge of moving the tabernacle, so now Korah, the head of his family and a contemporary of Aaron's, was taking orders from his brother's son.

This was all too much for him, so he gathered like-minded men around him and they protested to Moses and told him that they all should have a turn serving inside the tabernacle. Moses tried to tell them that it was God's plan he was following but they insisted on a showdown. So the day came when Korah appeared before the tabernacle with his men, ready to serve, and convinced that Moses was wrong. The earth opened up and swallowed Korah and the ring-leaders and their families. The rest of their followers were consumed by the fire of God.

It's a long stretch of time from Moses to King David, but David was a musician and he loved to write songs of praise and worship to God and perform them. When David became King, he began to use music as part of the way Israel worshipped God. David left his son Solomon with many plans for the building of a temple that would replace the tabernacle with a more permanent home for the presence of God, and David prescribed music for that temple. When Solomon completed the building of the temple, an array of musicians was prepared for service in the temple. Among them were, of all things, the Sons of Korah! Now, they would serve inside. Their family was redeemed, or maybe I should say, "Revived". And so we come to the 85th Psalm, the Psalm of revival, written most appropriately by the Sons of Korah

WHEN GOD TURNS

You, Lord, showed favor to your land; you restored the fortunes of Jacob. You forgave the iniquity of your people and covered all their sins. You set aside all your wrath and <u>turned</u> from your fierce anger.

Restore us again, God our Savior, and put away your displeasure toward us. Will you be angry with us forever? Will you prolong your anger through all generations? Will you not <u>revive us again,</u> that your people may rejoice in you? Show us your unfailing love, LORD, and grant us your salvation.   (Psalm 85, underscore added)

Here we read a simple, innocent, straightforward prayer to God to revive his people again, so that they can rejoice in Him. And here again we see someone asking God to turn from anger and wrath, and instead God is asked to restore and revive. Isn't that what we all want—to see God move wonderfully in our time and revive His Church, and reach the lost with an overwhelming presentation of his love, grace, and power so that people from every corner of the earth will come to him. Don't we also long to rejoice at such a wonderful awakening—to rejoice that our God has made himself understood again among the people of our lands?

So let each of us begin to ask with that same simplicity and innocence, "will you not revive us again?" Doesn't the Spirit testify in you right now that this is a prayer God wants to hear and answer if only His people will pray it?

The Sons of Korah were the experts on revival. Surely their family prayed this prayer and asked this question of God many times over the generations. God heard their prayer and they actually saw God bring about what Korah had wanted, that his line would serve inside the tabernacle. Of course it was now the temple, but none-the-less they were finally in it, and this time it was part of God's plan.

This is the confidence we have in approaching God: that if we ask anything according to his will, he hears us. And if we know that he hears us—whatever we ask—we know that we have what we asked of him.   (1 John 5:14-15)

PRAYING FOR REVIVAL

So, we know he hears our prayers too. Certainly asking for the salvation of others is within God's will. And the revival of God's Church would seem to be central to what God wants. What will Jesus do if he hears this prayer coming from all directions of his Church? Will he not revive us?

Andrew Murray (see pt. #2) says this about revival.

> Those who know anything of the history of revivals will remember how often both widespread and local revivals have been distinctly traced to specific prayer. An extraordinary spirit of prayer, urging believers to private as well as united prayer, motivating them to labor fervently in their supplications, will be one of the surest signs of approaching showers and floods of blessing.

It's time we prayed a prayer that Jesus wants to hear. It's time we "swipe the card" for God to turn and bring an awakening.

Aren't we all like the Sons of Korah? Needing redemption, searching for identity and purpose, and hoping to find meaningful service to God, who completes us in all these ways?

Let's be responsible for the next great turn of God. Let's pray it in.

Let's Pray-8

God Almighty, heavenly Father, hear this prayer and listen to our plea. Your people languish in compromise. In our wealth, we have found false comfort. In our education we have found false wisdom. In our science we have explained you away. With our technology we have made this world more efficient and connected, and yet loneliness and fear still thrive.

Father your people need to see you turn from the direction the Church has taken, and revive us. Will you not revive us, Lord? Will you not change the course we are on and start us on a new course?

You have called us to be life-giving, but often our works are dead. You have called us to share the Gospel with the world, but we have trouble getting out of our churches. You have called us to follow Jesus, but our commitment is half-hearted. You have called us to know your word, but so many of us rarely read it. You have called us to take care of the needy, but we mostly take care of ourselves. You have called us to be holy, and Jesus has indeed made us holy, but do any of us feel holy? You have called us to pray, and here we are, praying for you to revive us as your Church.

How long Lord before you bring your mighty hand and shake out your Church and breathe new life into us?

Let us see the day when the Church stands united and strong in our land.

Certainly there are some churches alive and on fire for Jesus, but for every one of those churches, there are ten that are dying. Very few churches are growing by winning the lost. Mostly the sheep just shuffle.

Oh God, bring power back into the Church. Drive us forward again with love and zeal. Stir our hearts and steel our minds to action. And as we act, move mightily and inspire us again by making your presence among us tangible, palpable, and undeniable. Turn your face toward your Church and shake the dust out of your sanctuary.

We know you God. We believe in you, but we settle for so much less than we should. Your word promises that you are with us always, but how seldom do we feel it? How seldom is the manifest presence of God with us in such a complete way that we are doubtless before you?

God, you are our Father. We need intimacy. Teach us to walk in faith—complete faith—so we can know you, see you, feel you, and believe afresh and anew.

Revive us Lord, and restore us as the organization on earth that represents you to the lost. Be so powerful on us that everyone we meet will know that our God is God.

We ask all this in the name of Jesus, the head of your Church, and the author of our salvation. Amen.

9. PRAYING FOR NATIONAL/REGIONAL BROKENNESS

Following the 9/11 attacks on the twin towers in New York City, the Pentagon in Washington D.C., and the apparent attempt on the Whitehouse which was thwarted when the passengers on that flight heroically counter-attacked, forcing their plane to crash that day, America saw something happen that hadn't happened in a generation. We saw people going to church who usually don't.

If you are old enough to remember those first few days, all flights were cancelled except military. The media shared with us what our leaders believed – that we may immediately see many more incidents of terrorism because our intelligence agencies didn't know how many more "sleeper cells" of terrorists within our borders may be activated for more acts of violence. Senators prayed on the floor of the senate in the name of Jesus, and major network anchors admitted that we were a nation united in prayer. We prepared for the worst, and we went back to God.

After a month or so, people began to raise their heads and look around. We didn't see more violence. Occasionally we heard about a plot being stopped, but no more skyscrapers fell, and we gradually went back to our previous lives. And Church attendance went back to usual too. We knew the danger wasn't over, but it seemed like our government had a handle on it.

America is seldom afraid like that, but when we are, we still have a knee-jerk reaction to run to God, and for the most part, that means the Judeo-Christian God. As I first began to pray for God to bring revival, I also began to wonder if I was inadvertently praying for some kind of national disaster that God would use to draw people to himself.

- When the Japanese bombed Pearl Harbor, America prayed.
- During the Civil War both sides saw a revival of faith, and there was no end to the prayers of Abraham Lincoln.
- The Great Depression was a long walk with God for many.

WHEN GOD TURNS

- During the Revolutionary War, many of the Founding Fathers authored prayers in public and in private letters.
- The first colonies were established by those who wanted to seek God on their own terms.

It is in our roots to turn to God, and God desires brokenness.

- *My sacrifice, O God, is a broken spirit; a broken and contrite heart you, God, will not despise.* (Psalm 51:17)
- *He heals the brokenhearted and binds up their wounds.* (Psalm 147:3)
- *The Lord is close to the brokenhearted and saves those who are crushed in spirit.* (Psalm 34:18)
- *Has not my hand made all these things, and so they came into being?" declares the Lord. "These are the ones I look on with favor: those who are humble and contrite in spirit, and who tremble at my word.* (Psalm 66:2)

There is a possibility that as we pray for God to turn and bring an awakening, He will orchestrate human events in such a way that people will cry out to him again. However, in the examples where we see God turn in both the Bible, and in the history of the Church, God doesn't create disasters to cause brokenness. Instead, we see God turn when people are not broken at all. He turns, and suddenly people can see Him again, they recognize what they're doing, and the brokenness comes from sudden conviction.

This is the brokenness we pray for—brokenness resulting from conviction, not brokenness resulting from fear. As we have seen, brokenness from fear doesn't last long, but brokenness that comes from seeing God's truth and love, and realizing how we have fallen short of it – this is the brokenness we pray for.

Still, while we may not be praying for a national disaster, we may be praying for some strong discipline from the Lord.

And have you completely forgotten this word of encouragement that addresses you as a father addresses his son? It says, "My

> *son, do not make light of the Lord's discipline, and do not lose heart when he rebukes you, because the Lord disciplines the one he loves, and he chastens everyone he accepts as his son."*
>
> *Endure hardship as discipline; God is treating you as his children. For what children are not disciplined by their father?*
> (Hebrews 12:5-7)

There may well come a hardship from God that will cause people to question the direction their lives are taking, and it will cause them to change course. Most believers have walked out these hardships and look back on those seasons as the defining moments of their lives. These hardships, or trials, may come first to the Church. After all, if we are to be prepared for a revival, we need to become the Church Jesus calls us to be. We must be strong in Spirit and rich in flavor. We must shake out of comfort, compromise, and complacency, and press on to take hold of the rich inheritance we have in Jesus, so we can have everything we need as a Church, to receive revival.

> *Praise be to the God and Father of our Lord Jesus Christ, who has blessed us in the heavenly realms with every spiritual blessing in Christ.* (Ephesians 1:3)
>
> *His divine power has given us everything we need for a godly life through our knowledge of him who called us by his own glory and goodness.* (2 Peter 1:3)

If the Church is not actively pursuing these things of God, completely sold out for this provision from Jesus as a body of believers, then we need to be corrected, disciplined, and reoriented toward Jesus.

I watch for the correction of the Church to come with great joy. Not with a big "I told you so" waiting to spring from my lips, but rather with a big "here we go again, finally" in my heart. If the Church needs a wake-up call, then I'm part of the problem, because I've been in the church for over forty years, and in leadership of some sort for most of those years.

I would give a wakeup call myself, but I find that God has better timing, better motivation, greater influence, reaches a wider audience, and in general is just more effective than I am. So I pray for him to do it. But I am broken.

We must be broken by conviction if we are to pray for the brokenness of the Church, or our nation. If it's true that revival begins when the first person says, "Let it begin with me", then the first evidence of revival may be the brokenness of those who are called to pray for it. I'm sure that by now, you know I'm talking about you and me.

LET'S PRAY-9

God in Heaven, glorious Father, your Church is broken. Jesus, you know how far we have fallen short of what you have called us to be. We are losing influence, and we are failing to represent you in our time and our culture, the way you have called us to stand.

We are compromised because we are too much of this world. We have affluence and we enjoy the things of this world too much. We are fat and lazy from enjoying the wealth and the prosperity that has existed for all our lives in America. Few if any are left who lived in the great depression. Few of us has lived in a time when the future of our country was seriously threatened. We are used to being comfortable and safe, and we think we are safe because our country is strong.

Bring us back to the realization that you are the only safety and security in this world. If indeed our nation is safe, it is because our forefathers sought your favor and found it. If we are strong, it is because we based and founded our nation on your principals and statutes.

We pride ourselves on being a free society, and we celebrate our freedoms as outlined in the Bill of Rights, but the greatest freedom, Lord, is freedom from sin, and only you can offer it.

We pride ourselves on having free enterprise where the business with the best product and the best customer service at the lowest price will thrive. But you, Lord, said that you came to serve, not

PRAYING FOR REVIVAL

to be served. You established this principal. We no longer give you credit. Our whole idea that government should serve people is based on the idea that the son of God serves people. Yet we now think that it was our idea and not yours.

Oh God, how we pray that our country would once again be broken-hearted, and come back to you. How we pray that the pride and arrogance toward your way and your wisdom would be humbled and silenced by the realization that you are indeed the creator, the deliverer, the redeemer, and the only Savior of all humankind.

Let justice roll down on us like thunder and rain, until our nation is contrite and broken before you.

But let justice roll on like a river, righteousness like a never-failing stream! (Amos 5:24)

Let the waters descend upon us until we give up on our own abilities to save ourselves, and turn to the God of all power and glory to make us safe and strong again. Cause us to cry out and to recognize our need for you again, dear Lord. For we have become a nation that has grown to think that we can take care of ourselves. We are prideful and we have mostly forgotten the ways of the God who built us.

And, in this nation, your Church is a shell of what we should be. We are compromised, lukewarm, and distracted. Too few of us gather to praise you, and most of those who do gather, are not the strong and vital people you have called us and empowered us to be.

Revive your Church, Father, and grow us again into the life-giving, humble, and powerful Church you have always called us to be. Jesus, take control of your Church and bring us back to overwhelming faith and commitment.

Break us all, dear God, and remake us into a nation and a Church that humbly bears your name and stands for you as a genuine example of what you do in the human heart.

How many times in the past have you turned, Oh God, and restored your people and reclaimed the nations whose people have cried out to you? Please Father, take us, brake us, and make us yours. Only you can do this, Father, and we call upon you to do it again, before this generation passes away having never known you.

We need you God, and we are broken in prayer for your deliverance. Spiritually we put on sackcloth and ashes in recognition of our fallen estate. We are hopeless before you, and even though many do not recognize it, we are broken even now.

Revive your Church, Oh Lord, and bring an awakening to our land. Don't wait any longer, Father, because the hearts of your children ache to see you revered and revealed, and loved again. We long to be your people in power and strength, and we wait to see you bring us to brokenness at your feet. We ask in Jesus' name, Amen.

10. PRAYING FOR MORE REVIVAL HELP

Then he said to his disciples, "The harvest is plentiful but the workers are few. Ask the Lord of the harvest, therefore, to send out workers into his harvest field." (Matthew 9:37-38)

Most of the sermons I've heard based on this scripture, are aimed at praying for people who will share the Gospel, often in the hopes that the listeners will not just pray but also step up themselves and share the Gospel. This is a good message, but I think it misses a larger point that Jesus was making when he said it. Let's look at what Jesus was seeing that moved him to say this.

Jesus went through all the towns and villages, teaching in their synagogues, proclaiming the good news of the kingdom and healing every disease and sickness. When he saw the crowds, he had compassion on them, because they were harassed and helpless, like sheep without a shepherd. (Matthew 9:35-36)

Here we see Jesus moved because the people are like sheep without a shepherd to guide and protect them. I once asked a pastor I had just met, "Do you call yourself Reverend, or Pastor, or what?" He said, "I prefer the title under-shepherd." I asked, "Why under-shepherd?" and he replied, "It's just a more accurate name for what I do."

I think when Jesus said to pray for workers, he was thinking of people with a larger job description than just sharing the Gospel. I think he wanted under-shepherds who could share and teach, but also correct and direct people with humility and love the way He did. Jesus wants us to ask for workers who can gather people, counsel with them, and meet their needs as they come to know the Lord. These workers should also be savvy enough to ward off the enemy with a little spiritual warfare too.

> JESUS WANTS US TO ASK FOR WORKERS...

In other words, the Church needs to be prepared with people who are well-rounded in their faith, with enough maturity to stand against the Devil, and humbly and gently love people into the faith. And the Church needs to supply these workers with resources enough to meet needs wherever they exist. This is what we should be praying for when we pray for workers, and this is what we should also become. Because, when you pray for God to send workers into the harvest field, you are probably praying for yourself to be sent as well!

But let's not stop at praying for them to be sent. Let's also pray to empower them, and bless them. Let's pray for their abilities, their outcomes, and their protection and their safety.

Moses prayed like this for the tribe of Levi, who were the under-shepherds of Israel, when he was blessing all the tribes of Israel at the end of his last book. Moses was a salty veteran and this short prayer contains some of the nastiest spiritual warfare in all of scripture. In this passage he is praying for all of the Levites by praying for Aaron their leader. He prays for their ability to be the priests of Israel, and then he says this.

> *O Lord, bless Levi's substance (ability), and accept and take pleasure in the work of his hands; crush and shatter the loins of*

> *those who rise up against him, and of those who hate him, so that they do not rise again.* (Deuteronomy 33:11, AMP)

Take a minute to revere this prayer in its power and perfection, and it's devastation to the enemy.

First Moses prays for the skills and ability of these Old Testament priests, or shepherds of people, if you will. If God blesses someone's ability, will their ability not become everything they will need to achieve His goals for them? And so it was in the early years of the tabernacle. The priests did their ministry, not perfectly, but faithfully, and the people followed God and were blessed.

Next Moses prays "outside the box" by asking God to be pleased with the outcomes of the ministry, and that God will predetermine to take pleasure in the efforts of these priests before they have even started. Remember when "outcomes-based goals and objectives planning" was all the rage for executives and CEOs? Moses did it first. If God is already certain to enjoy the work of their hands, then they can't miss.

Now comes the nasty part, crush and shatter the loins of their enemies. In sports I was taught not to hit below the belt. In self-defense I WAS taught to hit them in "the loins". Women know that a blow well landed in the loins will not only discourage an attacker, it might also take away the attacker's ability to complete a sexual assault. The attacker could become sexually incapacitated. One of the most painful experiences of my life involved the accidental "smiting of my loins" at close range during a snowball fight. So why does Moses go all graphic here?

First, it takes the enemies of the under-shepherds out, so that they cannot rise again. It's a blow that ends the attack.

Second, the loins are the reproductive organs. Israel would struggle throughout the Old Testament with foreign gods. I believe that Moses prayed this way to prevent the enemy (the Devil) from reproducing his own false idol worship through the ministry of these priests.

Once we have asked God for workers that can shepherd people with a degree of completeness, then we must pray like this for their success.

- Pray that God will bless all their abilities and gift them wonderfully and powerfully so they can supernaturally meet the needs of the people they share the love of God with, and shepherd them in every way as they share the Gospel.
- Pray that God, himself, will totally be pleased and take pleasure in the work that these God sent workers will do. Let's gain that assurance in prayer before they set foot in the harvest field.
- And, pray against the attacks of the Devil by asking for God to strike the loins of every foul demon spirit that lifts a finger against them, as well as any opposition they might encounter in this world. Banish every road block. Fill up their funding. Keep their good health. Fill them with fresh vision and encouragement. Strike the enemy in the name of Jesus until the Devil is so tired of being beaten up by your prayers, that he rises no more to mess with the workers you have asked God for.

It has been a long time since God turned in such a powerful way that an awakening occurred which was so great that the Church couldn't keep up. Maybe God is waiting for us to pray and ask for the human resources, and the spiritual protection, so we can handle it. There is a scriptural point made by some, that God sometimes limits himself to what we pray for. Let's find out. If God is just waiting for us to ask with faith for the things he longs to do. Let's ask.

> MAYBE GOD IS WAITING FOR US TO PRAY AND ASK FOR HUMAN RESOURCES AND SPIRITUAL PROTECTION.

Let's Pray-10

Oh God, heavenly Father, creator of all good things, hear this prayer and be attentive to our requests. Send us building block people. Send into the harvest of souls, those ordained people who are made and called by you to reach the lost with the Gospel message and shepherd them into the faith. Send them, Father, in incredible numbers that we might see a massive revival in your Church as they come among us in power and authority, and send them to begin that great awakening which will finally reach millions in this generation with the life-giving message of Jesus.

And, as you send them Lord, predetermine that they will be so successful that you will actually take pleasure in their accomplishments on your behalf and by your great power. Bless their skills and abilities supernaturally, so that they cannot help but bring people to you by the thousands. Bless them as you did Peter who preached on the day of Pentecost and saw thousands receive you as Lord and Savior.

God send us these under-shepherds in amazing numbers so we can receive the masses through them and know again that you are God and there is no other like you.

Also, Lord God, smite the loins of those who rise up against them.

In the name of Jesus, I command you, Devil, to get your filthy hands off of these under-shepherds of God. You may not bring any harm, distraction, or ineffectiveness to them in any way. I loose you off of them in the name of Jesus, and I bind them to God's plan for them, which is filled with success and salvation for this present generation. Devil, you may not replicate any of your heresy and lies through them. Instead, God will take great pleasure in their efforts as they add massively to his family in heavenly realms.

In the name of Jesus, I strike you, Devil, until you rise no more against the God-given leaders of this great awakening. You are a defeated foe, Satan, and I require you to coalesce and retreat in the face of these people whom God has raised up for such a time as this.

God, bless them in every way, and see to it that they are successful in our time.

We realize, Lord, that we who pray may also be the people we are praying for! Indeed we may be the under-shepherds that you are sending into the harvest field. We too may be the ones that are blessed by you, whose hands will do the work that brings you pleasure. We may be the ones you protect so fiercely by striking the loins of the Devil and this world when they opposes us.

If we are the prayer warriors and the under-shepherds, then convict us as we pray, and give us the boldness to step out in the name of Jesus to reach this generation with such God-given effectiveness that the world will surely be shaken by your glory. Amen!

11. THE SOUND OF HEAVY RAIN

I have mentioned the example of Elijah on Mt. Carmel a few times because it is one of the best examples of what can happen when God turns. Now I would like to revisit this event with an eye to what we can learn about prayer and how to pray for that move of God.

After watching the 450 prophets of the evil god Baal pray for him to accept their sacrifice by burning it up, and after seeing the prophets of Baal cut themselves to encourage Baal and exhaust themselves in vain, Elijah prepared his offering. Then he allowed the Baal worshippers to pour water on it time and again. And when they had done all this, Elijah prayed this short simple prayer.

> *At the time of sacrifice, the prophet Elijah stepped forward and prayed: "Lord, the God of Abraham, Isaac and Israel, let it be known today that you are God in Israel and that I am your servant and have done all these things at your command. Answer me, Lord, answer me, so these people will know that you, Lord, are God, and that you are turning their hearts back again." (1 KINGS 18:36-37)*

When God turns, the next thing that happens is, people turn to him.

Of course, Elijah's prayer is so short in contrast to the prophets of Baal and their lugubrious prayers over so many hours of toil and stress.

Elijah's life is on the line here. He knows that king Ahab and his Queen Jezebel are ready to have him put to death as soon as he fails, but Elijah has complete faith that God will consume his soaking wet sacrifice, and the fire of God does come down and consume even the rocks and the dirt around the offering.

Can we ever find that much faith for our prayers? Can we ever have that certainty that we see in so many of the great prayers of the Bible?

Elijah's faith for God's answers to prayer was not over. After the climactic overthrow of Baal, Elijah says something remarkable to King Ahab, whom he still respects even though Ahab was a horrible King who wanted him dead.

> *And Elijah said to Ahab, "Go, eat and drink, for there is the sound of a heavy rain." So Ahab went off to eat and drink, but Elijah climbed to the top of Carmel, bent down to the ground and put his face between his knees.* (1 Kings 18:41-42)

There isn't a cloud in the sky, and it hasn't rained in Israel for three years. They have been suffering with both a spiritual drought and an actual drought. The spiritual drought has just been broken and the hearts of the people have turned back to God. Now, Elijah is so connected with what God is doing that he can hear rain that doesn't yet exist, and it's a heavy rain. So, Elijah sits down to pray again for something he is certain about. He prays for rain.

At first, it looks like it's not going to happen.

> *"Go and look toward the sea," he told his servant. And he went up and looked. "There is nothing there," he said. Seven times Elijah said, "Go back."* (1 Kings 18:43)

So strong is Elijah's faith that even with one bad report after another, he prays on, undaunted. Can we have this kind of fortitude? Truly Elijah is evidence of what we learn about faith in Hebrews 11:1" Now faith is confidence in what we hope for and assurance about what we do not see." Certainly Elijah is sure about what he cannot see. Of course he can hear it supernaturally, but his faith is just over-the-top and it is startling in its certainty.

PRAYING FOR REVIVAL

> *The seventh time the servant reported, "A cloud as small as a man's hand is rising from the sea." (vs. 44a)*

Now he gets the meager report that some tiny cloud has appeared and again his faith is so strong that he knows it's the beginning of God's answer. He is so sure that heavy rain is almost upon them that he actually sends his servant to warn the King of the impending flood! All this from a dinky little cloud that wouldn't even show on today's weather radar.

> *So Elijah said, "Go and tell Ahab, 'Hitch up your chariot and go down before the rain stops you.'"*
>
> *Meanwhile, the sky grew black with clouds, the wind rose, a heavy rain started falling and Ahab rode off to Jezreel. The power of the Lord came on Elijah and, tucking his cloak into his belt, he ran ahead of Ahab all the way to Jezreel. (vs. 44b-45)*

Now he even gets super powers so he can run like "Flash".

Friends, I want faith like that. I want faith like Elijah had. But wait! It's really hard to believe what happens next.

Queen Jezebel sends Elijah a message threatening his life and Elijah panics?!

> *Elijah was afraid and ran for his life. When he came to Beersheba in Judah, he left his servant there, while he himself went a day's journey into the wilderness. He came to a broom bush, sat down under it and prayed that he might die. "I have had enough, Lord," he said. "Take my life; I am no better than my ancestors."*
>
> *(1 Kings 19:3-4)*

WHAT? What just happened to the guy with the OMG faith? He just performed fearlessly in the face of insurmountable odds with nothing but his faith in God to get him through, and now he runs away and hides and whines and feels sorry for himself, because he just can't take it anymore?

So, is Elijah a hero or a coward?

He's both.

There is only one conclusion I can take away from these two pictures of Elijah. He is human like the rest of us, and God gave him the faith he needed to do the good works that God had for him to do.

God has lined up some good works for you and me to do, too.

> *For we are God's handiwork, created in Christ Jesus to do* ***good works****, which God prepared in advance for us to do.*
> (Ephesians 2:10, emphasis added)

So, since God has good works for us too, then he must be ready to give us the faith we need to believe for those good works, or else we'll just sit under a bush and whine like Elijah. In fact, Paul writes about how the Holy Spirit gives us the gift of faith when we need it to help build up the Church.

> *To one there is given through the Spirit a message of wisdom, to another a message of knowledge by means of the same Spirit, to another faith by the same Spirit.* (1 Corinthians 12:8-9a)

Now keep in mind that Paul is writing about how the Holy Spirit gives these gifts to believers – they already have faith in Jesus for salvation. They have already been justified by grace through faith in Jesus Christ. So this gift of faith that the Holy Spirit hands out is not the faith that all believers have, it's a spiritual gift of faith to be used to build up the Church and perform the good works that God decided in advance for us to do.

Now let's pull all of this together. If we are convicted that we should pray for God to turn and bring revival to ourselves, and the Church, and this land of ours, and if this prayer is one of the good works God has planned for us to do, then the Holy Spirit should give us the gift of faith, like he gave Elijah, so we can pray with the certainty and assurance and perseverance that Elijah had.

There's just one last step. We need to ask for the gift of faith.

Paul tells us: "Now eagerly desire the greater gifts (1 Corinthians 12:31).

PRAYING FOR REVIVAL

Jesus tells us: how much more will your Father in heaven give the Holy Spirit to those who ask him!" (Luke 11:13b).

Let us ask for the Holy Spirit, and for Him to give us the gift of Faith so we can pray with power for the salvation of our generation and the restoration of the Church.

I want to pray to break spiritual draught like Elijah. I want to hear the sound of the heavy rain of an awakening. I hope you too want to give yourself to this endeavor in the knowledge that God has led you to this point, and he has called you to this prayer. Can you see it? Can you hear it?

I asked God once; "What is the sound of Revival? What is the sound of the restoration of God's glory among the people? What is the sound of warfare against the enemy? What is the sound of a spiritual draught being broken?"

This is how God answered me.

"It is the sound of anointed worship, the sound of certain prayer, the sound of cries of joy. Also, it is the sound of my voice calling you to pray for revival."

If you hear the sound of His voice calling you, then we share something deep and meaningful in common, and we are joined together to pray for the lost, and for the Church, with all our hearts, and with the gift of faith.

Let's Pray-11

God, has it not been too long since the sound of heavy rain was heard in our land?

Is it not time for you to do what you have done over the many centuries, and turn, and draw people to yourself?

Give each of us the gift of faith so we can pray like Elijah on Mt. Carmel, and know that the Lord God Jehovah is ready to move and claim a people to Himself.

WHEN GOD TURNS

Certainly there is so much more aligned against you now Lord, than there was in the days of Elijah, and yet we know with certainty that you are more than capable of defeating this present darkness, and declaring yourself to this present generation with clarity and authority, until your name is again revered, and your salvation becomes again the hallmark of our day.

We who pray to you live in a fallen world, and we are part of it. But we pray to our risen Savior who has triumphed over this world, and who leads His Church with power. Come, Lord Jesus, and vanquish the walls that separate your salvation from this generation. Come and make known among the nations that you alone are the King of kings and the Lord of lords.

Jesus, defeat the rulers and the principalities that work against the knowledge of God. We tear them down in your name, and we lift up the truth of your sacrifice as the evidence that our God loves all mankind, and is calling them into His family.

Let us hear the sound of heavy rain. Let us know that the spiritual draught which engulfs our nations with the dryness of propaganda and the emptiness of human effort, will be replaced with your truth, love, and power, until a great flood of revival sweeps through your Church, and an awakening dawns upon this generation that cannot be denied or resisted. Add to your family, and establish your kingdom on earth as it is in heaven.

God, let your prayer warriors hear the sound of the heavy rain of your turning. Bless us with the gift of faith to believe for a revival in your Church, and an awakening that will rock this world with salvation and intimacy with you. Give us the vision, and the spiritual eyes and ears to see it, hear it, and know that your turn is upon us. We ask for this in the precious name of Jesus, and because we love you so much that we are desperate to see your move in our day. Come to us now, and do not make us wait, for the draught is long, and we thirst.

12. ALL REVIVAL IS PERSONAL

Can I ask God for revival in my nation, or my region or my church, and not for myself?

I've heard a teaching that says you can't lead people where you've never been yourself. I'm sure that's not true. Our forefathers gave us a nation unlike any before it. Somebody has to be the first. Submarines, bifocals, the Bible in English, and baseball—some people do lead us "where no man has gone before". (Thank you, Gene Roddenberry.)

However, shouldn't a person praying for revival be revived themselves? If we are going to ask God to turn and change the direction of human events, mustn't it burn first in our hearts? Moses was driven to see the Israelites unite with the God that he had already met. He wanted them to experience God the way he did—on the mountain. It drove him, it motivated him. He didn't need vision, he was full of the presence of God, and he knew everything he needed to know in order to get them there.

I figure that every person who will pray for revival deserves to have one themselves. A section of this book is devoted to your personal revival, but we must also pray for the personal revival of each person who will join us in praying. It starts with this verse.

> "I live in a high and holy place, but also with the one who is **contrite** and lowly in spirit, to <u>revive</u> the spirit of the lowly and to <u>revive</u> the **heart** of the **contrite**.
>
> (Isaiah 57:15, emphasis and underscore added)

What makes our hearts contrite? Isn't it when we see the results of our sin? When we see the loved ones we've hurt and the damage we've done, we get contrite. When others see us at our worst, that can shame us too. When we stumble over the same sin time and again, our spirit gets low. We don't want to go back to God again and repent. We already tried that and it didn't work. It's not too hard to get it touch with those times in our past or present when we fit the description of contrite and lowly. These things take us to the place where God will revive us.

WHEN GOD TURNS

There is a story told about Robert Bruce, the King who led Scotland to freedom from British rule. In the story, Bruce had fought three battles and lost them all. Before each battle he had prayed and believed that God was with him and wanted his army to fight. But now, alone in an open field, he was beaten in spirit. He had lost heart, and he couldn't bring himself to pray again for victory. Maybe he was just fooling himself, and God really wasn't there at all. He resolved himself not to pray.

But as he knelt in the field in despair, he noticed a spider trying to set the first main strand of thread for a web. It was quite an expanse between two tree branches and the wind was gusting. Each time the spider would climb and try to stretch that first strand, it would snap before he could reinforce it. As he watched, the persistent spider tried three times and failed. Bruce wondered if the spider would try again, or just move on and look for another spot a little less ambitious. Then, Robert Bruce made a deal with God. If the spider tried again and made it, then he would take it as a sign that God would grant him victory too in the next battle. But if the spider moved on, or failed in a fourth attempt, then Bruce would be done, too.

Of course, the spider made his web, and Robert Bruce would lead his country to victory at Bannockburn.

I give you this legend, because it speaks to those moments we all have when we are down and low and then God revives. Most of us have been there, and we must go there again to those times when we were broken and crying out for God's help and he revived us. But now let us find, from God, a revival in ourselves of lasting proportions. Let God give you the calm assurance of his desire for your prayers. See if He will not build in you the quiet confidence of His intention to turn and receive your prayers and move. This is a revival for those whom God calls to pray.

King David wasn't always right with God. He had gigantic falls from grace, but he knew what to do when he was contrite of heart and low in spirit. Here's what David said to God in these times.

PRAYING FOR REVIVAL

Let me hear joy and gladness; let the bones you have crushed rejoice. Hide your face from my sins and blot out all my iniquity.

Create in me a pure heart, O God, and renew a steadfast spirit within me. Do not cast me from your presence or take your Holy Spirit from me. Restore to me the joy of your salvation and grant me a willing spirit, to sustain me. (Psalm 51:8)

He's wrestling with God here. He's asking for God to turn from His wrath, and have mercy on him, and revive and restore him. We pray under a better covenant than did king David, but we need that revived, steadfast, willing spirit. We need that renewed heart. We must have the strength of heart and spirit to pray with confidence.

(The following portion is reprinted here from Chapter 2 on Personal Revival.)

I want you to have revival for yourself. I pray for you to have it. Christians always want the rest of the world to have what we have because it blesses us so. So I have decided that, you have come to this point in my book, and you should now have revival.

> **WE PRAY UNDER A BETTER COVENANT THAN DAVID DID.**

- Will you <u>hope</u> for it now?

But those who hope in the LORD will renew their strength. they will soar on wings like eagles; they will run and not grow weary, they will walk and not be faint. (Isaiah 40:31)

- Will you ask for it now?

<u>Ask</u> *and it will be given to you; seek and you will find; knock and the door will be opened to you.* (Matthew 7:7, underscore added)

- Will you believe for it?

If you <u>believe</u>, you will receive whatever you <u>ask</u> for in prayer.
(Matthew 21:22, underscore added)

It's not like we're asking for something outside of God's will. Praying that we might experience a revived heart and spirit is central to what God does. We are simply asking God to be God. This is the appetite He wants us to have, and it's the thirst that Jesus died to quench by providing for us living water.

- Because you are the righteousness of God…

*God made him who had no sin to be sin for us, so that in him we might become the **righteousness of God**.*
(*2 Corinthians 5:21, emphasis added*)

- …you are at peace with God,

*Therefore, since we have been justified through faith, we have **peace with God** through our Lord Jesus Christ.*
(*Romans 5:1, emphasis added*)

- …and you may have this revival in your heart and spirit.

*His divine power has given us **everything we need** for a godly life through our knowledge of him who called us by his own glory and goodness.* (*2 Peter 3:1, emphasis added*)

- I need this revival in me, and I need you to have it too. Ask for it now in hope and faith and receive it even right now.

*Now **faith** is confidence in what we **hope** for and assurance about what we do not see.* (*Hebrews 11:1, emphasis added*)

As you begin to walk in this revived state, you will find that you have a confidence that God wants your prayers for Him to turn, revive His Church, and bring an awakening to this generation. And, you will find that it has already started in you.

Now let's pray like it's 32 AD!

Let's Pray-12

Father, it is so important for those of us who pray for an awakening in our land to have that awakening in our hearts. If we are going to ask with assurance for the Church to be revived, our spirits and hearts must first be revived. How else will we have the strength, endurance, and insight to pray with passion for you to turn, unless you have turned in our lives?

Father, we know you to be a God of love and grace. Let grace do its work in us. We look at this world and our hearts are often troubled. We look at the Church and are spirits inside us burn low. Give us the grace that revives our hearts and spirits within us so we can call upon you to do for this world and this Church, what you have done in us.

Surely, Father, we are only asking for what your word says you will do. We ache to see you turn and change the direction of our lives by pouring new meaning into our hearts—the meaning and purpose that come with revival.

Jesus, you are the head of the Church and the author of eternal life through your blood. Breathe into our spirits now, as you breathed into your disciples. Renew us in spirit and create in us a heart that swells with the love of God. You call your Church to be many wonderful things. Make each of us into those things right now, simply because we ask. You call us to pray. Fill us with those prayers you desire. You empower us with every good thing. Now motivate us with your love. You want us all to serve. Gift us right now with all we need to be effective. You have given us the Gospel so we can share eternal life with this world. Now send a wave of revival, like we have never seen, that will carry us into the harvest field with such momentum that this generation will be swept along.

My life in you has been good, Lord, and I'm not complaining at all. But if I am to persevere in prayer until that day when you turn, then I need this spiritual upgrade. I need the heart of the Lion of Judah, and refreshing in the Spirit of the one true God. I claim them in the name of Jesus, because I know that, with these, I too can pray the prayers that will cause the Lord God Almighty to turn from wrath, and bring a great light into this world again, and reinvigorate His people.

We each pray this prayer, Lord. And I also pray that those of us who are called to pray for these things will be knit together in prayer, like a spiritual gofundme.com so that our joint prayer will fund your turn, and all that it will bring to humankind. Amen.

13. THE ANOINTING OF BOLDNESS
(for Terri)

How bold are you in prayer? Do you confront God with your concerns and needs? Do you pray for safe things or do you take risks in prayer and ask for things that, should you get them, you might be uncomfortable and challenged?

The early Church prayed risky prayers. One of the first prayers recorded by the early Church is in chapter four of the book of the Acts of the Apostles. Peter and John, two of Jesus' disciples, had the boldness to ask God to heal a well-known crippled man who had been regularly begging at the entrance to the Women's Court in the Temple at Jerusalem, apparently for decades. God healed the man instantly and it caused a sensation because they had performed this healing in the name of Jesus, the one who had been recently put to death at the insistence of the religious leaders of the Temple. Peter and John and the man who was healed were all brought before the Sanhedrin (the gathering of Jewish religious rulers) and they were interrogated.

Peter and John told these leaders that they had killed the Son of God. The Jewish leaders warned Peter and John to stop teaching about Jesus, and threatened them greatly if they were to continue.

> *But Peter and John replied, "Which is right in God's eyes: to listen to you, or to him? You be the judges! As for us, we cannot help speaking about what we have seen and heard."* (Acts 4:19-20)

After further threats were made, Peter and John were let go and they went back and reported all of these threats to a gathering of the Church. Then the Church together prayed an amazing prayer. Here is what they <u>didn't</u> ask for.

- Protection from the threats of beatings, death, and exclusion from the Jewish faith.
- Safety and provision for their families.
- Comfort in times of trial.

Instead, they prayed against the alliance of the Jewish religious leaders, their King Herod, and the Roman government, which had set itself up against Jesus. And, they asked God to do more miracles, even though it would stir up their persecution. And, they prayed for God to give them boldness to continue their witness in the face of these threats!

> *Now, Lord, consider their threats and enable your servants to speak your word with great boldness. Stretch out your hand to heal and perform signs and wonders through the name of your holy servant Jesus."* (Acts 4:29-30)

This is a risky prayer, and it's just the kind of boldness we need now in order to boldly pray for God to turn, to move, to change the direction of human events, and to get us out of our comfort zones and into the fight for the salvation of the lost. This boldness is essential to our prayers. It's necessary for every generation that would see the Gospel take flight and reach the lost.

But, does God like this kind of prayer? Is it the type of thing he answers? Or, is this kind of prayer just a dramatic momentary expression of human emotion that God doesn't answer because He's waiting for us to settle down and pray more practically? The next verse tells us how God feels about prayers for boldness.

> *After they prayed, the place where they were meeting was shaken. And they were all filled with the Holy Spirit and spoke the word of God boldly.* (Acts 4:31)

They got what they prayed for, immediately and miraculously.

Will it work today? The Church in the book of Acts was at the beginning of an awakening that would move through much of the known world in a generation. They asked for boldness at the risk of their own lives.

So, pause for a minute and count the cost of praying for boldness. Are you willing to receive boldness from God to pray and to act for this awakening? We can't know where God given boldness might take us. You may find yourself in a third world country exposed to malaria, a corrupt government, street thieves, and an opposing faith system that seeks to silence you. You may find yourself sleeping on a cot in a dingy room with little critters crawling around you and water that you don't trust to bathe in or to drink. You may find yourself meeting with members of a tribe that has no electricity, or plumbing, and you will insult them and ruin your witness if you refuse to eat the meal they have prepared for you.

I pray for boldness, and I have been in these situations. Will you risk comfort and safety in order to pray and act with boldness? A fellow from our church recently returned home from a mission trip with malaria. He had taken all the prescriptions and precautions, but they just weren't enough to protect him. He was hospitalized for a time, but now he's restored. He would do it again in a heartbeat. That's boldness. If you're worried that you may not have this same drive to be bold, consider what the very bold Apostle Paul writes;

> *It is written: "I believed; therefore I have spoken." Since we have that same spirit of faith, we also believe and therefore speak.*
> *(2 Corinthians 4:13)*

You see, we who believe in Jesus all share that "same spirit of faith" that Paul, and every other believer has. So Paul says "we also believe and therefore speak." Our ability to receive boldness from God to speak, or in our case to pray for this awakening and act on it accordingly, comes to us from the same Spirit who has brought boldness and humility to believers since Pentecost.

You <u>can</u> pray this prayer and you must. It is time for this anointing of boldness to sweep through the Church again, and that includes you.

Boldness in prayer is central to the Christian experience. Traditionally Jews were afraid to be in the presence of God because they believed it would kill them. They would avoid speaking His name, and if they had to write it down, they would leave out the vowels. Even that one time each year when the High priest would go into the innermost chamber of the Tabernacle or the Temple, where the presence of God resided above the cover on the Ark of the Covenant, that priest would bring a censor which burned incense, and that smoke screen protected the high Priest from the direct presence of God.

> **BOLDNESS IN PRAYER IS CENTRAL TO THE CHRISTIAN EXPERIENCE.**

How bold we Christians are by comparison. The veil that separated the innermost chamber from the rest of the Temple was torn in two when Jesus died and now we have access through our faith in Christ to the presence of God in prayer.

> *In whom we have boldness and confident access through faith in Him [that is, our faith gives us sufficient courage to freely and openly approach God through Christ].* (Ephesians 3:12, AMP)

I say pray first for boldness to pray. Then pray for boldness to act. In Christ you were born to be bold. And, I pray this for you, that when you go home to be with the Father, the Church will remember you the way we remember Paul.

> *He proclaimed the kingdom of God and taught about the Lord Jesus Christ—with all boldness and without hindrance!* (Acts 28:31)

That's a legacy worthy of the life God has given us. I have already prayed for your boldness, now pray for yourself, and for everyone else that will join us.

Let's Pray-13

God, enable your servants to speak your word with great boldness.

Jesus, we are tired of being weak, afraid, timid, polite, benchwarmers. Breathe into us an anointing of boldness. Crank us up! Get your Church moving in power and wisdom, but get us moving, Lord.

WHEN GOD TURNS

You, Jesus are the head of the Church, and we take our orders from you. I know that you send us into the harvest fields, Lord, but so many of us are reluctant to go. We make excuses why we don't share. We see others in the Church who seem to have the ability and we leave it to them.

Jesus, I'm tired of "them" doing everything. I want "us" to get going. Light a fire under us, Jesus, a fire that cannot be denied or ignored. Break our hearts for the lost, and instill in every one of us the knowledge that we each have a story to tell and a Savior to share. Help us to realize that each of us is just the right witness for someone who doesn't know you.

Don't let your Church sit on the sidelines. You never gave us an example like that, Jesus, and it's clear from Church history that ALL of your true disciples went throughout the known world to reach the lost. In contrast, many of us struggle to tell members of our own families.

Please, Jesus, don't let any more time pass until you shake your Church into action. You have given us the greatest gift in the world, the Gospel message, which you provided at the cost of your own life. How can we not take up your call and share it. I know that every believer sees the need for the world to know you. So we are asking you now, God. Turn. Revive your Church. Wake us up. Renew your call and recharge our batteries. Give us the zeal of the early Church. Make it contagious as it grows and spreads through the Church.

And give us success, Lord. Drive us in the knowledge that we have caught the wave of your move. Help us to sense, as we go out as "fishers of men," that we are stepping deeper into your will, and achieving your purpose. Let us know the satisfaction of being good servants.

May it be said of our generation that we were bold in sharing the Gospel, and that we labored joyfully in service to Jesus.

Amen

14. DON'T GET KNOCKED OUT
(for Greg)

One phenomenon of the Christian faith is that our enemy attacks us with greater force as we press into serving God with greater effectiveness. Am I saying that the devil comes after believers with more fervor as we grow in our commitment to Jesus? Yes.

As a pastor, I see it all the time. Someone finds it in their heart that they believe in Jesus, they pray a prayer of salvation and join the Church, and then things go wrong for them. They lose their job. They suddenly have family problems or health problems. The attacks are predictable and well designed to discourage the new believer. One of my pastors put it this way, "If the Devil can't keep you from getting saved, then he'll do everything he can to make you ineffective in bringing anyone else to the Lord." This concept is extremely well illustrated in the book, *The Screwtape Letters*, by C. S. Lewis, which I highly recommend.

The same thing is often true each time we take steps forward in our service to God. We know some things about the devil. Jesus taught this.

> *The thief (the Devil) comes only to **steal** and **kill** and **destroy**; I have come that they may have life, and have it to the full.*
> *(John 10:10, emphasis and parenthesis added)*

And, Peter also speaks of these things.

> *Be alert and of sober mind. Your enemy the devil prowls around like a roaring lion looking for someone to devour. ⁹Resist him, standing firm in the faith, because you know that the family of believers throughout the world is undergoing the same kind of sufferings.*
> *(1 Peter 5:8-9)*

Faith in Jesus is our defense against these attacks. Paul makes this clear in his famous teaching about the armor of God.

> *In addition to all this, take up the **shield of faith**, with which you can extinguish all the flaming arrows of the evil one.*
> *(Ephesians 6:16, emphasis added)*

Paul, who was perhaps the most effective servant of Jesus' Church in his generation, was uniquely qualified to teach us about how to handle the attacks of the enemy. Paul, out of necessity, became an expert in warding off these attacks.

Listen to this brief litany of some of what he suffered in service to Jesus.

> *Five times I received from the Jews the forty lashes minus one. Three times I was beaten with rods, once I was pelted with stones, three times I was shipwrecked, I spent a night and a day in the open sea, I have been constantly on the move. I have been in danger from rivers, in danger from bandits, in danger from my fellow Jews, in danger from Gentiles; in danger in the city, in danger in the country, in danger at sea; and in danger from false believers. I have labored and toiled and have often gone without sleep; I have known hunger and thirst and have often gone without food; I have been cold and naked. Besides everything else, I face daily the pressure of my concern for all the churches.*
>
> (2 Corinthians 11:24-28)

When Paul says that our faith is the antidote for the attacks of the Devil, he should know. What are the attacks you have run up against? Have you applied your complete faith in the deliverance of Jesus from these things? Even in Jesus' model of prayer he coaches us to pray for deliverance.

> *And do not lead us into temptation, but deliver us from evil.*
>
> (Matthew 6:13, NASB)

Newer translations render this verse even more accurately.

> *And lead us not into temptation, but deliver us from the evil one.*
>
> (Matthew 6:13 (NIV)

This is the picture that Jesus, Peter, and Paul are all pointing us toward. We must have faith in Jesus for deliverance from the plans, attacks, whisperings, and confrontations that come from the Devil and his demons.

PRAYING FOR REVIVAL

Not everything is from the Devil, I get that. There are many things in this world that are just plain inconvenient and we have to endure them. I'm talking about things like; red lights, taxes, aging, politics, bad jokes, bad breath, rudeness, and whatever other pet peeves you care to include. These are the conditions of the fallen world in which we live. We move through them in faith, but faith rarely delivers us from them. Sometimes it's unclear to us whether or not an obstacle shows up as a result of the enemy or just the world. Our faith is still our ally, and so are endurance and submission. Endurance keeps us moving when the going gets tough, and submission to others keeps us from stumbling over people who might otherwise offend us.

Submission is a great weapon for those who seek to serve Jesus because it puts us in the right relationship with the people we meet. We are their servants. Jesus has said so.

The greatest among you will be your servant. For those who exalt themselves will be humbled, and those who humble themselves will be exalted. (Matthew 23:11-12)

It's a great attitude because it keeps us from feeling taken advantage of by others. Instead, we serve Jesus by serving them. We remain humble, "speaking the truth in love," and it keeps us from many of the entanglements that can otherwise slow us down. We become more Christlike—ready to forgive and build other people up in the Lord. It's not the easiest spiritual discipline to adopt, but it's the right one, and it helps us to negotiate those relationships that can sidetrack us.

Endurance is also a Christlike attitude, and again, Paul is an expert.

We are hard pressed on every side, but not crushed; perplexed, but not in despair; persecuted, but not abandoned; struck down, but not destroyed. We always carry around in our body the death of Jesus, so that the life of Jesus may also be revealed in our body. For we who are alive are always being given over to death for Jesus' sake, so that his life may also be revealed in our mortal body. So then, death is at work in us, but life is at work in you.

> *It is written: "I believed; therefore I have spoken." Since we have that same spirit of faith, we also believe and therefore speak, because we know that the one who raised the Lord Jesus from the dead will also raise us with Jesus and present us with you to himself. All this is for your benefit, so that the grace that is reaching more and more people may cause thanksgiving to overflow to the glory of God.*
>
> *Therefore we do not lose heart. Though outwardly we are wasting away, yet inwardly we are being renewed day by day. For our light and momentary troubles are achieving for us an eternal glory that far outweighs them all. So we fix our eyes not on what is seen, but on what is unseen, since what is seen is temporary, but what is unseen is eternal.*   *(2 Corinthians 4:8-18)*

This is a great synopsis of how the Church is supposed to operate. We see self-denial, spiritual vision, commitment, and victorious revival being shared with the world. And all of this acted out with great faith and sacrifice for the benefit of reaching those who are yet to be saved.

So I say, "don't let yourself get knocked out of praying for an awakening. Certainly you will be attacked as you pray for things that God wants and the enemy does not want. And, this world will seldom cooperate, so counter these things with faith, endurance, and servanthood so you can stand against all this and pray."

> *Therefore put on the full armor of God, so that when the day of evil comes, you may be able **to stand** your ground, and after you have done everything, **to stand**.*   *(Ephesians 6:1, emphasis added)*

After all, you are not an unarmed wimp who is pushed around by the devil and the world. No, you are a child of the living God. He gives you everything you need, so you have your enemy outnumbered!

> *Because greater is He who is in you than he who is in the world.*
> *(1 John 4:4b, NASB)*

PRAYING FOR REVIVAL

Let's Pray-14

God, deliver us from evil, deliver us from the evil one. Jesus, we know that the Devil and his minions seek to knock us out of serving you. The evil one does not want great prayers for the revival of the Church or an awakening in this generation. For those of us who are called to pray for these things, the attacks of our enemy are inevitable.

But equally certain is our deliverance from them when we rely in you God, in faith. You have always been the final authority on earth and in heaven, Father, and we count on your protection.

We put on your spiritual armor as a way of understanding spiritual warfare, and also as a way of activating our faith in You. When we lift up the "shield of faith", it simply means that we are actively believing in you to nullify the attacks of the enemy, the devil.

We have seen how discouragement, distraction, and lack of focus, can cause us to loose heart and fall away from all that you have for us to do. So we are praying now for ourselves and all those that you have called to pray for you to turn. Let us be consistent and faithful to our call. Keep us from the plans of our enemy so we can realize this purpose in our lives. Don't let us get knocked out of your purpose for us. Instead, destroy the plans of the enemy. His defeat is imminent since your victory on the cross. We put our faith in you to enforce his defeat whenever he seeks to deny us our service to you Father.

When you turn, Father, and we can see the light of salvation sweep across our land, then we will rejoice that we were not prevented from praying, but instead we were the effective and persistent servants of the Most High God, who came to us with His hand of protection during our time of service.

There is no other like you. There is none other who can defeat our foe. Only you, Father, can do these things. So we call out to you in true faith that your answer will always be with us. Deliver us from evil. For thine is the Kingdom, and the Power, and the Glory forever. Amen

15. HELL AND JUDGEMENT AS MOTIVATION
(for Steve)

What does the word of God say about people who die without believing in Jesus as their Lord and Savior? Will they really go to a place called hell?

Jesus teaches that there is a place called hell which has:

- "Fire that never goes out" (Mk. 9:43).
- "Eternal fire, prepared for the devil and his angels" (Mt. 25:41).
- There will be "weeping and gnashing of teeth" (Mt. 13:42).
- A place of "torment" for humans who go there (Lk. 16:23).

Other New Testament authors agree about hell and point out that it is the destination of:

- Those who disobey the gospel and are eternally separated from God (2 Thess. 1:5-9).
- It is not God's desire for people to go to hell (2 Pet 3:9).
- People who go to hell have rejected God's grace and salvation (Ro. 1:16 – 2:10).

Everyone continues to exist after death either with God in a glorious place, or without him in hell. It is human nature not to like this fact. Many choose not to believe it. But not believing it doesn't make it go away. God's truth and his way of doing things are not up for a vote. God does things his way—that's it.

So, have you really thought about this? People you and I know will spend their eternal lives in hell. Folks that we meet every day will reject Jesus and wind up in eternal torment. They will weep and know unspeakable pain and anguish.

PRAYING FOR REVIVAL

Let's not consider, for right now, people who live in a foreign country who never heard of Jesus or a valid presentation of the Gospel. Let's just consider the people right around us who have social media and computers and access to the Gospel—people who can walk into a life-giving church whenever they want to, and they choose over and over again to ignore it.

We've all run into it one way or another. We have family members who don't want to hear it. We have friends who are great, but they never bring up the subject. It's just not for them, or, they'll get around to it someday. My church is on a busy street in Aurora, Colorado. I don't know how many thousands of people drive past my church on a normal day, but it saddens me to wonder how many of them will wind up in hell.

> "When sinners are careless and stupid, and sinking into hell unconcerned, it is time the Church should bestir themselves. It is as much the duty of the Church to awake, as it is for the firemen to do so when fire breaks out in the night in a great city. Sleep! Should the firemen sleep and let the whole city burn down; what would be thought of such firemen? And yet their guilt would not compare with the guilt of Christians who sleep while sinners around them are sinking stupid into the fires of hell,"
> (Rev. Charles Finney – 1835, from *Lectures on Revival*)

When I first started pastoring in the 1980's, I was called to the bedside of an old man who was nearly 100 years old. He claimed to be the oldest living member of John Phillip Sousa's Band! I was, at the time, still a school band director myself, and I pastored on the weekends. I was thrilled to meet him, and I asked him how I could help. He told me that he wanted to get baptized and accept Jesus as his Lord and Savior. He had recently learned that he didn't have long to live, and he had promised his mother that he would get saved before he died. I questioned him to make sure that he was seeking baptism because he believed in Jesus and not just because his mother wanted it.

He was adamant that he had believed in Jesus, as the Son of God who died on the cross for our sins and had come back to life on the third day, for most of his adult life. So I asked him why he had waited so long. The answer came very matter of fact. He had never wanted to live a Christian life. He enjoyed drinking, and women, and a few other things I won't mention. He hadn't accepted Jesus before this because he didn't want to live a hypocritical life, having agreed to follow Jesus but knowing he wouldn't! But now that he was near death, he wanted salvation from the one he believed could offer it—Jesus.

His faith seemed real, not that it was my place to judge. Alarms were going off in my head, but I could think of no real reason to deny him baptism. He died about ten days after I baptized him.

I tell you this story because, (1) it's so rare that anyone who puts off salvation ever comes around to it later, and, (2) so many people see Christianity as having to give up things they don't want to give up, instead of seeing the freedom, the meaning, the empowerment, and, yes, the sacrifice, which is all so rewarding.

When talking about the judgement of the good and bad things we have done, which all believers will face upon entrance into heaven, Paul writes this:

> *If what has been built survives, the builder will receive a reward. If it is burned up, the builder will suffer loss but yet will be saved—even though only as one escaping through the flames. Don't you know that you yourselves are God's temple and that God's Spirit dwells in your midst?* (1 Corinthians 3:14-16)

I've always figured that the old bandsman that I baptized was one of those guys who had to escape through the flames. If only he would have received the Holy Spirit decades earlier, who knows what he might have built that would have survived judgement? How much more of a father and husband would he have been? What mark might he have made on this world for Christ? We will never know.

I don't know if the threat of hell motivates anyone to get saved anymore, but it ought to motivate believers to pray for those who are headed that direction. Parents pray for their children as they are growing up, because the parents realize that their kids aren't yet wise—they don't see the danger, they don't respect the consequences they will suffer. We must pray like this for the lost. How we need to see God turn and change the direction of billions of people who are otherwise going to hell.

Maybe, praying for the lost is a work that will survive the fire when we are judged. I think all of our valid, fire-surviving, work falls into three categories:

> THE THREAT OF HELL SHOULD MOTIVATE BELIEVERS TO PRAY FOR THOSE WHO ARE WITHOUT CHRIST.

1. Our love and actions in our relationship with God.

2. Our love and actions in building up the Church.

3. Our love and actions in reaching the lost.

Everything else just gets burned up.

Let hell and judgement sink in to your thinking and motivate you to pray. One day Jesus will return, and it will be too late. Until that day God tarries, waiting for the few that will come to him. You and I know all of this. If we don't pray, who will?

LET'S PRAY-15

God, maker of Heaven and Earth, in your wisdom you have created hell, and have made it the eternal destination and consequence for all people who do not enter into a saving relationship with Jesus, your son. I fear that His sacrifice is wasted on the vast majority of the people in this world.

Some reject Jesus regularly, and others know very little if anything about Jesus.

Still, the constant reality of hell remains in place.

God, have mercy on the lost and revive your Church. Since you have chosen to reach non-believers through us, the believers, then you must arouse us to action. Keep the remembrance of hell on our hearts as we go about our lives, not so we will become fearful, but so we might share your broken heart for the plight of those who are headed there.

I also fear that many of us in the Church don't want to think about hell. It's not an enjoyable thought, so we don't consider it. Give your Church the courage and the wisdom to recognize the realities of hell—the tortuous eternal life separated from God without hope, filled with regret and pain of all kinds. We must embrace this truth if we are to be motivated by it to reach all those difficult people.

Jesus, hell is not believed in very much in today's America. Our culture sees hell as an antique idea used to manipulate people into our churches. The idea of a devil and hell are considered archaic. We need true wisdom from you to know how to present this truth. We also need the Holy Spirit to convict people about judgement.

I don't know if believers in Heaven regret the people we might have saved from hell, but I want, from this point on, to live for the salvation of others. After all, if people are saved, we have to be saved from something. And you have made it clear, God, that we are saved from hell.

As much as we Christians are motivated by love, it seems that love should take the form of compassion for those who drive by our churches on their way to the fires of hell. It sounds dramatic to think this way, but the truth of hell is far more dramatic.

May the reality of hell light a fire under us to renew our efforts to share the Gospel with those who are still in danger of eternal torment. I ask in Jesus' name, Amen.

16. FISHING WITH JESUS / JOINING THE FAMILY BUSINESS

A clear expectation for all believers is that we will work together to reach the lost with the message of salvation. Jesus made this clear to his disciples often.

> *"Come, follow me,"* Jesus said, *"and I will send you out to **fish** for **people**."* (Matthew 4:19, emphasis added)
>
> *Therefore go and make disciples of **all nations**, baptizing them in the name of the Father and of the Son and of the Holy Spirit.*
> (Matthew 28:19, emphasis added)
>
> *And the gospel must first be preached to **all nations**.*
> (Mark 13:10, emphasis added)

What may not have been quite as clear to these first disciples was the partnership into which Jesus invites us all. Earlier in this section we discussed that the Holy Spirit is the one who convicts people of their sin condition, their need of Jesus as Savior, and the coming judgement. But now let's realize that Jesus has a very specific role in addition to Savior when it comes to fishing for people.

There are two different times when Jesus caused some of the disciples to catch miraculous numbers of fish. The first time was early on in His ministry, when he was gathering disciples (see Luke 5:1-11), and the second time was after his death and resurrection (see John 21:1-14). The stories are quite similar.

- In both stories, the men had been fishing all night and caught nothing.
- In both stories, Jesus tells them to try again and then they caught more than they could handle.
- In both stories they are using boats and nets to fish.

There are also some interesting differences between the two stories.

- In the first story, two boats are filled. In the second, they can't pull all of the fish into the one boat.
- In the first story, Peter reacts to the catch by telling Jesus he is a sinner. In the second, Peter is restored by Jesus for denying Him.
- In the first story, the nets break. In the second, the nets hold up.

Most importantly, in both stories, Jesus tells the men to try again and then they make their big catch. Clearly the one thing that changed between when they were unsuccessful and when they did so well, was Jesus. Jesus caused the fish to be gathered together so they could be caught. The men still had to fish, but with Jesus, they became great fishermen.

Jesus also made it clear that fishing for fish was analogous to saving the lost. So let's investigate that analogy.

1. You have to get in the boat and go where the fish are, and we are all called to do it. Everybody wants to save the lost in the comfort of their church. But that's like fishing with a pole on the shore. You might catch one or two, but it's not what Jesus was talking about. He wants a net full. We've got to go where the fish (the lost) are.

2. Fishing without Jesus is a waste of time. We must apply faith in Him to draw the fish together for us to catch. This is done in prayer.

3. The net we use is the Gospel message. In the first story the net began to break, in the second story the net held. I believe this happened because the first story occurred before Jesus went to the cross, so the gospel of Christ was incomplete, but by the second catch, the net held because Jesus was resurrected and the Gospel was complete.

Okay, so we might agree that Jesus caused the fish to gather for these miraculous catches, but does it truly indicate that Jesus will gather unbelievers for faithful followers to reach? Jesus says so.

*And I, when I am **lifted up** from the earth, will draw all people to myself.* *(John 12:12, emphasis added)*

Jesus does indeed draw people to himself, so we should never go fishing without our partners – Jesus the convener, and the Holy Spirit, the agent of conviction.

This is why I like to call it, the family business, because we are all to be involved in it.

People who fish with nets have a variety of techniques for casting the nets, or lowering them from a boat, or suspending the nets between boats. The nets usually have weights on the parts of the nets that are supposed to sink, and sometimes they have floats too. Fishermen have spent centuries figuring out how best to use their nets.

We too should practice techniques for sharing the Gospel. There are so many arguments we can prepare for, and so many methods of getting people to talk about what they believe. Section seven is dedicated to an overview of many approaches to sharing our faith with others. But the good news here is, we are not alone in this fishing expedition. Instead, we set out to sea as part of the family of God—the Father, Son, Holy Spirit, the believers, and you.

Please don't let me leave you with the impression that you are not qualified to "fish" until you have studied for years. That's not true at all. So often it's a family member or a friend that sets our feet on the path to Jesus, and they may have very little formal training. Jesus will use whoever he wants.

> *Do your best to present yourself to God as one approved, a worker who does not need to be ashamed and who correctly handles the word of truth.* *(2 Timothy 2:15)*

> *But in your hearts revere Christ as Lord. Always be prepared to give an answer to everyone who asks you to give the reason for the hope that you have. But do this with gentleness and respect.* *(1 Peter 3:15)*

These two scriptures talk about how each of us should do what we can to prepare to fish for people. I recommend that you start by sharing how you got saved, how you found Jesus, how you became a Christian. We each have a story, but until you practice sharing your story, you won't feel ready. In my church, we start off on most Sunday morning services with one of us taking just a few minutes to share how we got saved. It's amazing how well people can tell their stories. I know that some of them are nervous, and others can't wait, but it doesn't matter which kind you are. Because you have Jesus, you have a valid story.

WE EACH HAVE A STORY THAT NEEDS TO BE TOLD.

Jesus has some fish for you to catch, starting with our own children, brothers and sisters, and family and friends. Beyond that, there are so many around us who do not know the love of Christ, and the power of his salvation. You may be their best chance at eternal life. You too can fish. It's in your spiritual DNA since the day you met Jesus. Even when you feel like you have nothing good to say, remember this promise from Jesus.

> *On my account you will be brought before governors and kings as witnesses to them and to the Gentiles. But when they arrest you, do not worry about what to say or how to say it. At that time you will be given what to say, for it will not be you speaking, but the Spirit of your Father speaking through you* . (Matthew 10:18-20)

We can't fish without faith. But with faith, we are the greatest fishermen that ever lived.

Let's Pray-16

Jesus, you call us to reach the lost with the message of salvation. We who have fallen in love with you want to share salvation with those who don't yet know you. You have called us to be "fishers of people." Indeed we want to see the millions who live in darkness see your light enter them and fill them as it has with us.

In this effort, you must gather them, Jesus, and we put our faith in you to draw them to us, so that we in turn can bring them to you.

How good it is to go to work with you every day, Lord. And how wonderful it is when you bring us those people that we can love into your kingdom. We can feel no closer to you, Jesus, than when we plant the seed of salvation in another as we work hand in hand with you. It is the ultimate team experience.

Jesus, many of us have been hesitant to try. Some of us have been hurt for trying to share our faith. Some of us have been timid to try. Some of us have gotten frustrated when it didn't seem to work, and some of us just avoid the idea of sharing our faith, as if it were optional.

We know it's not optional. But it's also not natural for most of us. So, Jesus, please move on us to share. Holy Spirit, just as you convicted us that we needed a Savior, convict us now that we need to share our Savior with others. And as we share, we put more faith in Jesus to draw the people to himself through us.

Jesus, you once turned some fishermen into disciples. Now turn us, your disciples, into fishermen who fish for people, lost people. Without you, Jesus, we waste time and effort and become hurt and frustrated. With you, we can offer life in heaven to people who don't yet even know that they need you. We will go out and share, and trust you to gather and draw them. When our time on earth is done, and we go to be with you, Lord. May we be known as the people who never quit fishing with You. Amen

17. WE ARE THE WATCHMEN

I have posted watchmen on your walls, Jerusalem; they will never be silent day or night. You who call on the LORD, give yourselves no rest, and give him no rest till he establishes Jerusalem and makes her the praise of the earth. (Isaiah 62:6-7)

Almost every formal military that has ever existed in human history has appointed sentries to watch over and guard the rest of the troops while they rest. We often see sentries guarding walled cities. Their job is to keep lookout for danger and raise the alarm if they see trouble coming. It is not uncommon for sentries who fall asleep to be put to death if they are caught. The job may be easy to understand, but it is vital to the survival of an army and the nation they serve.

These watchmen that Isaiah speaks about, however, are not raising the alarm to alert an army, they're calling on the Lord. They are going directly to God with what they see coming. They are asking God to protect their people.

Furthermore, Isaiah is urging them on to never be silent, as if he knows that the need for God's protection will always be constant. Isaiah even says that they should give themselves no rest, and neither should they give God any rest. Isaiah sees their duty as a never ending ministry before the Lord until "Jerusalem becomes the praise of the earth." So when will this happen, or has it already happened? Jerusalem was the dominant nation in their part of the world during Solomon's days as King, but that was before Isaiah's time.

I believe that Jerusalem will only achieve this status when Jesus comes again.

> *I saw the Holy City, the new Jerusalem, coming down out of heaven from God, prepared as a bride beautifully dressed for her husband.* (Revelation 21:2)

And, if the New Jerusalem is dressed like a bride, then it is a picture of the dwelling place of the Christian Church. It's not a Jerusalem for Jews, but a Jerusalem for believers from all over the earth, from every nation and tribe.

So we ask this question of our passage in Isaiah, "If this is the Jerusalem that Isaiah is talking about, who are the watchmen?" They are the believers, the Christians who take their turn watching out for the Church and the nations. They are you and me.

We are the watchmen, and we must sound the alarm before God day and night until he turns. We must tell him of every wrong and malicious thing we see when we gaze out upon our countries and our churches. We must cry out continuously. It's not hard to recognize the danger. It doesn't take great discernment to see the rebellion toward God, and the many ways that hatred and confusion divide us against each other. The schemes of the devil, and the selfishness of humankind, are a deadly mixture that brings death through discord, jealousy, racism, economic exploitation, mistrust, alienation, and apathy. We are the watchmen. But we don't just tell God what we see, we also beseech Him to change it until Jesus comes again. To this we were called since the day we met Him.

But will we go to our graves and our maker never seeing the change we hope for? Is this prayer simply an exercise in blessing some future generation when the scriptures will be fulfilled and our stored up prayers are finally answered? What if it's true that we won't live to see it? Are we so selfish that we won't pray for anyone but ourselves? Haven't believers been praying for Jesus to return ever since they watched him descend into heaven? And what if Jesus isn't coming for another 2,000 years? Will we not also pray for an awakening because the alternative will soon be an entire world living in darkness? According to Isaiah, our job is to raise the alarm day and night. And what does Jesus say?

> *And will not God bring about justice for his chosen ones, who cry out to him day and night? Will he keep putting them off? I tell you, he will see that they get justice, and quickly. However, when the Son of Man comes, will he find faith on the earth?* (Luke 18:7-8)

Quick justice sounds good. Of course no believer wants justice for themselves. God is just, and justice would mean punishment for our sins. But we do want God's justice to come and restore goodness and kindness and mercy where we now see hatred and growing contempt. So we pray for a great awakening that will transform hate into love, doubt into faith, discord and jealousy into harmony and sharing.

In 2013 the Aurora theatre shooting took place just a mile from our church. In 2014 we prayed against the spirit of lawlessness. A school and a handful of churches joined us. We prayed on our own and as a church. We handed out devotionals about this spirit. Here is the prayer devotional we handed out.

> *For the secret power of lawlessness is already at work; but the one who now holds it back will continue to do so till he is taken out of the way. And then the lawless one will be revealed, whom the Lord Jesus will overthrow with the breath of his mouth and destroy by the splendor of his coming.*
> (2 Thessalonians 2:7-8, underscore added))

Some Bible scholars believe that "the one who holds it back" is the Holy Spirit, while others believe it is the Church. Either way, since the Church is filled with the Holy Spirit, and we alone have been given the power to deal with evil in the spiritual realm, (see binding and loosing in Matthew) we need to get busy. This power of lawlessness is creating one tragedy in our society after another, and we here in Aurora have seen it.

This is the same power that the anti-Christ will use when it is no longer held back. But there is good news for us now.

- *I have told you these things, so that in me you may have peace. In this world you will have trouble. But take heart! I have overcome the world.*   *(John 16:33, emphasis added)*

- *But every spirit that does not acknowledge Jesus is not from God. This is the spirit of the antichrist, which you have heard is coming and even now is already in the world.*
  You, dear children, are from God and have overcome them, because <u>the one who is in you is greater than the one who is in the world</u>.   *(1 John 4:3-5, underscore added)*

- *For everyone born of God overcomes the world. This is the victory that has overcome the world, even our faith. 5 Who is it that overcomes the world? Only the one who believes that Jesus is the Son of God.*   *(1 John 5:4-5)*

It's pretty obvious that we are overcomers. We overcome this world's evil by our faith in Jesus. Therefore let us pray the way he taught us to pray for ourselves and the people we care about.

> In the powerful name of Jesus, we loose the power of lawlessness off of our church, our town, and our nation. Power of lawlessness, we command you to leave in the name of Jesus, and we ask for the power of the Holy Spirit to come in your place and bring about good works and acts of righteousness.

> Wherever lawlessness has worked in the hearts of people, we now use the name of Jesus to drive it out and replace it with the conviction of God's Holy Spirit leading to salvation.

PRAYING FOR REVIVAL

God we pour out our heart's desire to see goodness and kindness in our church, community, and nation. We bind ourselves to the power and influence of Jesus by his name, and we ask for the protection of your mighty angels to ward off all kinds of evil, and keep safe the people who love you, and the people we care about in our city and nation.

God, deliver us from evil, especially the power of lawlessness. And make us strong of heart and mind as we stand against it and restrain it in your name Amen.

In the fall of 2015, the City of Aurora finally published crime statistics for 2014. The local paper reported that, while violent crime was on the increase in many parts of the nation, Aurora had seen a downtick in violent crime. We quietly rejoiced and gave the glory to God. Like Jesus said, we got justice, and quickly.

It CAN happen that we will get what we pray for. God does move in response to prayer. It stirs up Holy Spirit activity every time a believer hits their knees and goes before Him. We are the watchmen.

LET'S PRAY-17

Father in heaven, let us know your call upon our lives. Let us each know that we are the watchmen that you have appointed to stand on the wall and protect both your people and all of the other people you love who don't yet know you. Let the responsibility of it sink deep into our hearts, that we might find it in ourselves to cry out to you day and night and never give You, or ourselves, any rest because the enemy comes in at us like a flood.

> *When the enemy comes in like a flood, the Spirit of the Lord will lift up a standard against him.* *(Isaiah 59:19b, NKJV)*

So many people live to do harm, while others seek to do good, but they don't know what good truly is. You, O God, must intervene. Only you can bring about the lasting change that will save this generation. There is no worldly cure for the strife we see when we look over the wall. All of the worst traits of human endeavor are on display. What is there of this world that can solve greed and envy? What can stop hatred? How can a person hope to change the massive momentum of anger and discord between races, classes, nations, and religions?

Only You, God, can make such a change. Only you can rescue people from themselves. Only You can change the heart of a person, or a church, or a nation. So, as someone whom you have posted on the walls of the Church and the walls of America, I say HELP. Move now, Father of Lights, and shine the light of Jesus into this mess. Renew your call to salvation. Restore your Church to effective service. Rebuild the understanding of your truth and your word. We who call upon you would see our neighborhoods transformed into loving communities, and our nations become storehouses of help for the hopeless.

Maybe, Lord, revival is the best of words, for in it rests our hope for the lost and our hope for ourselves. We are the watchmen, but what good are watchmen when their alarms go unanswered? In the name of Jesus we sound the alarm to you, Father. Once again we pray. Turn from your wrath, Jesus, and change the very direction of this generation. Revive your Church and awaken this generation. Quicken us with passion for intimacy with you, Lord. Fill us with your Holy Spirit so that your influence in us is complete. Jesus lead your Church into the fray with love, humility, and quiet assurance that your will is being done on earth like it is in heaven. As always, dear Lord, be thorough and complete. Leave no stone unturned and no heart untouched. Present yourself anew in undeniable, irrefutable ways, so that the questioning and uncertain people of this world will find the richness of your love, the completeness of your salvation, and the excitement and fulfilment of your purpose for their lives.

As new parents rejoice when their first child is born, will you not also rejoice in adding vastly to your eternal family the hundreds of millions of people who do not yet know your love? Of this I am certain—we are not asking you to do something you don't want to do. Therefore, I am also certain you will hear our prayers and will answer from heaven, for we ask it all in Jesus' name. Amen.

I have given you, in this section, 17 approaches to praying for a revival in the Church, and for an awakening that will reach this generation. So many times God turned when only a very few were ardent in prayer for it. Are you one of them? Are you a watchman/prayer warrior/intercessor/believer/child of God?

JOIN US

And as you pray, keep this thought in mind. It's quite possible that your salvation was an answer to a prayer for revival that was prayed by someone you never met.

This is the confidence we have in approaching God: that if we ask anything according to his will, he hears us. And if we know that he hears us—whatever we ask—we know that we have what we asked of him. (1 John 5:14-15)

**WOULD THAT GOD
WOULD SET THE CHURCH
ABLAZE WITH HOLY FIRE.
SUCH A REVIVAL WOULD SPARK A
DIVINE REVOLUTION
ACROSS THE LAND,
AN AWAKENING
THAT WOULD INFLUENCE
THE FUTURE OF THE NATION,
THE CHURCH,
AND THE SAINTS TO
THE GLORY OF GOD.**

—J. ROWAN SAMSON

CHAPTER 7

EQUIPPING THE CHURCH FOR REVIVAL

I heard a missionary say once, that it was not the local church's primary job to develop missionaries, because less than 3% of any congregation would ever become missionaries. Instead, he said that the main goal of the Church should be to develop support for the few that go. This seemed to me to be a sad thought that 97% of believers should be cultivated for only financial support and prayer. It feels like paying someone else to do our job. I've read the "Great Commission" at the end of the books of Matthew and Mark, and it doesn't read that way to me.

> *Therefore go and make disciples of all nations, baptizing them in the name of the Father and of the Son and of the Holy Spirit, and teaching them to obey everything I have commanded you. And surely I am with you always, to the very end of the age.*
>
> (Matthew 28:19-20)

It sounds like all members of the Church should be involved in reaching the lost, and not just through financial and prayer support. As I read it, we all have mission fields appointed to us, and we should all support each other in our various fields of endeavor.

When I was studying to become a High School Band Director, I was taking a class from a very popular professor at the University of Colorado. He was a great composer/arranger of music, and he said to a classroom of public school music teachers, "Most of you will be lucky to teach one or two students who go on to make their living as professional musicians. Therefore, the real goal of teaching music is to create an audience for those few who make it." This seemed to me very similar to what that missionary said, in that so few will become missionaries or professional musicians. But as I continued to compare the two statements, I realized that professional musical performance in America continues to grow and thrive and expand in every form from Ballet to Bluegrass, but missions support nationwide is falling off.

It's easy to say that those who go to concerts and fill their devices with downloaded music are buying something for themselves, while those who swipe the card for missions are buying something for someone else, and therefore selfish motives will always win over voluntary sacrifice. We could let the comparison die there, but please, let us take it a little bit further.

We know this—for every musician in America who makes a living performing, there are thousands who perform at multiple levels of ability, from semi-pros playing for good money in bars on the weekend, to four-year-olds singing *Jesus Loves Me* in Sunday School. We see musicians in the Church, and on the sidewalks of big Cities. They play at weddings and funerals. They play Happy Birthday and Christmas Carols. They sing in choirs at all levels. They put on shows at old folks' homes. We see them at festivals. They play in the military bands and choirs. They play Jingle Bells at family gatherings, and they are all through our public schools. Some take lessons, some learn online, and some just pick up an instrument and play. Anyone who has ever tried to master an instrument, or sing in front of an audience, has a built-in appreciation for the professionals, the rock stars, and all those who make and perform the music we love.

But is there a parallel to this organic global experience of music, in the Church's effort to reach the lost? If the missionaries are the professionals that the Church sends out to reach the lost, do we admire them the way that someone who played flute in H.S. Band admires the Celtic Women in concert when they play the flute and other similar woodwind instruments? Does the Church have an entire infrastructure of believers who experience reaching the lost through multiple levels of amateur practice the way music does? Do our children's programs teach the fundamental "first notes" of sharing their faith? Like the different styles of music, do we have many different flavors of outreach in which Christians can participate? Are there many levels at which everyone

> CHRISTIANS MUST LEARN THE "FIRST NOTES" OF SHARING THEIR FAITH.

can perform and grow? And, how do the supporters of missionaries get to enjoy their "music"?

Let's take a lesson from musical pedagogy and consider a system where all believers can grow into sharing their faith at whatever level they can perform.

1. If the goal is that every Christian shares their faith with others, then the good news is, EVERYONE ALREADY HAS AN INSTRUMENT TO PLAY! Because every believer, by definition, has faith in Jesus. <u>Faith is the instrument</u>—we just need to learn how to play it for others.

2. In Band Class, everyone learns how to play the first few notes on whatever instrument they have. Then they practice together, and perform for their parents in a concert at school. (This is a very safe audience. Parents love whatever their kids can play. So does God.) For believers, we talk about how we came to be saved and accept Jesus as Lord and Savior. Once we've gotten comfortable with putting this first part of our story into words, we share it with other believers before God. This is our safe audience, and as each one shares, it builds our collective confidence.

3. Some kids pick musical performance up faster than others. That's OK. They help to move the class forward. They may jump to Advanced Band sooner than others. Some people are comfortable sharing in front of people and others are not. We will soon look at local outreach that these folks can jump into. However, believers who are not so comfortable are still greatly valued. Remember, Jesus chose the weak ones of this world to humble the proud. Sometimes a few awkward words spoken with love and sincerity, at a key moment, can do more good than the pastor's sermon on Sunday. And, the person who struggles the most to learn an instrument, is often the one who appreciates the accomplished artists the most. And, the person who wrestles the hardest with sharing their faith, will also be one of the most supportive of those missionaries.

4. Just as we have seen that opportunities to sing and play instruments exist at every level of our society, so must we have a menu of opportuni-

ties for people to engage in the sharing of faith at all levels of ability. Here are some possibilities;

- Home groups where non-believing neighbors and friends can study the Bible alongside believers.

- Non-believers nights at church where all their questions can be answered by some of your strongest sharers.

- Events in the local park where you may have free hot dogs as you share, or maybe a full-blown Sunday service. These events can give service opportunities that range from the clean-up crew to witnessing. These events let people of all levels and abilities find ways to help and support. One of the things I like most about competitive Marching Band is that every member of the band got a uniform and they played the whole game. You didn't win based on how well your top few band members performed. You won based on how well your entire band stayed in line, in step, in tune, and together as they collectively performed. It's the purest form of team competition. Your entire church can dig in at a church-in-the-community event.

- Our church is pioneering an outreach booth that will pay for room at large outdoor community events. This traveling booth will be staffed by folks who really love to witness for Jesus. They will hand out Bible based pamphlets and Bibles, and they will engage walkers-by with a gospel message. Our Booth is not aimed at Christian events, but rather secular events like, The People's Fair, Cinco De Mayo, Craft fairs, Flea Markets—any time the public gathers.

5. Some kids take private lessons from an expert on their instrument. After all, the Band Director only specialized on their primary instrument in College (mine was percussion). They can't know as much about each instrument as someone who majored in that instrument. So how do believers get private lessons in sharing their faith? Offer a class on sharing your faith. I really like Max Anders Book "<u>What You Need to</u>

<u>*Know About Sharing Your Faith*</u>". It's a perfect introduction for believers in Witnessing 101. Also, consider recruiting a pastor or promoting someone to Deacon of Outreach or some similar position for the purpose of driving these programs and teaching some of these classes.

(For more witnessing materials and resources, visit ekgministries.org and click on the printables tab.)

Once believers have successfully shared their faith, and had the joy of seeing Christ inhabit their efforts and enter the life of the people they spoke with, then they become life-long ardent supporters of missionaries around the world, and they become part of the entire Christian chorus of witness, and they will add to the congregation's drive to reach the lost.

Just as we hear live music in all facets of society today, we could see Christians share their faith at all levels of capability, and in every corner of society, if we will teach every Christian to play their instrument.

THE POWER OF YOUR PERSONAL STORY

There's an old Church term not much used today—testify. It's used all the time in court when witnesses of an event are questioned under oath they testify about what they know. In the old Church context, to testify was to get up in front of the congregation and explain how God has saved you from your sins. That meant sharing the details of your sin, and God's mercy, so God could receive glory for the turnaround in your life. Similar sharing often happens in support groups that help people fight addictions or overcome difficult circumstances in life. It seems that when others hear us tell our story, with its failures and successes, it helps everyone.

You have a story. You may not think that it's interesting enough or dramatic enough to share, but keep in mind that God is the author of your story, so it's the only one that fits you. I guarantee that you will be surprised at how many people will be touched by the story of your salvation when you share it.

Looking unto Jesus the author and finisher of our faith.
(Hebrews 12:2a)

WHEN GOD TURNS

God didn't just write your story. He also commands you to get ready to share it!

> *Always be prepared to give an answer to everyone who asks you to give the **reason** for the **hope** that you have. But do this with gentleness and respect.* (1 Peter 3:15b)

> YOU HAVE A STORY TO TELL—SOMEONE IS JUST WAITING TO HEAR IT.

Of course it's good to be able to give a scriptural reason for the hope that you have. But many unbelievers want to know your truth—how it works for you—what's happened to you personally as a result of believing in Jesus.

Pastors are taught that personal experience should never eclipse scriptural truth. We are taught this so that if we, or someone else has an experience that conflicts with what we understand in scripture, the Bible should carry more weight. For example, if I had a dream that God said it was OK for me to cheat somebody, I should not assume that God has changed his mind and cheating is now acceptable. The scriptural truth must not be suspended by an experience.

What if your horoscope in the newspaper said, "Don't make any important decisions today." So you avoided some decisions and it turned out to be a good idea. Does that mean that you should consult the paper for your decision making from now on, or should you go to God? You get the idea. Biblical truth wins out over personal experience.

However, when it comes to sharing Jesus, your experience is crucial because that's what people want to know. They don't yet believe in the Bible, but they may be willing to hear how it all works for you. They don't always want the quotes and the rules and the road to salvation. They want to know why you bought in to it.

Of course the story of your salvation, and your walk with Jesus since, should reinforce the big ideas in the Bible. It's the genuine story of love between a heavenly Father and his children. Only you can tell it, but you have considerable help.

> *But when they arrest you, do not worry about what to say or how to say it. At that time you will be given what to say, for it will not be you speaking, but the Spirit of your Father speaking through you.*
> *(Matthew 10:19-20)*

I think this same thing happens often when we step out to speak up for God—He speaks through us. This includes witnessing, testifying, sharing, and any form of communication about our God.

What are the elements of your story? What has happened between you and God that would be good for others to hear? You should make a list and practice sharing with one of those "safe" audiences I mentioned earlier in this section.

TIME FOR A LITTLE SELF-ASSESSMENT

Have you ever told someone about the time when you got saved and accepted Jesus as your Lord and Savior?

Do you know why Jesus died on the cross?

Can you explain to someone else what they need to do to be saved?

Do you have a collection of stories about your personal experiences as a Christian? These might include:

- Answers to prayer.
- Times when God kept you safe.
- Provision from God.
- How you know that God loves you.
- When God has corrected you.
- Comfort in failure.
- Unexpected success.
- Direction from God when you weren't sure.
- Healing.
- How God speaks to you – in prayer, dreams, through others, in life's moments, your conscience.

WHEN GOD TURNS

- God's call on your life.
- Help getting rid of sin habits.

Can you answer some of the big questions that non-believers ask? Like;

- Why does God allow evil in the world?
- Evolution vs creation.
- Jesus was a good guy, but was he the Son of God?
- What happens to people when they die?
- Why would God allow people to go to hell?

Can you start a conversation about your faith with a stranger, a friend, or a family member?

It's my experience that most Christians can't give strong positive responses to many of these questions, but with a little effort, most Christians could master these few basics, and much more. There are many great books and videos of sharing the Faith, witnessing, and Christian Apologetics (which is a big seminary term for defending the Faith). Search online. Check YouTube® and Christian websites. Visit a Christian bookstore. Let your networking begin.

> ANYONE CAN MASTER THE BASICS. IT'S JUST A MATTER OF ONE'S CHOOSING.

Please realize something. You are valuable, unique, and your story has an audience designed by God to be impacted by it. You can do this, and it's invigorating when you do. No doubt there are some people "out there" whom only you can lead to Jesus. A polished performance is never the goal. Rather, it's the honest and sincere sharing from the heart that helps the most. You have an incredible deposit in you from God. Please prepare yourself to share, because someone needs you.

(I have touched on this next idea earlier, but now it is developed more fully.)

GOD'S PLAN - PART ONE – PLAN A

It's also good that we can share God's story. What I will develop here is one strong understanding that covers a lot of ground when it comes to reaching the lost. If you can explain and defend God's Plan, then you can go a long way toward reaching the lost.

We start with the Garden of Eden. And again I say that whether you believe that the Garden of Eden is an historical and scientific fact, or whether you believe that is just a story given to us by God through Moses to teach us things he wants us to know, it doesn't make any difference. Either way we still learn many important truths.

First, we realize that God created this world to be perfect! There was no disease or death, no sadness or tears. All the world was at harmony and humankind (Adam and Eve) had a beautiful relationship with God. This was God's plan. This was how He wanted it. There was no evil (except for the snake). There was peace, love, and joy. All was good.

Why is this important? Because, it answers that question about evil in the world. It was not part of God's plan. If humankind had resisted the evil, it would not have been able to flourish. It was humankind that chose to let evil in. I'm sure that God knew it would happen. He knew what Adam and Eve would do, but he started with perfection so all of us throughout time would know that it was not God's choice to introduce sin and corruption and death into this world.

Some will argue that it's still God's fault that evil is in the world because He knew it would happen. However, we can respond that God could have avoided this problem and He could have kept the world perfect by not allowing us to have our own free will. Most people value their right to choose for themselves. They don't want to be automatons with no voice and no choice. They can see God's dilemma. He gave us choice, and we've been choosing sin ever since.

So, why did God give us free choice or free will? Knowing that all of us will make some terrible choices that set us apart from Him, why does

God allow this? To understand why God gives us this free will, we have to understand love.

Most of us, when we were young, had a crush or two on someone that didn't work out. We wanted them to love us and we wanted to love them, or at least to love them with our limited knowledge of love. As we grew older, we were still drawn to certain people, and we wanted so much for them to choose to love us—to approach us and let us approach them in the hope that something wonderful might happen—that we might fall in love. It doesn't take long for this new love to be tested to see if there is enough caring for the two to make sacrifices for each other. If they can grow through these sacrifices and trials, they might even get married and live a life of sacrifice for each other.

God wants this too! He wants people to love him. Out of all the other distractions and attractions in the world, God waits to see who will choose to love Him. Of course God is already busy loving us. He has given us life, and something of himself in every person, so we might respond when our spirits first sense his approach. So few people do respond to God's love by loving him back, but when it does happen, God knows that it's real. He knows our love for him is real because he gives us free will! We could choose anything else in the world to love, including all kinds of evil and wrong-doing. So, the ones who come to God with love for him are genuine. He's not forcing them. It's our choice to love God, and that choice is so important to God that he will tolerate all the bad choices in the world, just for the few that choose him. But now there's a slight problem.

GOD'S PLAN – PART TWO – PLAN B

So our free will knocked out the perfect garden, but a few people still choose to love God and embrace his love with some of their own, but here's the problem. These people who choose to love God are not perfect. Yes, they love God, but they have also made some really bad choices, and even after they choose God, they keep making those bad choices too.

Let's recognize something about God. He's perfect. He's holy, undefiled, glorious, righteous, and completely honorable. Sin is so far from

God that we can't imagine how pure and noble and complete He is in His perfection. This is God's character, and no sin can come near him. As Christians today, we often don't spend enough time recognizing how vast and unquestionable is the perfection and the righteousness of God.

And while we're talking about God's character, let me also mention that God is just. He is committed to justice. Doing wrong things will reap a reward that ultimately could lead to death in the place we call hell. This might be defined as eternal separation from God. There is more I could write about hell, but I think that missing out on God is the worst part.

Why would God, whose essential nature and most dominant characteristic is love, create hell for those who don't believe in him? Because He is just and is obligated to punish wrong doing. Any thoughtful member of a society recognizes that without punishment, criminals will not stop taking unfair advantage of people. It is human nature to expect that those who intentionally harm others should be punished. God follows through. Nobody likes punishment, especially for themselves, but it's so important for this world to realize that God follows through whether we accept Him or not. But God also provides a way out of punishment—a way to avoid His Justice. It will require faith in God, and a loving commitment to him.

What is God going to do so the people that love and believe in him can have a relationship with him? They're now quite sinful and cannot approach his holiness. So, God begins a new plan—Plan B. He will offer the people who love him a way of getting rid of their sin so they can have a successful relationship with Him.

PLAN B WORKS LIKE THIS.

God starts with Abram and Sarai, much like he did with Adam and Eve, and He builds a relationship with Abraham and his family. God promises to bless him and vastly grow his family if Abram will follow Him. Abram becomes Abraham and his descendants (Isaac, Jacob/Israel, Joseph, etc.) grow to be millions of people, but few are very faithful to God. Still, they have the mind-set to pray to God in times of need, but they are really struggling with their sin condition. Now comes the centerpiece of Plan B. God has had this relationship with these people for a few centuries and they are ready to receive from him a way to free themselves from sin —God's Law.

Moses gets the Law from God and gives it to the people. The Law has a lot of do's and don'ts, but whenever they break this Law, they can offer a sacrifice to God and the sin is forgiven! Now they can approach God free from their sin. The loving relationship has a chance to grow. It's the best thing humankind has seen since the Garden of Eden. God and the people are back together again. Well, maybe.

Problems arise with Plan B. Under God's Law, an animal must be sacrificed when a person sins or breaks the Law. When we consider how often people sin, this becomes an arduous task, and an expensive one. The Children of Israel now struggle to fulfill the requirements of the Law. So many animals must die, as well as paying support to the priesthood and other offerings of grain and the like. The Law is often seen by the Old Testament followers as too strict and cumbersome. It's too hard to keep.

As they wrestle with God's Law over the next few centuries, they have some wonderful moments as God's people, but they also have some colossal failures, and God follows through on punishment. Even to the point of allowing the entire nation to be conquered and enslaved.

During these centuries under God's Law, the people learn a few basic understandings.

1. The blood of a sacrifice atones for sin.
2. When they turn away from God, things get worse for them.
3. Without their relationship with God, they are unprotected and they do not prosper.
4. The Law is next to impossible to keep.
5. God gives them his word, warnings, and directions, through prophets that speak under the influence of God's Holy Spirit.

GOD'S PLAN – PART THREE – PLAN C

This is the part we've been waiting for. The stage is set. At the close of the Old Testament, God's Law continues but the priesthood is cursed by God because they hated to do their jobs. So, God curses their sacrifices. Nothing good will happen through the observance of the Law, and those who devote themselves to following it, tend to get bent and twisted. Now comes Jesus!

Jesus says: "Do not think that I have come to abolish the Law or the Prophets; I have not come to abolish them but to fulfill them." (Matthew 5:17)

Plan C is much better than B, because Jesus keeps God's Law for us. He qualifies us for a close relationship with God. We simply have to believe in Him as Savior and Lord, and we receive all of the benefits as we devote ourselves to following Jesus.

Let's look at how the understandings gained from Plan B play out in this new Plan C.

1. The blood of a sacrifice atones for sin.

However, now the blood sacrifice is Jesus, the Lamb of God. His blood takes away all sin, from this point forward, for everyone who believes in Him.

> *The next day John saw Jesus coming toward him and said, "Look, the **Lamb of God**, who takes away the sin of the world!*
> *(John 1:29, emphasis added)*

2. When they turn away from God, things get worse for them.

For people who believe in Jesus under the new covenant of Plan C, even when we turn away from God, have doubts, or try to hide, God never lets go. He stays with us through every dessert valley, trial, failure, and test. We may experience hard times designed to turn us back toward God, but our salvation is secure.

> *But Christ is faithful as a Son over His [Father's] house. And we are His house if we hold fast our confidence and sense of triumph in our hope [in Christ].*   *(Hebrews 3:6, AMP)*

3. Without their relationship with God, they are unprotected and they do not prosper.

Under Plan C, our relationship with God is not hindered by our sin or our ability to keep God's Law. Jesus' sacrifice has taken away our sin, so God's protection and blessing are secured for us by our faith in Jesus, and we can approach God without fear of rejection.

- *His divine power has given us **everything we need** for a godly life through our knowledge of him who called us by his own glory and goodness.* *(2 Peter 1:3, emphasis added)*

- *The Spirit you received does not make you slaves, so that you live in fear again; rather, the Spirit you received brought about your adoption to sonship. And by him we cry, "Abba, Father." The Spirit himself testifies with our spirit that we are God's children.* *(Romans 8:15-16)*

4. The Law is next to impossible to keep.

Again, we have good news. The Law required that people offer sacrifices for their sins, but seldom did people have a change of heart to turn away from sin. But now under Plan C, not only does our faith in Jesus forgive our sins, but it also helps us make the change of heart so we can grow to turn our backs on sin.

*Because through Christ Jesus the **law** of the **Spirit** who gives life has set you free from the **law** of sin and death.* *(Romans 8:2)*

5. God gives them his word, warnings, and directions, through prophets that speak under the influence of God's Holy Spirit.

One more, great component of Plan C is that the Holy Spirit is no longer reserved for a prophet or a priest here and there, but instead the Spirit is in every believer! We can all now receive directly from God His warnings and direction.

*Peter replied, "Repent and be **baptized**, every one of you, in the name of Jesus Christ for the forgiveness of your sins. And you will receive the gift of the Holy **Spirit**.* *(Acts 2:38, emphasis added)*

In order for anyone to embrace Plan C and believe in Jesus so they can receive God's grace for salvation, there are some things that must first be understood about Jesus.

Jesus is not just a great teacher who loved people and died for them. Jesus is God. This truth causes many to stumble, but it is crucially important. Many religions believe in Jesus the teacher, but not Jesus as God. Muslims see Jesus as a teacher and prophet, but they deny him as God. Mormons stumble on this one, too. Many of the off-shoots of Christianity do not accept Jesus as God, but we Christians would insist that a person cannot call part of what Jesus taught as great truth, and then say that what he taught about himself was a lie. Jesus didn't suddenly go insane each time he said that He and the Father are one (John 10:30). A person can't pick and choose which part of Jesus' teachings they like, and then deny the rest. As C. S. Lewis once wrote, Jesus is either "Liar, Lunatic, or Lord".

And, Jesus must be God or he would not have been perfect and free from all sin so he could qualify to die for the sins of the world. If Jesus were just a good man, then he would have died on the cross for his own sins, "for all have sinned and fallen short of the glory of God" (Romans 3:23). But Jesus was sin free and so he could then take on the sins of all humankind.

> God **made** him who had no **sin** to be **sin** for us, so that in him we might become the righteousness of God.
>
> *(2 Corinthains 5:21, emphasis added)*

And, Jesus taught that he was God, and so does the Bible.

- *Jesus answered: "Don't you know me, Philip, even after I have been among you such a long time? Anyone who has seen me has seen the Father. How can you say, 'Show us the Father'?* (John 14:9)
- *But he continued, "You are from below; I am from above. You are of this world; I am not of this world. 24 I told you that you would die in your sins; if you do not believe that I am he, you will indeed die in your sins."* (John 8:23-24)

WHEN GOD TURNS

For in Christ all the fullness of the Deity lives in bodily form.
(Colossians 2:9)

While we wait for the blessed hope—the appearing of the glory of our great God and Savior, Jesus Christ. (Titus 2:13)

FOUNDATIONAL CHRISTIAN TRUTH: JESUS CHRIST IS GOD.

The Christian Faith is founded on the truth that Jesus Christ is God. Yes, He comes to earth as the Son of God, which he is, but Christians also believe a larger truth—the Father and the Son and the Holy Spirit are all God. Sometimes Christians refer to God as the "three-in-one God". Every believer must know their Bible to be able to understand this truth, but it behooves us to know God in these three ways much like we might know a good friend by their appearance, and their mind, and their spirit. To relate to God in these three ways is powerful, wonderful, and sometimes overwhelming. Jesus is God. Amen.

What I call Plan C, is God's plan for our salvation based on the sacrifice of His Son, Jesus. The blood of Jesus washes us clean so we can approach God free of sin. Thanks to Jesus, we meet the righteous standard of a perfect and Holy God, and we can approach him as our Dad anytime. It's both startling in its simplicity, and powerful in its effect. Some people are offended by the free nature of this gift, which we call grace. They feel like we should have to do more than just believe to earn this wonderful salvation. But the definition of grace is undeserved, un-earnable, unmerited, favor from God for salvation and all kinds of blessings.

We can see that all of history was orchestrated by God and it was aimed at this one moment in time when Jesus would die that sacrificial death. But there's one more part to God's plan, and it's not Plan D!

GOD'S PLAN – PART FOUR

God's not done. Jesus is coming back, and the sequel will be spectacular, because the final part of God's plan is that Jesus returns us to Plan A. What? Yes, it's true. Evidently God is stubborn and he's determined to get things back to that perfect world he always wanted. So when Jesus comes back, he will bind up the source of evil for a time, while He rules the world the way it was meant to be. Then, God will do something more spectacular than we can even imagine.

> Then I saw "a new heaven and a new earth," for the first heaven and the first earth had passed away, and there was no longer any sea. I saw the Holy City, the new Jerusalem, coming down out of heaven from God, prepared as a bride beautifully dressed for her husband. And I heard a loud voice from the throne saying, "Look! God's dwelling place is now among the people, and he will dwell with them. They will be his people, and God himself will be with them and be their God. (Revelation 21:1-3)

It's really not just a return to Plan A. It's more like Plan A 2.0.

I know this—I don't want to miss it. And, I don't want anyone else to miss it.

There's nothing else like God's plan in all of the world. Although the world has many problems, thanks to humankind's free will, God continues to execute His plan flawlessly. In order to have faith in God and His plan it takes your hearts experience of Him. It's not head knowledge, it's heart knowledge that brings faith. It comes from drawing near to Him with hope.

A CHALLENGE

> The Jews there were amazed and asked, "How did this man get such learning without having been taught?"
>
> Jesus answered, "My teaching is not my own. It comes from the one who sent me. Anyone who chooses to do the will of God will find out whether my teaching comes from God or whether I speak on my own. (John 7:15-17)

Do you see the challenge here? Jesus is challenging you and me. He's thrown down the gauntlet. He's calling us out. Let's make sure we understand it.

- First Jesus says that his teaching comes from God.

- Next Jesus says that anyone who does the will of God will find out that the teaching comes from God.

The one question is, what does Jesus mean by doing the will of God? Does He mean <u>all</u> of the will of God? No one can do that, so no one can find out where Jesus' teaching comes from?

I don't believe that Jesus is talking about doing <u>all</u> of God's will in this passage. It seems to me that Jesus is talking about teaching. When we share about God with others, we are teaching them in a very personal way. I believe that Jesus is saying that when we do God's will, by trying to share about Him with others, then our teaching will come to us from God, and we will realize that's how it works for Jesus, too. When we step up to risk sharing and teaching about God, He gives the ability and the very words we need. And we will know that it comes from God, because it will be so much more than we had planned to say. When we take the challenge to try, we become vessels pouring out Jesus with every word.

This is the challenge I leave you with. I've already asked you to pray, but now I ask you to take the challenge and share you story—your one-of-a-kind story. When you do, the same teaching that Jesus got from God will come through you to the people you are reaching. They may or may not receive it, but you will know that God is moving through you, and you are doing His will. After all, Jesus said you will only find out when you take the challenge.

ONE MORE THING—COUNT IT ALL JOY

Consider it pure joy, my brothers and sisters, whenever you face trials of many kinds, because you know that the testing of your faith produces perseverance. Let perseverance finish its work so that you may be mature and complete, not lacking anything.

(James 1:2-4)

Is James serious here? I mean, we shouldn't let trials knock us off course with God, but does he really mean that we should be "joyful" when we suffer?

I say, yes! In fact, I think that joy during hardship and struggles is a secret weapon in scripture. If we think about it for a moment, being joyful while suffering is the ultimate sign of complete and mature faith. Joy when your bank accounts are empty shows faith in God's provision and plan for your life. Joy when you're struggling in your marriage clears your head so God can lead you to be the best spouse possible. Joy when you have suffered great loss shows that you trust in God's redemption and that you have hope for the future. Joy when the Devil is attacking you must be a great frustration to him. Joy when you are dying shows that you are certain of God's promises for you.

So many times in my life, when I have had the presence of mind, and the faith, to count it all joy when I am going through a trial, the trial clears up. Maybe it's because joy shows that we've learned our lesson and we have grown through the struggle all we can. I believe in this scriptural command for joy, and in practice, it has been uncanny how well it works. I pray for the self-discipline to use it more often.

The author of Hebrews says a similar thing about joy.

> *You suffered along with those in prison and **joyfully** accepted the confiscation of your property, because you knew that you yourselves had better and lasting possessions. So do not throw away your confidence; it will be richly rewarded.* (Hebrews 10:34-35)

Not only is joy a strength in the face of adversity, and an antidote for suffering, it's also motivation for service to others. The joy that comes from blessing people is an appropriate desire and a reward that Christians are encouraged to seek. Indeed Jesus knew this same motivation when he came to the cross.

> *Fixing our eyes on Jesus, the pioneer and perfecter of faith. For the **joy** set before him he endured the cross.*
> (Hebrews 12:2a, emphasis added)

Joy is set before us, too, both in this life and the next. We ought to be able to connect with it during those hard to handle times when life turns cold and our options are limited. But please understand, I'm not talking about silliness. I'm not talking about being happy when a close friend finds out they have cancer. Happiness is how we feel when things are going well. Joy is a choice we make based on the fact that God loves us, and has given us this life to live.

Let's say you've had a fight with your boss and you are frustrated and angry. It's one of those times when you are running the fight over and over in your mind thinking up things that you wish you'd have said to make your point even stronger. If, in this moment, you can count it all joy, it will change your inner discussion, defeat your need to win, and put your focus on how good God is. Now you've really won. Now you are free from self and ready to hear from God about strong steps you can take to fix the problem.

But how does it work? How can a person just start being joyful?

Here's how it works for me when I move into joy mode during a struggle.

I remind myself that God has given me an abundant life, and this pain, conflict, attack, or difficulty, is part of the life God has planned for me. I should be grateful for it, whatever it is:

- Grateful that I knew the friend I just lost.
- Grateful that I am still alive this day, and filled with His hope.
- Grateful that I have a spouse to fight with, and that God will use this fight to draw us closer.
- Grateful for the times when I fail to be joyful, and God forgives me.
- Grateful that I have a cantankerous boss who will see the peace on my face and know that it comes from my God.
- Grateful that the joy set before me helps me endure this world with joy.

I have found that joy will accommodate certain emotions. I have felt both joy and sorrow, occasionally joy and pain, joy and respect for another, joy and happiness, joy and awe, joy and sincerity, even joy and exasperation.

But I have also found that joy will not share itself with any of these emotions;

> ...bitterness, **rage** and anger, brawling and slander, along with every form of malice...   (Ephesians 4:31-32, emphasis added)

You get the idea. Joy is a fruit of the Holy Spirit and an evidence of spiritual maturity. It leaves when we allow the inappropriate.

You can choose joy—all the time. You can start right now. But you must choose joy when you witness for Jesus to others. People sense joy in others. Think of the folks you know who tend to be joyful. I hope you know some. Aren't they great to be around and talk with?

That's why you must count it all joy when somebody rejects your witness, so you won't get jaded, disappointed, and fed up. When I get slammed on, sworn at or rejected when I witness to someone, I try to thank God for letting me drop that seed and share a small piece of my faith. I'm just glad I'm in the game.

You can consider it pure joy, and as you grow into this most wonderful form of God's grace, the quality of your own existence will vastly improve. But even if it doesn't – count it all Joy.

WHEN GOD TURNS

About the Author

CHARLES W. CLARK

Pastor Charles W. Clark lives in Aurora, Colorado with his wife Jackie. For 17 years he was a High School Band Director while often pastoring small churches. In 1999 he joined the staff at New Life Church in Colorado Springs (then Colorado's largest church) as Children's Church pastor. He holds a Bachelor Degree in Theology, a Bachelor Degree in Music Education, a Masters Degree in Gifted and Talented Education, and a Masters Degree in Educational Leadership and Administration. He is currently Senior Pastor of Aurora Hills Church, and has been a member of the faculty of Christian Life School of Theology since 2001. For the past several years Pastor Clark has studied the classic revivals of Christianity through the writings of Charles Finney, Andrew Murray, Charles Wesley, and others, along with the revivals of the Old and New Testaments of the Bible. His previous books include "Able to Teach", and "Redeemed for a Purpose".

www.ingramcontent.com/pod-product-compliance
Lightning Source LLC
Chambersburg PA
CBHW071655090426
42738CB00009B/1528